Solution-Focused
Therapy Theory, Research & Practice

Solution-Focused Therapy

Theory, Research & Practice

2nd Edition

Alasdair J. Macdonald

Los Angeles | London | New Delhi
Singapore | Washington DC

SAGE Publications Ltd
1 Oliver's Yard
55 City Road
London EC1Y 1SP

SAGE Publications Inc.
2455 Teller Road
Thousand Oaks, California 91320

SAGE Publications India Pvt Ltd
B 1/I 1 Mohan Cooperative Industrial Area
Mathura Road
New Delhi 110 044

SAGE Publications Asia-Pacific Pte Ltd
33 Pekin Street #02-01
Far East Square
Singapore 048763

Library of Congress Control Number: 2011920873

British Library Cataloguing in Publication data

A catalogue record for this book is available from the British Library

ISBN 978-0-85702-889-1
ISBN 978-0-85702-890-7 (pbk)

Typeset by C&M Digitals (P) Ltd, Chennai, India
Printed by MPG Books Group, Bodmin, Cornwall
Printed on paper from sustainable resources

Contents

*An additional case study is available at www.sagepub.co.uk/macdonald

With thanks to Celia and my colleagues

About the Author

Alasdair has been a Consultant Psychiatrist in the NHS since 1980. He currently holds a part-time contract with Children's Services in Dorset County Hospital Foundation Trust, and has experience in all aspects of psychiatry including secure care. Alasdair's psychotherapy training includes psychodynamic, group and systemic approaches and he is registered as a family therapist and supervisor with the United Kingdom Council for Psychotherapy. He has been the Medical Director of two Trusts and Project Director of the Mental Health Institute at St Martin's College in Carlisle and Lancaster, and is Research Coordinator and former President and Secretary of the European Brief Therapy Association. Alasdair works as a trainer and supervisor and as a management consultant. Training workshops include solution-focused therapy, solution-focused approaches to mental health and organisational skills for finding cooperation in the workplace. He is the Service Director of Dorset Child and Family Counselling Trust and a Trustee of the Dorset Trust for Counselling and Psychotherapy, both local charities.

Teaching and training in solution-focused brief therapy has been Alasdair's chief interest for 20 years. He has taught in the USA, South Africa, China, Singapore and Australia, as well as most of the countries of Europe. He has special experience in the application of these ideas within the mental health setting and with offenders. Alasdair's main research interest is the study of process and outcomes in therapy and he has over 40 peer-reviewed publications and numerous other published pieces. His book *Solution-focused Therapy: Theory, Research and Practice* was published in 2007, and he is on the editorial boards for a forthcoming book on solution-focused approaches and for two journals. Alasdair is also the Scientific Advisor for the Helsinki Psychotherapy Institute.

For further information see www.solutionsdoc.co.uk

Praise for the Book

'Ideally, every clinician, supervisor and trainer who aspires to excellence would have unlimited access to a wise, supportive mentor or colleague with a wealth of practical clinical experience balanced by extensive knowledge of all the most pertinent research. This eminently useful and satisfying book comes close to approximating that experience! Macdonald provides a generous spectrum of practical solution-focused techniques that readers will be able to readily apply to a wide range of clinical, supervisory, coaching and educational settings balanced by a clear and satisfying overview of the solution-focused approach in the context of current, state of the art research.'
Yvonne Dolan, Director of the Institute of Solution-Focused Brief Therapy, Chicago, Illinois

'Whether you are an experienced practitioner in solution-focused therapy or an absolute beginner, this scholarly, yet accessible, text has everything you need. It explains not only what solution-focused therapy is but where it comes from, how it differs from other therapies, where it can be used, when to use it and when not to, and how and why it works. This revised edition has all the hallmarks of a classic text.'
Judith Milner, solution-focused practitioner (www.judithmilner.co.uk)

'The second edition of Alasdair's book is a must for both introductory courses in solution-focused approaches to therapy and for those established practitioners interested in the developing research from this field. Solution-focused skills are usefully illustrated with therapist–client vignettes that bring the practice of therapy to life for the reader. The updated research chapter offers a very helpful and contemporary critique of SFBT's growing evidence base, raising awareness of strengths, limitations and potential direction for future studies.'
Fred Ruddick, Senior Lecturer (Mental Health Studies) RMN, RGN, Adv Dip Counselling, MA Counselling, University of Cumbria

'Alasdair Macdonald's book is the go-to source for research and insights into solution-focused approaches. This new edition includes all the latest research studies and analysis, along with concise and usable ways to use SF in a huge range of situations from severe mental illness to workplace performance. The new chapters on ethics, commonly posed questions and future prospects are concise and sharply observed. Anyone interested in

evidence, research and application of the SF approach should have a copy to hand. Really.'
Mark McKergow PhD MBA, author of The Solutions Focus: Making coaching & change SIMPLE, co-founder of SFCT and SOLWorld

'This is a well structured and meaty text that presents SFT authoritatively, in a way that has to be taken seriously. It covers all the areas one would expect – a description and history of the model; ethics; research, settings and issues – and is an all-round excellent text.'
Colin Feltham, Emeritus Professor of Critical Counselling Studies, Sheffield Hallam University

Introduction

Solution-focused brief therapy was developed in the 1980s by Steve de Shazer and Insoo Kim Berg of the Brief Family Therapy Center in Milwaukee, Wisconsin. Both were social workers, among their other skills, and had met at the Mental Research Institute (MRI) in Palo Alto in California, where much of the early work on strategic therapy took place. After marriage they moved to Milwaukee, planning to form 'The MRI of the North'. They continued their research in their clinic, modifying existing brief therapies by using feedback from clients about successful outcomes. This process led to the gradual removal of many of the usual elements of psychotherapy because nothing was retained that did not show specific benefits for client outcomes.

As a consequence there are a number of differences between solution-focused brief therapy and traditional psychotherapy. The central assumptions are that the goals for therapy will be chosen by the client and that the clients themselves have resources which they will use in making changes. A detailed history is not essential for solution-focused work.

A solution focused interview will contain certain specific elements. Problems and goals are defined in practical terms, which enables the client to focus on solutions. Asking about pre-session changes, exceptions to the problem, scaling the problem from 0–10 and asking the 'miracle question' keep the focus on effective solutions. At the end of the session the feedback encourages change. Tasks such as 'Do more of what is working already' or 'It is time to try something different' help to maintain change after the session.

In solution-focused work, individuals, couples or families may be seen; the sessions follow a similar pattern with each. Clients find the method non-threatening and many enjoy the collaborative aspects of the process. Sufficient improvement is often achieved within three to five sessions, and about 25 per cent of clients require only one session. As with other psychotherapies, problems of long standing are less responsive to treatment. Medication and other treatments can be combined with a solution focus. Hospital stays and waiting lists are reduced when this approach is adopted since it focuses on empowering service users. Mental health staff have found that it gives them increased confidence in their work with clients.

The Author

My father was a physician and psychoanalyst and so I was exposed to psychotherapeutic ideas from an early age. During my psychiatric training I had experience of psychodynamic therapy with individuals and groups. I attended an analytic groups course at the Scottish Institute of Human Relations and underwent a personal psychoanalysis. My training in systemic family therapy progressed to strategic therapy and then to solution-focused therapy. I employed solution-focused approaches in psychiatric practice, in my role as a medical manager and in management consultancy.

This Book

This book is intended as a basis for introductory courses and will also describe ways of applying solution-focused skills in a number of specialist areas including mental health, child protection and organisational consultancy.

Therapists are often of a temperament that does not lend itself to research. However, within developed countries it is increasingly necessary to produce an evidence base for therapies. This means that therapies have to be shown to be effective within the scientific research paradigms traditionally adopted for the examination of medical remedies. This book contains an extensive review of the current research and evidence base. The historical roots of solution-focused ideas are also examined.

As the scope of this book includes the application of solution-focused approaches to organisational situations, I hope that it may be useful as a text for managers and management consultants in their constant search for more effective interventions.

The Structure of the Book

1 The solution-focused therapy model: the first session; Part 1 describes the development of the method and its introduction to mental health practice in this country. The core of the chapter is a systematic account of the basic solution-focused method and its application to a first session. This includes details of the question sets for identifying the problem, finding goals and exceptions and using scaling and the miracle question. There are extended commentaries on the micro-skills of interviewing. Chapters 1 and 2 are based on the teaching materials for an accredited course at the University of Cumbria and on the feedback received from trainees since the courses began in 1997.

2 The solution-focused therapy model: Part 2 completes the first session process, discussing the value or otherwise of taking a break and proceeding to the feedback element. The procedure for constructing feedback using acknowledgement, compliments and after-session activities is presented. The question set for subsequent visits is described. Each element is illustrated by vignettes of dialogue taken from an actual case. Applications in specific settings such as family practice, couples and families, teenagers and schools are discussed.

3 Case study: This chapter contains a full length transcript of the first interview with a couple. The wife is doing little in the home, and the husband is staying out and drinking more alcohol. They have come to seek assistance in restoring their joint satisfaction with their marriage and their life in general. This demonstrates the main features of the approach in a clinical setting. The transcript is annotated throughout with discussion of options. This material exemplifies the method described in Chapters 1 and 2.

4 Ethical issues in therapy addresses some of the common ethical issues in the practice of counselling and psychotherapy. Some of these are general, applying to therapists everywhere, and some are specific to the UK. Reference is made to the ethical code of the United Kingdom Association of Solution Focused Practice (UKASFP) and to the Health Professions Council. Other issues have been specifically raised in relation to certain therapies. Ethical issues specific to solution-focused brief therapy are then discussed.

5 The historical roots of solution-focused brief therapy. Solution-focused brief therapy is often described as a postmodern therapy that employs very different assumptions from other past and present approaches. However, there are numerous elements within solution-focused brief therapy that owe their origin to previous schools and techniques of therapy. This is of importance for practice, teaching and for future developments. This chapter places solution-focused ideas in the context of their historical development and describes their relationship to other current approaches. The development of psychodynamic theories of mind and behaviour is summarised with reference to their influence on many current schools of psychotherapy. The contributions of behavioural and systemic ideas are examined. An attempt is made to identify some of the elements that have been retained both by solution-focused and other postmodern therapies. The chapter ends with some conclusions about the position of solution-focused brief therapy in relation to other psychotherapies.

6 The research and evidence base for solution-focused therapy provides a summary of the large body of published research in numerous languages. Discussion of the existing process research is followed by a review of examples from the currently published outcome literature. The material is set in the context of current research findings about psychotherapy in general. Some of the limitations of current knowledge are considered. Unlike other therapies, solution-focused therapy has been shown to be equally effective for all social classes and with client groups usually considered unsuitable for psychotherapy.

7 Applying solution-focused brief therapy within mental health services: Since solution-focused ideas were first introduced there has been considerable experience in their application within the mental health field. This chapter draws on the literature and the author's personal experience. Although diagnosis is not directly relevant to solution-focused brief therapy, common categories are examined together for ease of reference. Anxiety, compulsive phenomena, substance misuse, eating disorders, personality disorders and other common issues are discussed. Self-harm, suicide, domestic violence, sexual abuse and child protection issues are included.

8 Solution-focused approaches to severe mental illness: Severe mental illness includes bipolar disorder and psychotic illnesses such as schizophrenia. Solution-focused brief therapy can be combined with other therapeutic approaches, including medication and other types of therapy. It can be applied in ways that improve collaboration with clients and compliance with treatment with both inpatients and outpatients. Specialist applications for this purpose are described from the author's experience and from work by international practitioners. Aspects relating to hospital admission and the application of solution-focused ideas in long-term mental illness, in rehabilitation and within secure units are described. A case transcript based on a patient detained under the Mental Health Act is included.

9 Solution-focused approaches in the workplace begins with the new topic of research into the effectiveness of solution-focused approaches within the workplace. It goes on to describe techniques for managers to use in crisis management. Approaches to resolving conflict within teams and organisations and ways to deliver constructive criticism in appraisal and elsewhere are described. Supervision and solution-focused reflecting teams are presented as tools for enhancing the use of solution-focused ideas within teams. Novel approaches are offered to deal with situations in which more powerful vested interests are putting employees or clients under pressure. 'Microtools' represent new thinking about how to apply brief question sets in combination with solution-focused language and attitudes, and some examples are given. A few ideas on how to deal with large organisations are included for completeness.

10 Common questions about solution-focused approaches: Certain objections and challenges to the solution-focused model are commonly raised during trainings. The place of emotions in this therapy model and its significant effectiveness across cultures are discussed. There are times when solution-focused tools are not a first choice, for example in investigating possible abuse. There may be times when the client can do better with another approach. Notwithstanding the importance of common factors, there are many variations in theory between therapies. Theory is not an essential factor in all therapies, and aspects of this are discussed.

11 Future directions in solution-focused therapy are given. Training and accreditation are reviewed with comment on the current official response to solution-focused approaches and to therapy regulation in the UK. The situation about training and accreditation is widely different in different areas of the world. Research presently in progress in Europe and elsewhere is described. The contribution of the European Brief Therapy Association in providing research grants and disseminating research findings is recorded. Some possible future directions for research are proposed.

Appendices

Appendix I: A list of website links and addresses.

Appendix II: Habitual or intermittent hyperventilation is a cause of symptoms resembling anxiety and a common accompaniment of true free-floating anxiety. Once recognised, its treatment requires a minimum of therapeutic intervention. Although solution-focused methods can be used for this problem, simpler approaches are often sufficient. This Appendix includes a paper summarising this condition and an instruction leaflet for its management.

The Solution-Focused Therapy Model: the First Session; Part 1

Contents

This chapter describes and explains the logic of the first session in solution-focused brief therapy, following the above sequence for reasons that will be analysed in the text. Chapter 2 pursues the break and subsequent sessions, followed by discussion of a number of specialist aspects of solution-focused work.

> All that is necessary is that the person involved in a troublesome situation does something different. (de Shazer, 1985, p. 7)

For Steve de Shazer, the essence of psychotherapy was that the client is helped to make a change in their situation. Following on his Mental Research Institute training, he realised that any change is likely to be beneficial. The only thing one can be sure of changing is oneself. The first interview in solution-focused therapy is the most important. For many clients this is when the majority of the work is done. Unlike other psychotherapies, the treatment process begins at once. No detailed history is taken.

To join with the client, talking about the problem describes issues prior to the first session, with attention to changes made prior to therapy. Then the focus moves to the here and now, examining goals and exceptions to the problem. The issues are defined using questions about scales from 0–10. The 'miracle question' encourages creative thinking and explores possible futures as a means towards developing plans. Structured feedback from the therapist looks at strengths and next steps towards the future, concluding the session. Second and subsequent visits follow a simpler pattern, looking at what has improved since the previous session, further use of scales and discussion of the next steps. The progression from past to future appears to be a useful sequence. This chapter and the next describe the interview process in detail, with examples.

The order presented has been chosen through clinical experience and through teaching accredited courses at St Martin's College since 1997. After learning the method, practitioners develop their own pattern of use and their own modifications and additions. However, like learning to play a musical instrument, it is necessary to start with basic skills before beginning to improvise. At the same time, the flow of the interview is important. If someone mentions a miracle or a scale or a percentage, then the therapist may choose to move at once to that topic rather than follow the usual sequence. The response to questions about goals or scales may be so detailed and positive that the miracle question is not needed. However, in my experience, asking the miracle question will almost always bring out additional aspects of their best hopes for the future.

Assumptions Affecting the Context of Solution-Focused Therapy

The central assumption is that the goals for therapy will be chosen by the client and that the clients themselves have resources which they will use in making changes. Therapists promote descriptions in specific, small, positive steps and in interactional terms. Descriptions favour the presence of solutions rather than the absence of problems; the start of something new rather than stopping something that is happening already. Therapists adopt a respectful, non-blaming and cooperative stance, working towards their clients' goals from within their clients' frame of reference.

A detailed history is not essential for solution-focused brief therapy. However, if a story has never been told before, then it may need to be heard before continuing. Safety assessment may require this in any event, if material is being disclosed that has implications for the safety of the client or others. 'Problem talk' and speculation about 'motives' or 'purposes' of symptoms are avoided.

It is preferable that any prior assumptions about hidden motives and unconscious mechanisms on the part of the therapist do not interfere with attention to the content of the client's discourse. In de Shazer's words (1994), the interview is 'text-focused'; that is, the information comes from the material offered by the client and it is their understanding and language employed. The alternative, applied in traditional therapies, is a 'reader focus', in which the reader/therapist has special knowledge and only needs enough from the client to make a fit with the preconceived ideas and plans of the therapist. This concept of therapy as text-focused links well with Wittgenstein's (1965) view of language as the essential tool for thought. The client has the text, and ideas in the mind of the therapist should not intrude on this material. The lack of technical language in solution-focused brief therapy is both a consequence of this view of therapy and an asset in communicating with clients.

Steve de Shazer carried this idea further to look at the effect of literally using some of the client's words or turns of phrase in every response that is made. This is an amazingly effective technique for building relationships with clients quickly. It is equally useful in other conversations with clients. This skill is conveniently referred to as 'language matching' and represents a way of staying connected to the client and their experience of their situation. Language matching ensures that the therapist is not only paying attention to the client's every word but that this is clearly recognised by the client. Ideally, the therapist will use words from their last response in each comment or question. If the response is monosyllabic or 'Don't know', then a word from an earlier reply can be used. The skill for the therapist lies in being able to ask the necessary questions while using something from their response to do this.

Psychodynamic therapists say that if an emotion is named in a session, then that emotion will soon appear, often accompanied by memories and experiences connected to it. This is comparable to the Stanislavsky method used by actors in portraying emotions. Therefore, it is unwise to introduce topics or emotions into the session unless the client has done so first. Dr Plamen Panayotov from Bulgaria has suggested that the sequence is thinking, then sharing, discussing and acting. So in our team we always ask 'What do you think about that?', not 'What do you feel about that?', because an answer about feeling will be less precise, less behavioural and less open to change by direct means. Feelings can be modified by hypnosis, eye movement desensitisation and reprocessing (EMDR) and by medications (including street drugs). All of these methods require some dependence on the therapist or on the suppliers of medication. Otherwise changes to feelings occur via cognitive or behavioural events.

A number of physiological and psychological studies have shown the influence of words on our functioning and behaviour. Hausdorff et al.

(1999) have shown that elderly people exposed to positive comments about aging showed fewer disturbances of gait thereafter than those exposed to negative comments. Bargh et al. (1996) showed that talking to older people about difficulties of later life reduced gait speed in the experimental group. In a detailed study, Rosenkranz et al. (2005) showed that when asthmatics heard asthma-related words such as 'wheeze', then their brain and lung functions changed towards patterns associated with illness. Van Baaren et al. (2003) found that a waitress who repeats the customer's order receives larger tips than one who does not. Seligman (2002) has developed Positive Psychology, whose whole premise is that using positive words and resources leads to more effective personal and emotional functioning.

The Structure of the First Session

When arranging the session it can be useful to tell your clients that family or friends can come to the appointment if it will be helpful. It is most productive to work with those who want to make changes or who can provide resources. In this, solution-focused therapy differs from family therapy because in most family therapy it is customary to see all family members even if they are disruptive or do not want to make changes.

It is also useful to ask clients to note what changes they make prior to the first session. To do so implies that change is inevitable and that clients will themselves be active in promoting changes.

Introduction

Introduction: Key Questions

Introduce yourself.
What do you like to be called?
What do you want to get out of being here today?

From this point on use the client's words and language whenever possible. The Mental Research Institute workers who constructed strategic therapy (Watzlawick et al., 1974) noticed that using the name given by the client to their problem was much more powerful than applying a professional title to it. Applying a new title usually gives the client the impression that they are being contradicted. It devalues their knowledge of the situation. Expert 'jargon' is best avoided unless it is introduced for a specific purpose.

Language in this sense includes non-verbal behaviour. In everyday speech 55 per cent of the information is relayed in non-verbal cues, such as dress and posture, 38 per cent is vocal, such as tone of voice and volume, and 7 per cent forms the linguistic content (Mehrabian, 1981). Also, language is itself a behaviour, so that a behavioural description may consist of reported conversations. If someone uses language to describe themselves doing something, then that behaviour is more likely to become part of their repertoire. So if someone says 'I could do that' then it becomes more likely that it will be done. This is a common element in all therapies that include talking about change.

Many therapists like to paraphrase or recapitulate the client's account, but the client could experience this as a contradiction. Therefore it is important to do this respectfully, making it clear that it is intended as a clarification that you are understanding the client correctly.

Problem

Information gained at this stage will also be useful in conversation about goals and exceptions (below). Having a baseline account of the problem makes it easier to assess progress later. Repetitive accounts of the problem are common, perhaps because people believe that therapy requires this. One of the bases of Freud's free-association technique (1895) was his belief that given enough opportunity to talk about the problem, clients would eventually exhaust their descriptive powers and would have to reveal new material. Having attended to the description of the problem at the start, it is easier to interrupt or redirect the conversation later if the client restarts talking about the problem.

A period of problem-free talk (George et al., 1999) is often a good beginning, especially if clients appear unsure of what they want from the session at the start. A few minutes' talk about something they enjoy or a skill that they possess allows them time to think about what they want. Another option is to collect factual information about what they do, where they live and what family they have at home or nearby. This is usually neutral or problem-free and provides valuable information about their social context and abilities. Similarly, if the session seems to be moving too fast for a client, a brief talk about a skill or pleasure helps to slow the pace appropriately. The questions below about exceptions often produce topics that can be developed in this way.

If more than one person is present, it is important to ask them whether they agree with the description of the problem and of any changes that have occurred. This will generate useful information and helps to encourage others in contributing to solutions.

Problem: Key Questions

How often does … happen? (days/parts of days)
How long has it been going on?
Has it ever happened before?
How did you deal with it then?

It is important to get a practical description in behavioural terms:

What is said/done?
Who says it/does it?
Who notices?
What happens next? And then what?
What else?

If the description is unclear you may ask 'If you made a video of … happening what would I see on the tape?' or 'If I was a fly on the wall what would I see happening?'

Therapist:	What do you want to get out of being here today?
Client:	Don't know. I suppose I just want you to help me stop all this drinking.
Therapist:	How many days in the week does the drinking occur?
Client:	Every day.
Therapist:	Do you drink the same every day?
Client:	Yes; four or five pints of lager both at lunchtime and teatime as well as wine in the evening plus spirits at weekends.
Therapist:	Lager and wine … What happens when you drink that much?
Client:	I go on drinking until I pass out.
Therapist:	When did you start drinking until you pass out?
Client:	I'd say it's been this heavy for about two years.
Therapist:	Two years … Who else notices that you are drinking so heavily?
Client:	My mum … I hit her last week when she told me off about drinking.
Therapist:	Who else notices as well as your mum?
Client:	Other family told me to get myself sorted out after I had hit my mum.

Clients sometimes say that there are many problems or that they do not know where to start. However, in the context of brief therapy, it is important to work with only one problem at a time. If the focus shifts back and forth between different problems it can be difficult for the client and therapist to make progress. The following example shows how this sort of response from the client can be handled:

Therapist:	Mostly we can only work with one problem at a time. Which is the biggest issue for you at present?
Client:	The drinking worries me most but it comes from the depression.
Therapist:	We can move on to other problems if necessary, after the drinking.

In practice it is rare to need to take up a second problem. Solving one large problem releases enough energy for clients to deal with the other issues themselves. This does not exclude the situation in which clients 'try you out' with a minor problem and then reveal a more major concern later. In that case it is necessary to clarify with them which is the problem that they want to work on first.

In solution-focused work Steve de Shazer said on many occasions that the word 'Why' should be avoided. 'Why' leads to speculative and general answers that do not usually clarify goals or behaviour. If more details are needed as to the process that leads to an outcome, which is usually what we mean when we ask 'Why', then 'How come ...?' is a good alternative, since it is more likely to lead to a behavioural description.

If you hear the word 'should' from a client, listen carefully. In English 'should' has two meanings. The concrete meaning is shown in statements such as 'The Finance Department should send your pay cheque.' This states that it is the correct responsibility of the Finance Department to carry out this action. The other, less concrete, meaning of 'should' is 'This action ought to be carried out'. This usually refers to an emotional action, which cannot or will not be controlled by the client. This meaning comes into play in 'I should forgive him ...' or 'I should stop worrying'. This may stand for 'I have been told that I should ...'. Thus it can be useful to ask 'Who says that you should ...?' Often this refers to one specific influential person in their past or present life. This person's opinion may be inappropriate or unhelpful in the present situation. Similarly, if there are remarks such as 'People think ...' or 'Everybody knows ...' it is useful to ask 'Who in your life says this/thinks this/knows this?' Again, it is usually one influential person. Sometimes engaging that person in the therapy can be helpful, or asking what this person will think about the miracle and other changes later in the session.

Rarely someone will present with a story of a problem that has never been told before. If this does occur, the issue is often sexual abuse in childhood or some other major family secret. In such a case it may be necessary to listen to the story before moving on to solution-focused work. Chapter 8 includes discussion of ways to manage these issues.

However, disclosure often is not needed for therapy to progress; it depends on the goals of the client. It can sometimes be useful to ask 'Suppose you pretend that you have told me already; how will things be different for you?' If a client insists on repeating a lengthy story, it can keep the narrative moving to say 'What happened next?' at every pause. This shows that the therapist is taking a constant interest, reduces talk about extraneous details and keeps the narrative moving forward.

Pre-Session Changes

Addressing a problem does not begin with seeing a therapist. Most people have tried other ideas first. Coming to see a clinician is usually a result of attempts to solve the problem, not the first step taken in problem solving. In Salamanca, Beyebach et al. (1996) have found that those clients who see themselves as able to influence events have often made pre-session changes and that this predicts a good outcome for their therapy (see Chapter 6).

Pre-Session Changes: Key Questions

Have there been changes for better or worse since you decided to take action? Who else noticed this?

Some clients will criticise previous treatments or therapists when asked about pre-session changes. This lets the therapist know what suggestions are likely to be refused when the time comes for feedback. If another clinician is criticised, a useful response is to say 'I have always heard people speak well of X until now.' This demonstrates respect for their opinion but signals that the therapist will not be drawn into any scapegoating or collusion.

Therapist: What changes have happened since you decided to stop drinking?
Client: I've actually cut down a bit already so I have managed to get four college assignments in, which was a relief.
Therapist: What else has happened as well as finishing your assignments?
Client: I'm also taking driving lessons and spending more time with some friends who don't drink, or at least who do not drink much. They are good friends for me!

Goals

Seek specific practical descriptions of goals. Check for reality, for example 'Will you *really* never argue again?' If the therapy is failing to make progress or if a client's actions do not seem to make sense, it is important to confirm what the goals are, or to ask: 'Your goal when you came here was to ...; How does this help you towards that?' For Mental Health Institute strategic therapists, a client with vague or poorly formed goals required careful thought because the interview method required specific information. With solution-focused work, a specific goal is less important because 'What will be different?', 'What will you be doing instead?' can often be clearly described even if the goal itself cannot be defined. The goals often relate to the problem and therefore may not be essential to the solution.

All the questions are framed using the future tense 'What will you be doing when ...?' and not the future conditional 'What would you be doing when …?' It is helpful to maintain this use of tenses throughout the interview whenever possible. It creates a constant assumption in the therapist and the client that something is definitely going to happen, not merely that a possibility exists that it might happen. This draws on the Ericksonian concept of pseudo-orientation in time, in which stories of a successful future are collaboratively constructed (de Shazer, 1988). The conversation makes this successful future easier to recognise and to achieve.

The question 'What else?' is invaluable. It implies that you are following the story closely and that you know that there is more to come. It is surprising how often clients will react to this simple query by producing more information and ideas. To avoid being repetitive, you can extend the question by adding it to their last response: 'As well as X, what else is happening then?'; 'As well as X, what else helps?' Linguistically, 'What else?' implies a continuous dialogue, so it helps to maintain the relationship with the client even if the therapist is not yet clear about the situation. The same phrase can be useful in dealing with distressed clients where little information has been forthcoming. Once new information stops or if time is precious, to ask 'Anything else?' will imply that this element of the discussion is coming to an end.

Another useful word is 'instead'. Any statement containing a negative can be reversed easily to 'So what will you be doing instead of X?' This one change can make an enormous difference to the information offered and to the atmosphere of the session.

Goals: Key Questions

What will it be like when the problem is solved?
What will you be doing instead?
When that happens, what difference will it make?
How will other people know that things are better?
Who will notice first? And then who?
What else will be different?
What else?
What else?

It is important to ask what they will be doing, not what will have stopped.

Therapist: So when things are better will you be doing these things?
Client: Yes, and I won't be drinking so much.
Therapist: So you will be drinking less?
Client: Yes.
Therapist: What else will be better when you are drinking less?

Client:	I will be spending more time doing things with my old friends from school and getting my work in on time for college. I won't feel so tired and fed up.
Therapist:	How will you feel instead of being tired and fed up?
Client:	Ready to take on anything!

To retain the focus on solutions it is important to break into or interrupt the client's 'problem talk'. Although this may feel uncomfortable at first, it is possible to show the client that you are still connected with their concerns by using language matching and talking about what they want to achieve in therapy.

| *Client:* | Talking about goals is no use while drinking is the problem. I've been drinking for years and I've … |
| *Therapist:* | You have told me about the years of drinking just now. This has been a problem for a long time and I want to understand it properly. It will help me to understand if I know what you want to achieve. |

Many responses in conversation can be summarised as 'yes', 'no' or 'maybe'. As soon as it is clear which one it is, the next question can be asked. As long as this is done respectfully and with language matching, it appears to be acceptable to clients. This can save time in sessions, as can not asking clients to dwell on painful topics unnecessarily.

Exceptions

Asking about exceptions is particularly useful with goals that are normally viewed as resistant to change, such as alcohol and drug misuse or domestic violence. Clients may be feeling quite hopeless about their ability to change or control their situation. They are surprised to find that there are small exceptions where they clearly control or delay behaviours. This improves their sense of self-mastery and their ability to plan further small steps.

Exceptions: Key Questions

What about times when the problem is not happening?
Or when it is less?
You mentioned earlier that some days/times are better. What is it like at these times?
What are you doing instead at these times?
What else is better at these times?

Who notices first when things are better for you?
And then who?
What do they notice at these times?
What else?

Again, as with goals, it is important to get descriptions of what they are doing, not of what they are not doing.

Therapist: Tell me about the other times when things are going better?
Client: I'm getting on better at home with everyone, especially Mum. I am enjoying college more and feeling a bit healthier in general.
Therapist: What else is different at college?
Client: I spend more time talking to people that I know when I don't have hangovers.
Therapist: Who else notices when you have no hangovers and are talking?
Client: My friends notice, and my family when I go home.

The following questions come from systemic family therapy rather than solution-focused therapy. However, the responses are often useful.

*   Who is the boss in your family?
*   How are decisions made?
*   Who makes which decisions?

Power issues are a reality of human affairs and these questions highlight them at the relevant level. Asking the questions causes these issues to be thought about, sometimes for the first time. The replies may not be verbal. For example, if everyone looks at the mother before saying 'There is no specific boss', then it is likely that the mother is the key decision-maker. For most families the important thing is that someone makes decisions that the rest can follow. A complete lack of effective decision making is usually not comfortable for any family or any group of people. If the boss in the family wants change to occur, it is much more likely to happen. If the boss of the family is alcoholic or an adolescent behaving in undesired ways, then it may be useful for others to recognise this. In one case, devoted new parents allowed their toddler to decide when it was teatime and bedtime, with the result that they might still be awake at midnight or not eat in the evenings. Once they recognised that this was a source of difficulty they decided to restrict him to being in charge of a more limited range of activities, with beneficial results for all concerned.

Scaling

Scaling questions are one of the great assets of the solution-focused therapist. They help the client to move from all-or-nothing goals towards less daunting steps. The scale has no reality outside the negotiation with the therapist but is an instantly usable means of tracking progress. Scales also increase clarity of communication with other professionals who may be involved with the client.

Scaling can also be used in other ways. For example, 'How confident are you of reaching the number you have chosen as a goal?' People who have come to therapy only as a last resort may be able to identify goals but initially have no confidence that they can reach them. In relationship problems it is useful to ask 'On a scale of 0–10, how confident are you that you will be together in two years' time?' Clients often learn from their own replies, whether the partner is present or not. If both are present, then the same question can be effective. If one says '2' and the other says '10', then they have learned something about how they are communicating with each other. It is not always necessary for the therapist to comment on this directly.

Scaling: Key Questions

Please think of a scale from 0–10 with 10 being the best. Nought is how you felt when things were at their worst. Ten is as good as things can be in relation to this problem.

Where are you now on that scale right now? [*pause*] Give it a number, for example 2 or 3.
If not precise, 'nearer 2 or nearer 3'?
How long will it take to get to 10? [*prompt if necessary to get a time – 5 years? More? Less?*]
Maybe 10 is too big a goal?
Is something lower more realistic?
What number will be acceptable for you?
How will you recognise when you are one point further up the scale?
What else will be different when you are one point further up?
Who will notice?
How long will it take to get one point up the scale?

Clients sometimes need some prompts to answer 'How long ...?' If you offer 'Maybe a year? Or longer?' they will often respond that they expect change to be sooner. You can then propose a shorter time. Clients' estimates of the time required are often wrong but the process demonstrates to clients that they have more predictions about the situation than they knew. It also shows the therapist what pace they like to use for making changes. If someone wants instant results, then in the feedback it can be suggested that this may be unlikely if the problem has been developing over a long time. If a person expects change to be very slow, then a longer gap between sessions may be appropriate. It is a good rule that the therapist should not be working harder than the client, or trying to go faster than the client can accept. The phrase 'solution forced' has been used to describe this phenomenon (Nylund and Corsiglia, 1994). Use 'will' not 'would' in questions whenever possible, as this increases the predictive effect of planning the future.

Therapist:	Where is the problem today on a scale where 0 equals the worst and 10 equals the best that you hope for?
Client:	I'd say maybe 4 or 5.
Therapist:	Nearer to 4 or nearer to 5?
Client:	5.
Therapist:	What will need to happen or change for you to go up half a point on the scale?
Client:	Sort things out with my bad drinking 'friends'.
Therapist:	How will you sort things out with them?
Client:	I'll tell them that I need to concentrate more on my college work.
Therapist:	As well as you concentrating, how will other people recognise when you are one point up on the scale?
Client:	They will see me happier, more in control of everything and that I'm noticeably drinking less. I'll be less short-tempered and rude to people, especially mum. I will just be nicer in general to be around!

Ask others present if they agree with the answers given. It can be useful to ask them if the client's number on the scale was what they expected.

It is sometimes suggested that solution-focused brief therapy ignores feelings. However, in practice it is very common for the first response to 'How will you recognise when you are one point further up the scale?' to take the form 'I will feel ...' Acknowledging this feeling, it can then be expanded into the behaviours that go with this feeling and the reactions of others to these changes: 'When you feel ..., what else will be different?'

'On a scale of 0–10, how committed are you to achieving what you want?' Answers to this question are often helpful in identifying strengths and resources, especially if clients are feeling pessimistic.

Therapist:	You say you are at 5 on the scale today. If we think about a different scale from 0–10, how committed are you to controlling your drinking? Give it a number?
Client:	How committed ... you mean how determined am I to sort it? I guess 8 or 9 out of 10; I don't want to be in this trouble in a few months' time.
Therapist:	What will help you to be out of trouble, since you are 8 out of 10 determined to sort it?
Client:	I have fixed things in my life before, and my mum and friends will help.

Steve de Shazer (2005) points out that goals are associated with the problem, while scaling and the miracle question are future-oriented and associated with solutions.

The Miracle Question

The miracle question is a common tool used by solution-focused therapists. Clients appear to experience pleasant emotions during their replies, which enhances their experience of therapy and is in itself another exception to their previous state. Creative thinking is stimulated. It is common for clients to start haltingly but suddenly come up with some completely new goal or ambition.

Miracle Question

I'm going to ask you a kind of strange question now.

Suppose [*pause*]
you go to bed and to sleep tonight as usual [*pause*]
and while you are asleep a miracle happens [*pause*]
and the problem that brought you here today [*look round all present*] is solved [*pause*].
But you are asleep and don't know that it has been solved [*pause*].
What will be the first small signs that this miracle has happened and that the problem is solved?

The work of Bandler and Grinder, the founders of Neuro-Linguistic Programming (1979), emphasises eye movements as an indicator of internal processes. Specifically, they state that for the majority of people with normal neurological organisation, envisaging new material involves a fleeting movement of the eyes upwards and to the right or that their eyes will unfocus briefly. It is a common experience when watching clients respond to the miracle question that this will happen. Either of these events are promising signs, suggesting that some useful response to the miracle question will be forthcoming. This applies even though Bandler and Grinder say that 50 per cent of persons are visually oriented, 30 per cent favour auditory information and 20 per cent favour kinaesthetic/somatic information. Nevertheless, such an eye movement is common to the majority of clients, not just 50 per cent. It may be that the miracle is a visual experience initially.

Common first responses are a silence or an 'I don't know'. This appears to be about a delay for thought as it is often followed by more detailed replies. Harry Korman, of Sweden, has identified from studying videos of therapist behaviour that it is important for the therapist not to move or speak for a short period during this first response. He suggests that if you move or make a sound, this implies that it is now your turn to speak, which will stop comment from the client. Steve de Shazer endorsed this finding; he suggested that a pause of six to ten beats is long enough. Bryson (1990) quotes linguistic studies which show that for the English language, four seconds is the longest silence that can be tolerated in normal conversation. If there is still no comment then the questions below can be used to prompt for information.

• Will you know at once that the miracle has happened? How will you know?
• What will happen next?
• Who else will notice?
• How will they tell?
• And who next?
• What happens next?

If necessary this can be expanded by enquiry about changes to breakfast, clothes, work and interests. Previously described goals and exceptions will provide ideas for this. Others present can be asked to comment about what the miracle will be like.

Small children may prefer 'If you could wave a magic wand' or 'Suppose magic happens and ...'.

Some followers of Islam may consider it presumptuous for humans to talk of miracles, which they believe to be the province of God. Some traditions of Buddhism will reject the miracle formula because the Buddha forbade miracles to his followers. Interestingly, he did so on the grounds that miracles were frequent and ought not to be used as a means of convincing people about any particular religious truth.

If the 'miracle' formula is not acceptable you can use 'When you meet us in five years and the problem is solved, what will you tell us is happening?', or 'When you send us a video of what you are doing in five years' time, what will we see on the video?', or Erickson's technique (de Shazer, 1985): 'If we could look into a crystal ball and see the future, what will we see?'

Therapist: I'd like to ask you a strange question: suppose you go to bed tonight as usual, and while you are asleep a miracle happens, and the problem that brought you here today is solved. But you are asleep and do not know that the miracle has happened; what will be the first small signs when you wake up in the morning that the miracle has happened and that the problem is solved?

> *Client:*   I don't know. No hangover? And … I'd feel happier. I would not drink in the afternoon.
> *Therapist*   Who will notice that this miracle has happened?
> *Client:*   Everyone! Especially mum!
> *Therapist*   How will you know that mum has noticed?
> *Client:*   She will tell me and she will smile at me instead of nagging.

Ferdinand Wolf and his colleagues in Vienna examined the use of 'will' as against 'would' in the responses to the miracle question. They found that the use of either tense by clients did not predict overall outcome or the likelihood that specific elements of the miracle would be achieved. They did not examine the use of these tenses by the therapist. They found that any response linked to the miracle question did predict a good outcome (de Shazer, 2005).

With some clients who have experienced a recent loss or bereavement, their miracle will be a restoration of the loss, such as 'My girlfriend will come back', 'My gran will not be dead'. This is evidence that they are still in the 'numbness' stage of bereavement and have not yet accepted their loss. Asking the miracle question is a quick way to determine if this is their situation. They will not be able to develop new visions of the future until they accept the loss, so further miracle details are unlikely to be useful at this stage. Possible responses are: 'Is there any chance that you will get together with your girlfriend again?' or 'It would be good if your grandmother could come back to life but I guess that this is not very likely to happen?' The focus then is on crisis intervention questions as below. Other useful questions can be found in the discussion of self-harm in Chapter 2.

Surviving the Present: Key Questions

How will you get through the rest of today?
How have you kept going so far?
What else helps?
Is there anyone else who shares this with you?
What were the happiest times with X?
Can you do any of the same things without X?
What can you do to keep their memory alive?
What would X want for you now?
What is happening now that you want to go on happening?

Sharry's (2002) scale from 1–10 can be useful: 'How confident are you that you can get through the day/the weekend? What would increase that by one point?' He also uses the interview to take stock of the effect of the event itself: 'Has this event made you stronger or weaker? Are there things that you are thinking now that had not occurred to you before? Is it possible that some good might come of this? If you look back in six months and see that this turned out for the best, what will you be doing then?'

The concept of 'resistance', found in many schools of therapy, assumes that if therapy is not making progress, then clients are failing to cooperate for conscious or unconscious reasons of their own. This largely absolves the therapist of responsibility and implicitly or explicitly blames the client. In an early paper on 'The death of resistance', Steve de Shazer (1984) criticised this position. He maintained that there is no such thing as resistance, only the client's unique way of cooperating. It is part of the therapist's task to seek ways to engage with the client successfully. If the client did not do a task, then the fault is with the task and its timing or presentation, not with the client. The Mental Research Institute also held this view of resistance versus cooperation.

Walter and Peller (1992) make the point that 'The meaning of the message is the response you receive (p. 26). In solution-focused work the question may appear clear to the therapist, but the interactional/socially constructed meaning is only apparent when the response comes from the client. This is contrary to the idea that it is the client's 'fault' for misinterpreting or resisting the meaning of a question. It is the task of the therapist to take the responsibility for clear communication. Equally, it is the task of the therapist to recognise and use the response that is given. If the response is unexpected, then it provides clues about the therapist's clarity in regard to this particular client and about the issues that are important to this particular client.

In the same vein it is important not to work harder than the client. The flow of the interview is important. Being 'solution-forced', jumping in with compliments prematurely or demanding answers to the standard questions, is not appropriate. This process is analysed by Nylund and Corsiglia (1994). They see it as a novice error, often linked to excessive enthusiasm and to heavy caseloads. They emphasise the importance of pace and timing in solution-focused interviews. In recent years Steve de Shazer (2005) said that if he had to lose one solution-focused question, he would rather lose the miracle question and keep the scaling questions. He suggested that it is easy to maintain the flow of the interview using scaling questions.

Conclusion

This completes the initial part of a first interview. The client has described the problem, identified goals and exceptions to the problem and used scaling questions as a means to measure change and to identify small steps forward. The miracle question has enlarged on this process and may have generated new possibilities. At this point many therapists will take a break for reflection, and this option will be explored in the next chapter.

Key Points

- Language matching is a major strength of solution-focused therapy.
- The sequence of questions may vary once the therapist feels confident about this.
- Maintaining the flow of the interview is important.
- Concrete and behavioural descriptions of events clarify the situation and make it appear more manageable.
- Talking about the problem is a means of joining with the client.
- Pre-session changes are important building blocks for progress.
- Goals are central to monitoring progress.
- Exceptions are common but often go unnoticed.
- Scales can be used in many different ways.
- The miracle question encourages creative thinking and some surprising changes follow its use.

The Solution-Focused Therapy Model: Part 2

Contents

In Chapter 1 the initial structure for the first interview was described. Chapter 2 completes the first session and deals with a number of specific settings for therapy. The points made about attention to language and the micro-skills of interviewing continue to apply in this later part of the session and in all solution-focused work.

The interview process itself encourages reflection and new thinking about the problem and about possible solutions. The information gained in the first part of the session is now used to generate an appropriate feedback message for the client(s). Compliments are the key part of this element as they help to build self-esteem and hope. Return visits follow a simple structure, which has many applications. These tools are useful in family practice and in work with teenagers. Work with more than one client and with institutions have specific aspects that can be added to the basic solution-focused script.

Breaks and their Purpose

The founders of brief therapy and many of those therapists who come from a family therapy tradition believe that it is useful to take a break in order to compose the feedback. It is a common experience that appropriate responses occur to us just after we have left a situation. The French philosopher Diderot (2001[1830]) describes this as 'L'esprit de l'escalier': the clever riposte that you think of only after you have left the room and are on the stairs going out. It is in the nature of human interaction that we are affected by one another's emotions and this is one of the pleasures of human existence. However, when clients are anxious and unable to reflect, we will be affected by this if we are in close contact with them. Leaving the room and/or entering another conversation with colleagues or supervisors allows us the cognitive space to think more clearly about their situation and about what comments will be the most useful. In traditional therapy this thinking takes place between sessions or in supervision. A break gives the clients the advantage of this process of reflection within the same session. Reflections delayed until their next visit are likely to be less relevant as events will have moved on for all concerned.

In our team, we see that more effective responses are composed if a break is taken. This appears to be a consequence of the team's joint reflections on the session and of the chance for the therapist to distance themselves briefly from the emotional atmosphere of the session. Some therapists ask clients on their return if they have remembered anything important during the break. This is best avoided because it restarts the exploratory dialogue instead of punctuating the end of the session. If conducting a session in someone's home the therapist can ask to go to another room briefly. In the past the tradition for the perplexed British family doctor was to say that he/she had to collect the thermometer from the car, thus giving some moments for calm reflection.

Some therapists regard a break as unnecessary and as causing an interruption in the therapeutic dialogue. If I am in a situation where a break is impractical because of time or the setting in which I am working, I say 'You have told me about a complicated situation. Please let me think for a few minutes before I give you some feedback about it.' Clients appear to see this as respectful of their situation and are content to sit quietly.

Before giving the feedback or before going for a break it is important to ask this closing question:

Therapist: Before we finish, is there anything you want to mention that we have not covered?

As well as punctuating the session, this is a safety question. It gives the client an opportunity to raise any matter at all, which may not be connected with the ostensible reason for attendance. They have had the duration of the session to decide whether the therapist can be trusted enough to reveal matters that they may not have wished to disclose previously. If their response requires further questions, about self-harm or danger to others, then this can be done at once. If the matter is less urgent, then it can be taken to the team and a comment included in the feedback. If a complete change of topic is produced, then it may need to be carried forward to a future session.

If the question is about future lines of treatment this can be viewed either as a genuine enquiry or as an expression of anxiety about what the team is going to say or suggest. Again, it can be taken back to the team and a comment may be included in the feedback.

Feedback

Each session ends with feedback to the clients. A structured format for this is useful to both clients and therapists. Watching many sessions shows that clients are anxious about what feedback they are going to receive. However good the initial relationship, they appear to anticipate criticism. As a rule this anxiety lessens in subsequent sessions.

Feedback: Key Elements

Acknowledge the problem briefly: specifically or in general.

This confirms to the client that the therapist is not ignoring or underestimating the seriousness of the problem.

Compliments

Give at least one compliment by name for each person present.

In some cultures it is acceptable to include some compliments during the earlier part of the session. However, this runs the risk of appearing to be underestimating the seriousness of the problem. In the UK it seems quite acceptable to give compliments only at the feedback stage. It is useful to make a mark in clinical notes during the session to highlight possible compliments for use in the feedback. Sometimes several small positives can be combined, for example talkative, attempted several pre-session changes and holds two jobs, could be combined into 'You are energetic' or 'You are a determined person'. It may be that compliments that identify enduring characteristics rather than single events are more likely to produce change. However, children appear to prefer compliments based on specific elements of behaviour.

The number of compliments is also dictated by local custom. In the USA people seem more accustomed to compliment each other and the compliments can be numerous. In the UK more than three compliments for one person seems to be regarded with suspicion. With couples or families one compliment for each person present may be sufficient, accompanied by an additional compliment about the relationship or family.

Suggest a Task

1　Think or discuss what in your present life you want to keep the same.
2　You have several good ideas already for reaching your goals. We think that you should continue what you are already doing.
3　You have tried many ideas already with limited results. It is time to try something completely new. You will know best yourselves what to try after you have thought about it.
4　Each evening predict where you will be on the scale tomorrow and check next evening if you were right.
5　Pretend on one day each week that the miracle has happened but do not tell anyone which day you have chosen.

According to Steve de Shazer and much psychotherapy research, clients expect therapists to give advice or provide suggestions. Therefore it helps the therapeutic alliance if this is done. Whether the clients take the advice or not does not affect outcome. Task 1 is useful if the situation is not clear or if there has not been time to complete the first session in full. It is safer than advising any change prematurely. It encourages thought about the positives in the present situation, while implying that change will come about soon. Clients will make changes in any event, even if you do not give any specific advice. It is in the nature of the human condition that change is constantly occurring and some changes may be for the better, especially if they are noticed and amplified. Most clients prefer advice to go slowly or not to act too soon (Watzlawick et al., 1974) and Task 1 has this implicit message.

Task 2 is used if there has already been useful pre-session change or if the clients have come up with ideas of their own during the session. It is also useful in later sessions if clients are progressing well.

Task 3 is used when pre-session changes have not been useful, or when clients are clearly highly motivated to have change happen soon. Clients come up with some remarkable and unexpected ideas when given this task.

Task 4 is helpful when clients are pessimistic since predicting a low number and being correct becomes a successful insight instead of a failure.

A good day is a success whether they predicted it or not, so that the overall chance of an exception of some kind is increased.

Task 5 can be useful for couples and families as they have to attend to each other to see if they can tell when the other is pretending that good things are happening. This leaves them looking for positives in each other's behaviour instead of negatives. In solution-focused brief therapy it is common practice to advise people to behave as if something has changed. This is based on the assumption that people can change themselves but not anyone else. Change in one person can have a substantial effect on the family system, and it is surprising how often changes by others will follow.

Sometimes a specific piece of behaviour may emerge from the client as a possible change. Less commonly, the therapist may have a specific idea to try, although it is rare for clients to act on these suggestions. Such a piece of behaviour can be suggested, framed as 'Try just once …' or 'As an experiment …' if attenders are uncertain. In the UK at present it is best to avoid the words 'task', 'test' or 'homework', all of which appear to have negative connotations for the public. It is sometimes appropriate to include normalising information as a part of the intervention, for example whether all toddlers are dry at night or whether most adolescents will be difficult at some stage in their maturation.

> *Therapist:*   [Acknowledging the problem] You have been worrying a lot about your drinking. [Compliments] I am really impressed that you have begun to cut it down. You work really hard and you know what you want out of life. You have lots of good ideas about how to cut down your drinking. You have thought of some practical steps such as not going out with drinking friends, working long hours at the weekend, taking less money when you go out and not mixing drinks while you are out. [Task] You plan to try some of these before next time.

Feedback: General Points

Watch for nods and open postures as signs of engagement with the intervention. Non-verbal responses are a much more reliable guide than verbal comments.

The Mental Research Institute found when developing strategic therapy that the first response to feedback is to make a comment that will disqualify it in some way. This seems more likely to happen if the feedback has successfully raised the possibility of change. In practice it is rare for anyone to return to these comments subsequently, which seems to support the Mental Research Institute hypothesis that it is a spontaneous reaction which is not relevant in the long term. In our experience, therefore, it is best not to allow any discussion of the feedback. If questions are asked, simply repeat a part of the feedback or say that they can revisit the topic at their next visit.

However, it is uncommon in solution-focused work for any comment to be made after the feedback.

Following the feedback, ask if they want to make another appointment and how soon that should be. Clients often want enough time to think about what has been said and to try out changes before they return. Anything other than a definite 'No' should be taken as a cue for making an appointment 'which you can cancel if you do not need it'. People often fail to cancel and simply do not attend. Nevertheless, this is a better course than failing to offer another necessary appointment. It is not useful for clients or therapists if someone must create a crisis simply to obtain another appointment.

It can be useful to send a written copy of the feedback to the clients if several have been unable to attend. Sending a copy to the referring agent can sometimes reinforce skills and compliments that have been identified. Sending such copies routinely has not been found to be helpful.

A discussion about the 'Yes, but ...' construction in the English language took place in 2005 on the solution-focused internet list (SFT-L; see Appendix I). The discussion is accessible in the archive of the SFT-L list. The consensus was that when this construction is used, everything said before 'but' can be disregarded. In other words, 'Yes, but ...' generally means 'No'. As such, 'I don't want to criticise but, but ...' means 'I am criticising ...'. In the experience of myself and other therapist colleagues, this understanding of 'Yes, but ...' is a valid and useful observation. As a therapist, if you find yourself using this construction, you can consider whether you can express your reservations differently and more clearly. For example, instead of saying 'You say that relapse will not happen, but it has happened three times already', it will be clearer to say 'Relapse has already been a problem for you' or 'What will you do if relapse does happen in spite of your hopes?'

Once the therapist is familiar with the model, many variations on the basic sequence of questions can be used. Harry Korman of Sweden is a child psychiatrist with many years of family therapy experience. He asks: 'What will tell you that being here today has been useful?' As soon as a symptom is mentioned he asks the miracle question in relation to that symptom. Then he explores exceptions and scales within the responses to the miracle question. He favours very small tasks or attempting something new only once before the next session.

BRIEF in London have been in solution-focused brief therapy practice for many years. Currently, their model is 'What are your best hopes for being here today?', followed by the miracle question and then enquiry about signs of the miracle that have happened already. The feedback includes advice on looking for further small signs of the miracle. They point out that the responses to best hopes, goal-setting or scaling may be so detailed that it is unnecessary to ask the miracle question specifically. However, in my experience, the miracle question has almost always brought out new or additional information or changed the client's mood in a useful way.

Subsequent Sessions

Return visits are commonly shorter than first sessions for individual clients. Couples and families usually require more time than individuals as there are two or more accounts of events.

It is important to give the client credit for all positive events. Similarly, it is helpful to speak as if negative events are external and not the fault of the client. For example, if a client reports having assaulted someone, 'How come that happened?' or 'How did that come about?' will uncover information, whereas direct criticism of their actions is less likely to do so.

It is best not to ask about the experiment recommended at the end of the previous session. They may report on it spontaneously, in which case it can be built on or repeated in the feedback if it was helpful. It is important to give the credit to the client and not to the therapist. If they did it and it failed, the therapist can apologise for choosing the wrong idea or the wrong moment for suggesting it. If they did not do it, asking about it will not improve cooperation; the issue is whether things are better, not what happened with the task. As much information will come from what they did instead. Accepting non-performance helps to build a cooperative relationship. It may be that tasks are not useful to this specific client (de Shazer, 1985).

Subsequent Sessions: Key Questions

What has been better for you since you were last here?

What else?

What else?

(If positive events have happened) How did you do that?

(If negative events have happened) How did that come about? How did you cope with that?

Where are you on your scale from 0–10 today?

What is the next step for you?

What comes next to be up one point on the scale?

(Get a practical description)

Feedback: acknowledge problem/compliments/task.

How soon should the next appointment be?

Are you better enough now to cope without coming here to see us?

Berg and Reuss (1995) suggest a structure for return visits for which the mnemonic is EARS: Elicit; Amplify; Reinforce; Start again.

EARS Questions

Elicit:

What's better?
What exceptions have there been?

Amplify:

More details of what is better and what exceptions there have been.

Reinforce:

Compliments and non-verbal encouragement by the therapist aimed at these improvements and exceptions.

Start again:

Repeat the process until no more improvements and exceptions are forthcoming. Then move on to scaling and next steps.

Berg and Reuss (1995) suggest that where setbacks are reported, these have usually occurred shortly before the session, after a period of relative success. Respectful enquiry after hearing about the setback can establish this and the EARS process can continue.

Therapist: Good morning! So what has been better for you since we last met?
Client: Hi. Things were going well but I had a really bad day yesterday. I really wanted to have a drink.
Therapist: What sort of bad day was it?
Client: I had a bad mark for an assignment and my mum was not pleased.
Therapist: How did you deal with that; your marks and your mum saying?
Client: I remembered that my last assignment was all right because I had not been drinking when I wrote it. I texted to my friend and she was nice about it. We agreed to go for a walk in the park before deciding what to do next.
Therapist: Was that one of the good friends that doesn't drink so much?
Client: Yes; she's an old friend; we used to walk to school together.
Therapist: Did the walk yesterday help?
Client: Yes; I managed not to drink in the evening.
Therapist: And you said you had not been drinking sometimes, like when you did the last assignment?

Client:	Yes; I have had some days without any drink or with none until the evening; and then only a few.
Therapist:	How did you manage to have days with no drink?
Client:	Just willpower, I guess.
Therapist:	What else has been better, as well as willpower?
Client:	If I do have too much to drink I pay attention when my mum tells me, and I stay in my room instead of going out in a huff.

It is unusual to remind clients where they placed themselves on the scale at their last visit, unless they ask specifically. The scale is an internal measure and so the numbers in themselves are not significant. What matters is the current score and the next step. If their score is the same on the scale or lower than at the last visit, then a reminder about this can be experienced as criticism. If they are higher now than before, then it is more important to explore this achievement than to make comparisons with the past, which cannot be changed in any case.

Therapist:	So on that scale from 0–0, where are you today?
Client:	I would have said 7 until yesterday; maybe 6 now.
Therapist:	So if it is 6 now, what will be different when you move up one point, or maybe half a point?
Client:	Dunno; I'll still feel bad about bad marks, but maybe I will read up stuff to understand where I missed things.
Therapist:	Who else will notice when you move up a little and are reading and such?
Client:	Mum and my friends. They notice if I am drinking as well.
Therapist:	What will you do if you feel like drinking too much?
Client:	I sometimes text or talk to friends, or stay in like I said, or stop having drink in my bedroom so I have to go past mum to get it from the kitchen.
Therapist:	And is that sort of thing, like having to go to get it, is that enough to work well for you?
Client:	Seems to be OK so far.
Therapist:	What will you do if it is not OK?
Client:	Phone you, maybe?
Therapist:	And as well as phoning here?
Client:	Maybe ask mum to help me.
Therapist:	Is there anything else that you want to mention today?
Client:	No, thanks.

It is valuable to give the clients the choice about how long it should be before the next appointment. As a rule they will ask for a longer gap than the therapist expects, revealing their own self-confidence about managing their situation for a while. Families will often say 'We need time to try things out before we see you again.' If they have chosen their own time interval it is less common for them to request earlier appointments or to miss subsequent ones.

In asking if they need to come back at all, it is best to assume that anything which is not an outright 'No' should be treated as a 'Yes'. It is safer to offer an appointment that is not kept than to fail to offer one which is needed.

Therapist: [Acknowledging the problem] You have had times when you drank a lot or wanted to drink more. [Compliments] You have managed this by having willpower and by using help from your friends and your Mum. You have successfully had days without any drink and other days without much drink. You are proud of yourself when you have good marks for your college work. You have good ideas for what to do if you feel like drinking too much. [Task] We think you should keep on doing the things that are working for you. How soon do you want to come back again? Do you need to come again?

Client: I would like to see you again … How about six weeks from now?

Therapist: OK. Here is the appointment card.

(In the event this client telephoned to say that all was well and that she did not intend to keep the appointment. She was not referred to the service again in the subsequent two years.)

Moving Towards Concluding Therapy

Once people have had time to review their progress, they often decide that a return visit is not needed. Unfortunately, it is rare for people to notify the clinic that they do not need the appointment until almost the last minute, so unfilled clinic appointments are not uncommon. Follow-up studies reveal that most clients have done well, but there is some initial anxiety for the therapist when someone fails to attend without notice. If no cancellation is received, then a standard letter is sent to the client with a copy to the referring agent along the lines of: 'We were sorry not to see you for your appointment today. We hope that this means that things are going better for you/both/all. We will not send further appointments unless we hear that it is necessary.' It is not appropriate to pursue non-attenders with offers of therapy unless other information suggests that safety assessment needs to be undertaken. This standard letter respects their decision and makes no criticism of their absence. It makes it clear to them and to the referring agent that they bear the responsibility for any further action, such as requesting another appointment.

Most clients will be ready for discharge when they have reached seven or above on their scale. Some studies have found that 25 per cent of clients only require one session. However, the average from all published studies of solution-focused therapy is that three to seven sessions are usual. Steve de Shazer suggested (2005) that 'If you tell the client there will be four to six sessions, then they will wait until session five before doing anything.' In many cases the gap between sessions can become longer as they move towards discharge from therapy. Many brief therapists work to a notional limit of 10 or 12 sessions. If success is not forthcoming after 10 sessions, it may be that solution-focused therapy or this therapist are not the best form of help for this client at this time. However, people make changes at different speeds, so a fixed limit is not always appropriate. Some chronic or long-term problems can require many more sessions. Steve de Shazer's rule is: 'Not one more session than is necessary.'

One strength of solution-focused brief therapy seems to be that it does no harm. Even if clients do not improve, the questioning process appears to be harmless and compliments are always appreciated. It is often easier to choose a suitable alternative treatment after solution-focused discussions about the client's goals and preferences. With other therapies it can take much longer to determine whether or not therapy is going to be effective. Solution-focused therapy can often be completed before the client has reached the top of the waiting list for other treatment. If they have not improved with solution-focused work they can move on to other treatments. This is another argument for early access to solution-focused work; in general, around 70 per cent of clients will improve with solution-focused work (see Chapter 6). Thus only those 30 per cent who do not respond to solution-focused brief therapy need to be passed on to specialists in other therapies, thus making better use of scarce resources.

In the case of clients who are clearly doing well but are reluctant to be formally discharged, it can be useful to propose that 'Because you have made changes so quickly, you have not used up all the sessions available. You have sessions in reserve, so if necessary you can call us directly to arrange another session.' This reassures many clients and it is rare for them to use the 'sessions in reserve'. In our clinic we usually close the case for administrative purposes if we have not heard from the client after six months.

Family Practice: Solution-Focused Work and the General Practitioner

The busy family practitioner is always short of time. There are some 30,000 treatable conditions in the medical literature and the family doctor may be the first medical authority to encounter any one of them. The allotted time in the UK for a routine consultation is 10 minutes. Family doctors working in this context have a natural interest in short and effective interventions and in time-efficient interview methods. The solution-focused interview structure lends itself to starting where the patient has started, to recording data in a way that is easy to pick up later and to pursuing the next step at the following consultation. General practitioners find it useful with emotional and mental health issues as well as with a wider range of conditions. The return visit sequence can be used in almost any medical consultation after the first contact.

Park (1997) gives a good account of the use of solution-focused methods in family practice in Korea. He identifies that family medicine includes the psychosocial elements of managing psychosomatic illness, long-term physical disease, bereavement and severe illness. He advises that a suitable approach has to be widely applicable, short-term, focused, of relatively low risk to the physician and the family, and to be usable with only a reasonable amount of psychological knowledge. In their experience they find that solution-focused therapy meets these criteria. They use it for short supportive sessions and for a few regular scheduled sessions for specific problems. Park's case examples illustrate the use of solution-focused conversation in combination with medication.

Unwin (2005) has published his personal experience of solution-focused thinking in family practice in England. He points to the value of having a waiting room which is full of heroes instead of being full of problems, to the merits of focusing on the present and the future instead of the past and to the value of avoiding harm by not emphasising or provoking negative memories.

Couples and Families

There is no research evidence indicating any difference in the effectiveness of therapy whether individuals, couples or families are seen. We encourage people to bring anyone that they think will be helpful to the first session. We assume that, whoever the other person is, they are there to be helpful. Sometimes, especially if a case is not progressing, we will ask for someone else to attend (e.g. a partner) or for people to be seen separately. Those who want change are not always the most powerful ones in the family. So, for example, a troublesome adolescent may not wish for change and their attendance at the sessions may be counterproductive. It is sometimes helpful to meet such a client once to show respect for the family and to offer the chance for all to be heard. Thereafter it can be more useful to see only those who want change.

Burns (2005) suggests that families have at least five useful roles. They can provide expert testimony about the client's previous skills and exceptions to the problem. Family members can be a source of compliments and can be partners in noticing and reinforcing exceptions. They are themselves existing resources for the client. They can provide the 'other person/best friend' who will notice changes and miracles. Burns identifies that self-esteem is a vital construct in recovery from both physical and mental disorders, yet it is less well studied than depression or anxiety. She recommends the use of the self-report VASES scale; 10 items concerned with self-esteem, each rated 1–5 by the client (Brumfitt and Sheeran, 1999).

The Milwaukee team reported that their interviews were longer for couples than for individuals and longer still for families. In comparison, our team found that the same time was required for any combination of attenders, provided some adjustment to the questioning process is made so that everyone could contribute some answers to some questions. We find that the therapy process is easier with couples because you can get immediate verbal and non-verbal feedback on statements made. By contrast, with individuals it is necessary to ask at key points: 'What will your partner/family think about that?' The necessity for this means that the therapy process takes longer. Families are usually run by a coalition of two, which may be the parents or one parent and a child together. So the work is often done by this couple while the others follow their lead.

The circular questions formalised by Palazzoli et al. (1978) can be helpful in clarifying the opinions of family members. Many people prefer gossiping about others to answering for themselves, so information is more forthcoming. Asking the husband where he thinks his wife will put herself on the scale, or whether he expected the answer that she gave, is informative for all about their relationship. The children of the family can often tell you what their mother or father are likely to say in response to your question. This allows them to contribute ideas without too much pressure to conform.

Milner has an ingenious variation on this technique with which to draw children into talk with the adults in their lives (2001, p. 139). She describes giving the child two pieces of paper with 'CORRECT!' and 'WRONG!' written on them. She then interviewed 'the mother as the child' and the child would hold up a piece of paper to show his view of mother's reply. 'What is the temper like?' 'Like a volcano. Exploding!' CORRECT! Then the therapist interviewed 'the child as mother' while mother held up the relevant piece of paper without speaking. To 'the child as mother', 'Does he use the f-word?' 'No.' WRONG! Both parties enjoyed the interaction. In the next session both child and mother answered as each other but had also become more able to negotiate their own joint answers directly.

The structure of conversation is based on sequences of four and a half to five minutes (Zunin, 1972). This is illustrated in social situations, where it takes some five minutes with a new person to decide if further contact is desirable. Conversations and relationships are made up of successive sequences.

This rule for interaction can be used as a tool in therapy. There are key moments in the day for close relationships. If these five-minute periods go well, then the character of the whole relationship can improve. For children and for adults who are partners the key times are in the morning before work or school and on return home. The other important time for children is following minor injuries, when five minutes can make all the difference to a child's reaction. Most people are willing to attempt to be amiable for five minutes on a few occasions in the day. The benefits often appear quickly, so this can be a useful task to offer to couples and families where the relationships are strained.

In working with couples or families their exchanges sometimes become heated, especially in the early part of the session when they fear that their point of view will not be heard. The therapist may deal with this in various ways. The simplest is to seek to have all conversation between each party and the therapist, not between the family members. This can be done by using the questions from the lists above, looking directly at the person and using their name: 'Bill, what do you want to see happening instead?' If one is speaking a lot, interrupt to ask the others 'Is that how you see it?' Another option is to ask them to slow down because they are giving you information too quickly and you do not want to miss anything which might be important.

If arguments between the clients become so heated that it is not possible to get answers to your questions, or so heated that violence will occur, then the session may need to be interrupted. It can be effective to ask 'Is this useful for you, because it is not helping me to understand?' Clients accustomed to relating through argument may not realise that the therapist is not party to this. If this does not change the interaction, it can be suggested that the session finish and that another appointment is arranged when the therapy process can continue. Remarkably, what has looked like a major domestic confrontation will sometimes stop instantly while appointment times are discussed.

With couples who are no longer attending to the questions from the therapist because they are arguing, it can be useful to say: 'I cannot follow this properly, I will need to talk with you one at a time while the other waits in the waiting room. Who wants to stay in here first?' Often both will cease argument and vie with one another to be the 'good' one who stays in the room first. With both couples and families, if there is a supervising team, one member can come in or telephone to support the therapist and to suggest something different. This interruption is often enough to change the conversation.

Occasionally, whatever training or skills or goodwill a therapist may have, there will be clients with whom they simply cannot work. Apart from the ethical issues, it is in the interests of both the client and the therapist to recognise the situation and to make alternative arrangements.

Teenagers

Teenagers are often difficult to engage with traditional therapies. Sometimes they have come to expect only criticism. Solution-focused work may be successful with them, because it respects their world view and pays attention to their wishes, as well as paying them compliments. Others are struggling for independence within their families of origin and see therapists as simply another adult seeking to hold them back. Being addressed as individuals encourages their independence and hoped-for adult status, while a focus on exceptions and miracles encourages competence, resilience and hope.

Some young people find considerable satisfaction in their activities and see no advantage in engaging with any reduction in these activities. It is society in the form of their parents, schools or the criminal justice system that wants to see changes in their behaviour. In terms of power relationships, it is those who feel themselves to be on the losing side who are seeking help from the therapist. In these families it is often more productive to work with the parents or the school rather than the adolescent. The focus remains on looking for positives, exceptions and talents rather than talking about negatives. It can be helpful to have one interview with the adolescent if they are willing to attend. Sometimes it is possible to engage successfully with the adolescent as described above. On other occasions the main benefit is that it strengthens the therapist's position with the parents and the other adults involved. It prevents work being undermined or disqualified by remarks such as 'You don't know what he is like'.

Use in School Settings

Ron Kral (1988) has developed a short form of solution-focused interview suitable for hard-pressed school counsellors and teens who are not ready to engage in formal therapy sessions.

- 'What's the problem that brought you here/had you sent here?'
- 'Where is the problem as a percentage, if lower is worse?'
- 'How do you feel about that percentage on a scale of 0–10?'
- 'Have you been higher or lower than that percentage in the past?'
- If higher: 'How did you get to be up there/stay there?'
- If lower: 'How did you get up to where you are now?'

Ron Kral says that if you ask teenagers to scale 0–10, initially they will reply using percentages to show their superiority to the adult world, therefore it is best to ask for a percentage first. Scaling or percentages can be quoted to measure progress quickly in the school setting because only the therapist and the client know what '76 per cent this week' or 'up 5' refers to. So a fleeting exchange in the corridor or playground can be enough to maintain progress.

John J. Murphy's (1997) textbook on school counselling includes a number of case studies of different school situations. In addition to the usual solution-focused questions, he devised the 5-E method for using exceptions effectively.

1 Eliciting an exception to the problem.
2 Elaborating the details and circumstances associated with the exception.
3 Expanding the exceptions to other situations and to a greater frequency.
4 Evaluating the effectiveness of the intervention.
5 Empowering and maintaining desired changes.

Under 'Evaluating', Murphy recommends the use not only of scaling but of objective tests, teacher ratings and single-case measures, whichever seems best suited to the particular case. He points out that solution-focused coun-selling is not wedded to any specific theory of development or of therapy. It is therefore legitimate to draw on any existing model or knowledge in order to assess progress or to furnish reframes and compliments which may assist in changing the views of the teenager or others.

FKC Mellansjo is a private day school for children with difficulties in Stockholm, Sweden. The whole organisation is solution-focused, providing therapy and consultation as well as education. Two of the senior staff have written an account of their application of solution-focused work in day-to-day practice within the school (Måhlberg and Sjöblom, 2004). Among other interesting aspects of their work, their chapter on 'The importance of language' makes several points that can be applied to work with clients of any age. To them, language can create possibilities. So, talk of 'problems' and you create problems; talk of possibilities and you create possibilities. Asking 'When …' instead of 'If …' enhances the likelihood that something will happen. They recommend that 'Do not …' be avoided because events described in words seem to happen even if we are talking about them not happening. Instead, they suggest phrasing advice in terms of positives: not 'Don't be offensive' but 'Be respectful'; not 'Don't be late' but 'Be punctual'.

Fletcher Peacock (2001) has suggested that everyone uses post-hypnotic commands in everyday life. Statements such as 'Don't drop the glass' pro-duce a mental image of dropping the glass. If the command instead is 'Carry the glass carefully' the image is positive, of success and not of failure. In the therapy room or the school, focusing on positives creates a positive picture of the future, so that both therapist and client are instilling productive post-hypnotic commands. Similarly, opening sessions by saying 'What is better?' creates a post-hypnotic suggestion that things are becoming better.

In the USA, Linda Metcalf has written a number of books for educators and parents about the use of solution-focused ideas in schools and in parenting

(Metcalf, 1997, 1998a). Her books contain many documents and worksheets for all stages of the process. She is also a specialist in solution-focused work with groups (Metcalf, 1998b). Her most recent work (2004) is a self-help book *The Miracle Question: Answer It and Change Your Life*. It includes worksheets and diaries to enable people to take themselves through the solution-focused process.

Rhodes and Ajmal (1995) describe their application of solution-focused ideas in British schools. They make the point that meta-cognition, the understanding of how we personally deal with information and new learning, is enhanced if we understand the methods that we use to do this. Thus skills used to learn existing skills such as football can be understood and transferred to spelling or reading. Their writing includes useful material about providing 'creative consultation' to teachers, a process with many similarities to supervision within therapy and to coaching in the business sector. They describe methods of structuring consultation in schools to assist with classroom management and organisational change. They used an initial questionnaire, which included identifying pre-session changes and exceptions. A planning meeting begins by clarifying the 'contract' for the work to be done, including how many meetings and when, who will be involved and who needs to know about progress. They then proceed to goals and exceptions. Review meetings include direct observation of the child or class, followed by the usual solution-focused elements of noting what is better and then setting goals and tasks for the next step.

Dr Cynthia Franklin (Franklin et al., 2001) has researched solution-focused approaches in the school setting. She is one of the major influences in Gonzalo Garza High School in Austin, Texas, which is run on solution-focused lines throughout. The initial impulse for this school's philosophy came from the observation that those students who do not complete high school have worse lifetime outcomes on a variety of measures. The school had already developed ways of addressing high school dropouts similar to solution-focused methods. This is the school's mission statement:

> Imagine a high school where students are in control of their destiny. Imagine a high school that believes that a student's environment and past history does not have to decide their future. Imagine a high school that teaches that a student's family problems, and poor neighborhood do not have to dictate their personal success in school or work. Imagine a high school that considers a student's personal adversities and life difficulties as strengths that they can harness for their personal betterment. Imagine a high school that inspires hope and teaches that the small steps that a student takes can lead to big changes in their life. Imagine a high school where each principal, teacher, social worker and staff member are convinced that every student has capacities that can be built upon to assure a positive outcome for that student. Imagine a high school where at-risk and dropout youth attend school, graduate from high school, and successfully transition to college and work. Imagine Gonzalo Garza Independence High School, a solution-focused high school, where dreams come true.

Information about this school and the project are available via Dr Franklin's entry on the University of Texas at Austin website (www.utexas.edu) or at the Garza High School website (www.austinisd.org/schools/website. phtml?id=024).

Young People in Residential Care Settings

Traditionally, residential care has relied on a deficit model of function for young people. A problem or an offence is the defining event for entry to the system. Even those who have been placed in care as a means of protecting them from abuse are likely to suspected of contributing to the problem and to see themselves as deficient because they have been taken from their homes. One result of this has been that residential care in social work and nursing in units for adolescents are famously difficult careers. Consequently it is difficult to recruit and retain staff, which can mean that the most inexperienced staff are caring for clients who are both difficult to help and at a crucial stage in their lives. Solution-focused methods offer hope for such young people and their care workers.

The effectiveness of solution-focused supervision is described by Triantafillou (see Chapter 5). Wilmshurst (2002) has evidence that residential settings can themselves be harmful to the residents even when solution-focused methods are employed. The work of Bob Bertolino and Thompson (1999) have highlighted the benefits of a competency-based model for residential care. They describe ways of building relationships quickly, altering problematic views of residents by staff and approaches to crisis management. In the book there are examples of forms and assessment tools that will help to create the possibility for beneficial change and development for staff and clients.

Solution-Focused Group Work

A number of workers have used group settings for solution-focused work. Most use mainly the standard form for solution-focused work, but there are many variations. One option is to use the group form for goal-setting, scaling and reporting progress, but to ask the clients to work in pairs to interview each other about their miracle. The miracle question may be asked by the conductor to each client in turn, although this diminishes the chance of group-centred interaction.

Another format was used by Britta Severin (2001), a Swedish social worker who was asked to conduct a group for sexual offenders serving long-term prison sentences. She interviewed each client separately while the other prisoners (and prison staff) acted as an audience. The groups were limited to four inmates at a time. She found that the miracle question was important, as was the closing statement for each inmate. The prison staff spontaneously began to encourage the inmates to pursue their ideas between sessions. There was a joint evaluation after every five sessions about which elements of the session were valued by Severin and the inmates. This work is of particular interest because many of the inmates were from countries other than Sweden and were not native Swedish speakers. Of necessity, their goals and small steps were very small because most of them had long prison sentences.

Ron Banks (2005) published a summary of his approach to solution-focused groups. He draws on Ben Furman's (Furman and Ahola, 1992) work as well as on the Milwaukee solution-focused model. Like Severin, he sees the process as being individual therapy in a group setting. However, in his work the group members ask the questions, with the conductor moving the group through the different stages and intervening to modify or prevent inappropriate 'pathologising' questions. He identifies six stages in the group process: the problem is introduced; details are clarified; the problem is acknowledged and positive aspects examined; miracle/better future is discussed; building on progress and sharing credit; next steps for the client. Throughout the process he uses the concept of the 'problem as friend': 'Did this make you stronger or weaker?'; 'How did you manage to get through that?'.

Solution-focused Groupwork by John Sharry (2001) is an excellent introduction to the topic. The book is unusual because it contains advice on the administrative and clinical preparations required when starting a group. Few texts on any variety of groupwork address these issues, and the information will be of value to workers of any therapeutic persuasion. Sharry also includes plans for sessions according to the setting and purpose of the group and discussion about the relative usefulness of facilitator-centred and group-centred conversations.

Restricted Progress in Therapy

Fletcher Peacock (2001) has thought about the concept of 'customers, complainants and visitors', terms used to describe the three possible initial relationships with clients. He suggests the alternative formulation of clients as being 'High speed', 'Medium speed' and 'Low speed'. High speed clients are ready to do things, medium speed clients can be asked to observe things or to suggest what needs to happen, while for low speed clients it is useful to advise them to take things slowly and to give compliments and positive feedback. The Mental Research Institute (Watzlawick et al., 1974) pointed out that people have their own speed or pace for doing things. This often emerges during scaling questions. It can also be identified by asking people if they like to act quickly or if they prefer to consider decisions carefully before acting. This gives the therapist useful information about how to recommend tasks and how to schedule appointments.

In some ways this resembles the stages of change described by Prochaska and DiClemente (1982). They suggested that different interventions are needed according to which stage of change the client has reached. The time intervals necessary have been studied and are well described in Prochaska (1999). So in *pre-contemplation* (i.e. not in the next six months), providing information may be all that is acceptable to the client. In *contemplation* (perhaps six months prior to change), information, thinking about resources and ways to approach the situation are possible topics. In *preparation* (weeks before change), how to make change and what resources to use become significant. In *action*, the process is under way. Prochaska suggests that this element takes about six months, which is in keeping with other research on psychotherapy generally (see Chapter 5). In *maintenance*, relapse prevention and relapse management are central. This stage is predicted to last between six months and five years, but can last a lifetime. Finally, *termination*, when the client has left the whole issue behind for ever.

The work of Yvonne Dolan (2000) includes her proposal of a sequence from 'Victim' to 'Survivor' to 'Authentic self'. The latter two are comparable with Prochaska's stages of Maintenance and Termination.

In solution-focused work, Prochaska's stages of Preparation, Action, Maintenance and Termination fit the model easily. However, it is important to recognise clients who are still at the Pre-contemplation or Contemplation stage, as they are not ready to make changes yet. There is a risk of becoming 'solution-forced' with such clients unless careful attention is paid to their goals and their responses to the miracle question. Replies to questions during the scaling dialogue about how long it will take to reach ten or other points on the scale can be useful here. Their time scale for change can be compared with the time sequence outlined by Prochaska and DiClemente above.

Hawkes et al. (1998) have identified some questions to use when clients have not made as much progress as they wished. They call this 'The non-miracle scenario'.

'The Non-Miracle Scenario'

- Is the change so far enough for you?
- What else needs to happen to move you a little more towards your miracle?
- Is there something else that I could be doing to be more helpful to you?
- Now that you have tried all this and feel that you cannot change your husband/wife's behaviour, what can you do to make things even a little better for yourself?
- While you are waiting for something to change, how can you look after yourself a little more?

These questions can help clients to find alternative goals if there has been no change or when they believe that someone else needs to do the changing, or if they consider that change is outside their control.

Some clients have long-term or chronic physical illness, so there are certain changes they cannot make. Many such clients know that their bodily disability will not disappear, and therefore find it difficult to use the miracle question constructively. For them, the most effective techniques are seeking for small goals 'which will be a first step for you', and to use exceptions and scaling. Nevertheless, Burns (2005) has used solution-focused brief therapy with patients who have major physical disabilities, and the use of solution-focused approaches has been recommended in UK guidelines for palliative care (NICE, 2004) and cardiac rehabilitation when accompanied by depression and anxiety (SIGN, 2002).

The Mental Research Institute identified that sometimes failure to progress in therapy does not imply a failure of therapy or therapists, but that the client is seeing the wrong sort of expert. Sometimes a relationship is beyond recovery, or the advice that the client seeks cannot be given by a therapist. Examples include couples who have come because one of them seeks 'counselling' to stop the other one ending the relationship; they may benefit more from good lawyers than from therapists. Sometimes a client will ask for a specific intervention other than solution-focused therapy. Such requests are legitimate and can be supported by the therapist. An example was an elderly married man, who said at his fourth session, 'You want me to actually do these things! I don't want to do them. I want to see an attractive woman regularly to talk about my life, as I did with my previous counsellor.' He was congratulated on his clear goal and referred to another team who might offer this service.

Other examples are situations where someone wants their state benefit confirmed, or where they want their doctor to prescribe certain pleasant drugs to them. These may be tasks in which the therapist cannot be helpful. There may be situations where, for ethical reasons, the therapist may not wish to be helpful, for example if the client asks for a favourable report to influence their probation officer, or an unfavourable report to support a claim for compensation. In justice to the clients, such requests are rare, although some will control the information that they give to the therapist in order to avoid unwanted difficulties.

If therapy is not progressing as anticipated, it can be useful to ask about the disadvantages of change as well as the advantages. It is usually possible for the therapist to suggest one genuine disadvantage, which allows the client to raise some more. For example, getting up every morning to go to work may be a difficult change after three years of unemployment or chronic disability, or the return of a partner may bring more housework as well as more support.

Conclusion

Many people who wish to try out solution-focused approaches find it hard to make the change from their previous style. There are various ways to make this process easier. Some like to begin by using scaling as a part of their usual approach and developing their skills from there. Others choose one client for a complete first session. Some colleagues began by telling an existing 'stuck' client that they had heard about a new approach and wanted to try it out. Most clients seemed to find this respectful and interesting. In training courses the trainees are advised to try the whole set of questions in succession, using each part of the dialogue with a different client. Once comfortable with the question sets, they proceed to conduct a complete first session with a single client.

Key Points

- Taking a break before feedback to the client can be a useful tool.
- Constructing a useful and complimentary feedback statement follows a logical sequence.
- Sessions other than the first follow a simple structure.
- Concluding therapy is usually straightforward.
- Solution-focused therapy can help in family practice, especially by looking for strengths and exceptions.
- The basic model is easy to adapt to work with couples, families and groups.
- Teenagers and schools: specific situations may benefit from modifications to the model or to its wider use.
- There are solution-focused tools to manage failure to progress in therapy.

Case Study

Contents

This case study is based on therapy with a married couple who had no previous experience of counselling or psychotherapy. The text is taken from a transcript of the first interview. Comments about the therapy process are derived from the contributions of the team who sat behind the mirror during the session.

A Melancholy Marriage

Their family doctor referred this married couple in their forties because the wife (Carol) was depressed.

AJM: Good afternoon. As you know from the appointment letter, we have a team here to help me to help you. I wonder what you would like to be called.

Bob: [*Looks at Carol*] Just Bob and Carol.

Problem

AJM: And it was your family doctor that suggested you come here today?

Bob: Well, I was trying to get Carol to go to the doctor because things in the house have not been right for some time. She has been behaving differently and I thought she needed some tablets or something to get her going again because she is sitting around doing very little and it is causing real problems at home.

AJM: Is that how you see being here today, Carol?

Carol: Yes, I guess, I don't really know.

AJM: So did you go to the doctor as well as Bob?

Carol: Well, we both went. Bob came and took me.

Bob: I took her down, sat in the car and waited.

AJM: So what would you like to get out of being here today?

Bob: Well, I want things to get back to normal. The way things were before.

AJM: When things are back to normal, what will that be like?

Bob: Well, Carol won't be just sitting about the house, eight hours a day, not doing anything. I come back from a long day at work and nothing has happened. The place is just a tip. There is no tea on the table, there is nothing tidy, it is just …

Carol: I do sometimes, I do make the tea.

Bob: Ah, well, if you call that snack we had tea, I suppose.

AJM: How long have things been like this then, Bob? How long have things been a problem?

Bob: Four months, I would say.

AJM: Four … Do you agree with that, Carol?

Carol: I would say it is the start of September, five months.

AJM: Five months, OK. And you say that sometimes things are done and you make the tea?

Carol: Yes, I think it is since Jane has gone to university in September that I have not really felt like doing things as much.

Bob: You can't pin the blame on Jane, Carol.

Carol: Yes, I know, I just think that we used to get on really well and used to do things with her.

AJM: You and Jane used to get on really well?

Carol: Yes, and I miss her really. She used to help me with the tea and we would often make it together because she finished her school. In fact, this summer we had quite a lot of time together.

Bob: What I can't understand though, Carol, is why, when she went away, why should things change? I mean, she has gone away to college. I mean you never talked to me about that very much anyway. All the decisions were made behind my back, really.

Carol: No, we did ask you but you were usually out or she had to fill in forms and that, and I helped her.

Bob:	Well, I was out at work.
Carol:	I know.
AJM:	You work quite long hours, Bob?
Bob:	I work very long hours. It is a very physical job. Sometimes getting in late, shift work.
AJM:	Do the shifts change very often then?
Bob:	Yes, they change.
Carol:	But your shifts at the club don't change. I mean you often go, after most shifts.
Bob:	Well, I go down there to escape a little bit, because there is nothing much going on in the house. You don't talk to me. You sit around and watch those programmes on the TV all the time and I am better off talking down the club.
AJM:	How many times in the past have you spent a lot of time in the club because of how things were at home?
Bob:	I think I have always gone down there but I have gone down there a lot more …
Carol:	You never used …
Bob:	… in the last five or six months now.
AJM:	Have there been times in the past, in past years, when you have had to do that?
Bob:	I can't really think of any. It seems to have crept up rather than happened all of a sudden. I would like Carol to get a bit of energy back and start doing things again and start talking to me.

The problem has been described in terms of time and behaviour by both parties. They have also given some information about their social context. Bob has begun to talk about his goals for change.

Pre-Session Changes

AJM:	Energy … Can I ask you what changes there have been since you went to see the doctor, but before you came here today?
Bob:	Well, it was a struggle to get Carol to go to do anything about it anyway because she did not feel that there was anything to do anything about, so I mean, just getting her through the door and sitting here was an effort.
AJM:	What other changes have there been?
Bob:	Well I suppose in a strange kind of way we have had to talk more. Yeah, just talking about coming here. Arguing but talking.
Carol:	Well, I didn't mind.
AJM:	Carol, what changes have you seen since going to see the doctor about coming here today?
Carol:	Well, I think he has been slightly more understanding.
AJM:	How has he shown that understanding?
Carol:	Well, because he is not getting at me as much. The doctor said that he was referring me here because he did not think that I was depressed.
AJM:	So Bob is more supportive and more understanding?
Carol:	Well he has not kept saying to me, you are really depressed, you are really anxious, you need to do this, you need to do that and he comes in a little

	bit sooner, not right after shift, but instead of being out, two, three, four hours he has only just gone for a couple of hours.
AJM:	He has come home sooner?
Carol:	Yes.
AJM:	Has that been helpful to you?
Carol:	Yes, because I am fed up being on my own and I miss my job. I have been looking for another job, but I cannot get one.
Bob:	Well you were certainly better when you were there, when you were at work.

Language matching is helpful in staying connected with the conversation in order to maintain the relationship and to make both feel included in the conversation. Pre-session changes may reflect motivation or energy to seek change. It is best to ask about such changes early in the interview, as they involve a focus on the past and not the future. If asked later, they can distract the client from any future focus which is developing.

Goals

AJM:	What things would you like Carol to be doing when things are better?
Bob:	Well, I would like her to be keeping the house sorted out. I would like her to be sorting out the bits she used to sort out, the bills, she really doesn't sort of keep track of that any more and we end up getting red letters through the post and stuff like that because she just can't be bothered …
Carol:	We have had two red letters.
Bob:	Two.
Carol:	Well, there are about 16 bills or 20 bills.
AJM:	Does that mean you have paid the other 16 bills?
Carol:	Yes, I paid them. He hasn't a clue how much I do because he has never taken an interest. I have always sorted the mortgage, sorted the shopping and done the housework. I had a part-time job, I virtually brought up Jane, I spent a lot of time doing things with her and, you do work long hours and I appreciate that, but I do too.
Bob:	I am not so worried about the 16 bills that were paid.
AJM:	Does Bob hand over the money to you then?
Carol:	We have a joint account, so that's been a bit of a problem because I am not working now. You get fed up, Bob.
AJM:	Is Jane your only child?
Carol:	Yes.
AJM:	So Carol, you used to work.
Bob:	She used to work, I mean that made a difference as well, brought a bit of extra money into the house.
Carol:	We don't need the money.
AJM:	How long is it since Carol stopped working?
Bob:	It must be maybe a year ago, something like that.
Carol:	I worked in a bakers and it closed down so I did not choose not to work. I really liked to work.

AJM: So, Bob, you look forward to when things in the house are sorted out and you are not getting red letters anymore.

Bob: Yes, that would be nice.

AJM: So is that the first improvement you would like to see? Or is there something else you would like to see before?

Bob: I would like to see Carol just do anything, because I think she has vegetated.

AJM: What sort of thing do you have in mind?

Bob: Do the dishes, wash a few clothes.

Carol: I do.

Bob: ... do the shopping, pay those two red bills that never got paid. Anything, any kind of movement like that.

AJM: What do you think, Carol? What is the first thing you would like to see improving?

Carol: I suppose him just understanding what it has been like for me.

AJM: And when Bob understands?

Carol: Stop having a go at me all the time, when he comes in later and later now after every shift. He immediately says this and that hasn't been done. He always finds the bit that hasn't been done. But I do do things. I admit it is not as tidy as it used to be, but you would think the way he is talking that we live in a tip.

AJM: So when things are better, what will he be saying instead of that?

Carol: What will he be saying? Well, 'Hello darling, have you had a nice day' would be nice even. Just instead of you haven't done this and you haven't done that and have you paid the bills. Most of the bills have been paid.

AJM: What else will be different when things are better?

Carol: Well just back to do talking and just about each other's day and having a meal together. I mean he is saying I don't. I do.

Bob: You need to cook it.

AJM: Having a meal together in the house?

Carol: Yes, but I do cook it, you are not in, so the food has been cold or going in the bin.

Bob: I get in, I am tired, I have been at work all day long.

Carol: And you have a skinful before you come in and ...

Bob: A couple of pints maybe.

Carol: ... and six packets of crisps or something and so you come in and say I am not hungry and I have made the meal. When Jane was home we always used to really make an effort to sit around the table, the three of us, or with my mum and dad. Most Sundays mum and dad would come, unless we were off for the day, because we always used to go somewhere on Sunday and if we did not do that mum and dad would come around or we would have, I would prepare the meal and they would come at night or they would sometimes ...

AJM: Those things like mum and dad coming around on Sunday, are those things going to be happening again?

Carol: Well they are happening still, well not the trips out, but mum and dad coming around because I do a Sunday meal still, but he is not usually here.

Bob: That's because I sometimes work on a Sunday as well.

Carol: And if you are not working, you are at the club.

AJM: So when things are better will Bob be coming to the Sunday meal as well?

Carol:	Well, yes.
AJM:	What else when things are better?
Carol:	What do you think?
Bob:	Well, apart from ...
AJM:	Let's check out with you, Bob. Is it right what Carol says that you are not at Sunday meals as much as you used to be?
Bob:	Well, the weeks that I am not working, we do that, that is not particularly a big issue for me.
Carol:	But you don't come, you are not there.
AJM:	What are the other things that you would like to see happening then?
Bob:	I would like to get back to the way that we used to talk to each other.
AJM:	You and Carol talking together.
Bob:	Well, I don't know, before Jane went away it always felt like it was the two of you and I was outside. I was on the outskirts of all this, you know. You felt close, I felt quite lonely in all that and I felt excluded a lot of the time.
Carol:	I did not know you felt like that. Because we did still talk.
AJM:	Let me ask a question. Bob, does that mean you and Carol did not talk so much together when Jane was at home and when things are sorted out you will be talking together? Will that be something new then?
Bob:	It is something, we have been there before, but I think we used to talk about Jane or to Jane or through Jane or whatever you want to say.
Carol:	That's not right because Jane would do stuff and then be out, I mean she was a typical teenager, you know, she was out most nights clubbing or if she wasn't she was in her room studying and when you came home we would talk over the day and I did not realise that you felt so kept out of things.
AJM:	You say that you used to talk together; that was you and Bob talking together?
Carol:	Yes, I mean we would have a meal together, we always sat down and we always talked about the day, we did something every weekend. We always have holidays together.
Bob:	And where has it gone?
Carol:	It has gone in the bloody club, down your neck in a pint glass.
Bob:	That makes it sound as if I am an alcoholic or something.
Carol:	No, because you are never at home, you are never at home.

The couple have described their goals. In this process they have also conversed between themselves instead of through the therapist. The couple easily return to problem talk. The therapist interrupts this at times.

Exceptions

AJM:	Can I ask you then, is that the kind of talking together that you and Bob would want to be doing more of in the future?
Carol:	Yes, yes.
AJM:	And Bob is saying that he would like to talk with you. Is that the kind of conversation that you and he had when Jane was not there?

Carol: Yeah, yeah. I miss that. I do not understand how you are saying that that did not happen.

AJM: Bob, do you think that the first thing you would like to see change then is that having the conversation together? Or to get the house things sorted out and the red bills paid?

Bob: Well, all of it really but …

AJM: Which is the first one you would like to see happen?

Bob: It would be nice if we could have a civil conversation. If we could talk about things other than constant arguing because that is just …

AJM: What do you think you will talk about when you have this conversation?

Bob: Well, when we first got married and in the years just after that, before Jane came along.

Carol: That's 20-odd years ago!

Bob: We had some wonderful holidays.

Carol: We had some wonderful holidays last year.

Bob: We did things together.

AJM: What do you think you will talk about now when you have these conversations?

Bob: Well, just about things that we may be planning to do. Things that we may be wanting to plan to do with our holidays. I mean I get about four weeks a year.

Carol: And we always go away and we have gone away every year, including last summer. It was our last family holiday with Jane, we had a great time, didn't we?

Bob: Well, last year wasn't so bad if you remember. I mean, it's this year, or even the last six months, in which you have become really into yourself.

AJM: What are the other things as well as the holidays that you will be talking about in these conversations?

Bob: Sorry?

AJM: What are the other things as well as holidays that you will be talking about during these conversations?

Bob: Well, just everyday kind of stuff.

Carol: Family.

Bob: Yeah, I mean we have got a big family; we have a family that live abroad. We have local family, you know, we are often getting invited to things but the last 12 months we don't take them up because, you know.

Carol: Why, tell the doctor why.

Bob: Well, one, I'm tired and I don't always feel like going but the other is that you haven't been a bundle of energy and what about those panic attacks that you have been having as well? That is why I wanted the doctor to give you some pills so that we could sort them out for a start, you know.

AJM: When things were better, would you be going out more together?

Bob: Together, I would like that to happen. I can't see how it can happen.

Carol: I can. If I go up the club with him that will be together. I refuse to go up the club, because it's all his mates, his drinking mates. I am not saying he drinks vast amounts. I don't think you are an alcoholic like you are accusing me of saying.

AJM: You say if things get better you will be going to the pub with him or going somewhere else?

Carol: No, go somewhere else. He never used to do this and we would go out to the pub together and we would have a cooked meal together or we

> would go around to friends and have a meal with a bottle of wine. It's not
> his drinking that is the problem, it's the fact that he is not coming home.
> He keeps saying I am depressed and I am not.

Bob: It sounds like, it is starting to sound like I have a problem here somewhere
along the line. I mean that is not what we came here for is it? You were
feeling on edge all of the time and you were feeling down and you know,
that is why we came in the first place. We never came to talk about my
drinking problem, which I apparently have.

Seeking for exceptions uncovers some pleasant shared experiences, in which
Carol has taken the lead at times. Steve de Shazer (1994) points out that
you only know what question the clients have heard once you hear their
reply. When a question fails to produce the information that you want,
or if it has been misheard, then it is useful to repeat it in exactly the same
words, which makes it easier to follow the second time. The repetition also
conveys that the therapist has a plan for the session and expects answers
to questions. This can reassure clients when it is perceived as competence.
The same technique can be used if a question has not been answered, as
it interrupts any inappropriate answer and is less disruptive than asking a
different question. If a question has been asked three times and no useful
information has come back, then it is best to change to a different form of
words or to another question.

Carol: And I meet some of my friends through the day and that is really …

AJM: Is that something new, meeting your friends or something you have
always done?

Carol: No, I have always done it but I mean, you don't even know that,
do you?

Bob: I don't know them that well.

Carol: No, but you don't even know that I meet them. I meet them maybe just
for lunch or they come around to mine and that is when sometimes I
have not got as much housework done because they have been around
but I have still tidied up and prepared the lunch and things and so I don't
want to stop seeing them, but if he thinks I am seeing them and not
doing stuff, then he gets annoyed, but I don't want to stop.

Bob: Well, that happens when I am out.

AJM: When things are going better then, will you be seeing more of your
friends or about the same?

Carol: If things were going that much better, we should be seeing more of each
other, that is what I want. My friends are there and I like them being there
but it's not the same.

Bob: The way you have been, it is a wonder that they do come around as often
as they do, because you are not the cheeriest of people, are you, at the
minute?

AJM: You have mentioned a number of times in the past about having more
time together and that you would both like to see more of each other
in the future. Have there been times in the past when you have been on
holiday that you did things that you don't have time for usually?

The therapist is disattending Bob's negative comments.

Bob:	We used to go deliberately to places where we could do a lot of walking.
AJM:	Like serious walking, walking on the hills?
Bob:	Yes, a bit of that. We like mountains and anywhere where we can sort of have a little bit of a challenge. We used to. We haven't done it for quite some years now.
Carol:	We did a little bit this year but not as much as normal because we wanted to try to spend a bit more time with Jane. Normally we would get a holiday club that we could do together, obviously as she got older she would just lie by the pool.
AJM:	Jane did not walk?
Carol:	No, we always did that together and if we went away with mum and dad, Jane used to just go and potter about and look in the shops.
Bob:	When Carol was working, we used to put her money away in a little holiday pot, so that we could go and do some things that we might not have been able to afford otherwise, but that has disappeared now.
Carol:	We go to the lakes.
AJM:	So has that disappearing restricted your choice in holidays?
Bob:	A little bit.
Carol:	No. We have to pay towards Jane, but she is very independent, so it's not like we are poor, well, up until the alcohol.
Bob:	But you have got to be up for it, haven't you? You have to have enough energy.
AJM:	But you are not saying it has restricted your choice on holidays and so on, now the money situation has changed?
Carol:	The money situation has changed now because he is spending the money that we don't have on the alcohol. I am not getting at you. It is just I am the one who sorts the bills.
Bob:	Yes, and I am the one who earns the money.
AJM:	Is there a holiday you would like to have that you can't afford at the moment that you still want to go to?
Carol:	Yes, it's not that we can't afford it. We have got money that we could have a holiday with, that is not really what the issue is. The issue is that we never seem to have the opportunity to talk about it because Bob works long hours and he is tired when he comes in but by then, he has just gone off to allegedly have his couple of pints to relax, then by the time he comes in I am in bed, so we have just not had the opportunity.
AJM:	Are there other things as well as walking that you do on holiday together?
Bob:	Museums, things like that. She used to choose places where there was a bit of local history. I don't think we are really into the sun-bed kind of, lying around all day long and baking.
Carol:	We would hate that, wouldn't we?
AJM:	Have you chosen quite a lot of holidays for walking and so on?
Bob:	We have done it but lately we haven't.
AJM:	So are these things you are likely to do again in the future?
Bob:	I would like to think so. I would like to think so.
Carol:	But what is stopping us?
Bob:	If we can get you sorted out, I think it would be possible.
AJM:	What sort of places would you like to go to in the future?

Bob: I have always wanted to go to Italy and we have heard some good reports of various places.

Carol: We have done a few Greek Islands and we love Austria because that is good walking.

AJM: So, is Austria somewhere you would like to go for holidays?

Carol: We have had some good holidays but we wanted to do something and the other thing is that for me, when we are with Jane, I would like to go somewhere where we could just go ourselves where neither of us have been.

AJM: Have you somewhere in mind?

Carol: Well, there are lots of European cities, there is Prague, we wanted to go to Bruges, we have been to Barcelona but a long time ago, so that we would like to go back there. We really want to do Italy. We have got relatives in Canada and we have got a lot of opportunities.

Bob: You can tell Carol likes travelling! She is a good organiser as well. She used to be good at lists, lists of things. She was good at getting things done. She used to be very organised. She used to, I mean she used to keep everything. She was spot on. She was meticulous about things, she really was and in terms of holidays, I think you can tell, Carol organised them and I tended to follow her lead. I was not bothered about that. It was quite nice for somebody else to arrange it.

Carol: But we always chose it together. I mean we always sat down and looked at the brochure.

Bob: Oh yes. If you really wanted to go somewhere, I was never that worried about it, you know, so that I would have argued.

AJM: You would have been involved for a short time in the planning and choosing and then Carol would deal with it.

Bob: Yes, but I was happy to let Carol get with it really and let it happen.

AJM: OK, so you would share the tasks like that?

Bob: Yes.

Carol: As he worked long hours I was quite happy to do that 'cos I only worked part-time so I had plenty of time to go to the travel agents and sort the money and that. He is right, I am, I mean I still think I am organised.

Bob: Well she was definitely better at that kind of thing than I have ever been. I miss that now because I think life is harder when …

AJM: That was her skill and you did not have that kind of thing.

Bob: No I was not as good at it, no.

Scaling

AJM: OK. I am going to ask you a slightly different sort of question now. If you can think about the difficulties that we talked about on a scale of 0–10, with 10 being the best. Where would you say that you are on that scale?

Bob: It feels like 2 or something like that.

AJM: 2. Carol, would you say 2?

Carol: No, I would not say it was anything like as bad as that. Somewhere in the middle. Maybe 5 or maybe 6.

AJM: Nearer 5 or nearer 6?

Carol: Probably nearer 6.

Bob:	Do you really feel that?
AJM:	Were you expecting Bob to say 2?
Carol:	I would have thought he would say −2 actually. Yes, I am being facetious there. I thought he would be lower than me, but I did not think he would be that low.
AJM:	OK. Were you expecting Carol to see things around 6?
Bob:	No. I did not think because things have been pretty dire and pretty desperate lately and I thought, I actually thought she might even be lower than me.
AJM:	Right, OK.
Carol:	You can't get much lower than 2.
Bob:	No, that's true.
AJM:	How long do you think it would take to get to 10 then? Is 10 a realistic place to get to? Is it where you would want to be all of the time?
Bob:	No, it seems too much for me. Not in a short time anyway.
AJM:	What would you go for then?
Bob:	6 sounds good.
AJM:	6, OK.
Bob:	6 sounds good to me. I mean any movement in a positive direction.
AJM:	OK, Carol, would you like to get to 10?
Carol:	I think if Jane was at home. I could think about and things were kind of a bit like they were before but I mean, that is not going to happen because she is making her own life.
AJM:	She is at college now, making her own life and she is being independent and managing?
Carol:	Yes, she is doing great and is really happy.
AJM:	And she is happy?
Carol:	Yeah, yeah, she has really settled in.
Bob:	We are both really proud of her, the way she has come on and the fact that she got into university. She does really well. I mean once she comes home the place is different. I mean, I still don't always feel included in things.
Carol:	But that is like it was really and that would be my 10, things to be like her home and everything.
AJM:	But is she going to be home again like that?
Carol:	No.
Bob:	And me not drinking.
Carol:	No, I am not saying that.
Carol:	I think I would settle for a 9 or something like that.
AJM:	How long do you think it would take to that?
Carol:	How long do you think?
Bob:	Well I don't think I would go for 9, but if I was going for something less than that, maybe a year.
Carol:	Oh God!
AJM:	Do you think it is too long, a year?
Carol:	No, I would hate to think.
Bob:	Well, I would hate to think it too.
AJM:	How long do you think it would take?
Carol:	Months really. I don't think it would take too much to sort things out really.
AJM:	So you are talking months, but not as long as a year, maybe six months?

Carol:	Maybe not. I am not getting at you so don't jump down my throat but I think that if he came home a bit more and didn't drink so much that would mean we would have a little bit more money in the bank and could plan a holiday. That would not have to be six months, it might be about four months, we used to go in June or July. It is something that could happen in a short time.
Bob:	If you could get out of the house a day a week or something and get back to doing something. You were always doing something and you were always better when you were doing that, but you stopped doing that.
Carol:	Yes, I have stopped but I am still looking for a job. I mean I am still applying for part-time jobs but I am not very skilled at lots of things, it was just the baker's I worked in.
AJM:	How long did you work at the baker's?
Carol:	Oh, eight or nine years. You got to know the regular customers and they were really good. I did quite a lot of knitting and sewing and so I used to do a lot of soft furnishings.
AJM:	A long time then.
Carol:	Yes, I mean it closed down, he retired. I would not have left.
Bob:	She had more life when she was doing things.
Carol:	I did a lot of soft furnishings and things. The customers got to know.
AJM:	So Bob, shall we talk about some of the things to move up one point on the scale from where we are now? How would you know when you had moved up one point?
Bob:	Well, I think we would have less arguments. We would be talking more about things that we used to, things that we used to enjoy, more often.
AJM:	When you say more often, do you mean every day?
Bob:	I think we would have to think about how we used our time because at the moment like I said, I just feel tired when I come in and …
AJM:	So talking more often. Would more often be like once in a week?
Bob:	No, I would hope it would be every day. I don't think it will happen on a Thursday or something like that.
Carol:	We could put it in the diary or on the calendar that we are talking to each other!
Bob:	I would like it to be an ongoing thing. It would be nice to have a little bit of time every day where we actually just talk rather than argue.
AJM:	So if you talk, is that moving up one point on the scale? If something as good as that was to happen every day would that be just one point up the scale?
Bob:	Well, even first thing in the morning. Because Carol tends to get up early, I am not sure whether she goes back to bed as soon as I have gone out the door but she tends to get up and we do spend half an hour or so together first thing in the morning before I go working.
AJM:	Is that talking together?
Bob:	Well, it hasn't been, but it could be a time when…
AJM:	So would you be up one point on the scale?
Bob:	Well, for me that would be significant. That we were talking in that kind of way again, that would be really something very significant.
AJM:	What do you think, Carol? What would it take to move just one point up the scale?
Carol:	For Bob to just come home after his shift.

AJM:	So if he came home once in a week immediately after his shift, that would be enough to move you up one point?
Carol:	No, I am sorry, I would want him to come home more often. I mean he does five shifts in a week so three of them.
AJM:	So would that be enough to move up one point? How often?
Carol:	Three times ... he does five shifts a week. I feel it would be enough.
AJM:	If that just happened in one week, would that be enough to move up one point?
Carol:	Actually one shift would be good, it's not enough but even if that happened. If you were to ask me that tomorrow and he came home tomorrow night.
Bob:	But if we were like that I would want to come home if we were talking more. That is the reason I am not there.
Carol:	But we can't talk if you are not there.
AJM:	OK, if I can ask you a different question, on a scale again of 0–10. We talked about six months to a year. How confident are you, Bob, that you will have moved up a point on the scale of 0–10 in 6 months' time?
Bob:	It sounds OK.
AJM:	So how confident are you? 10 out of 10?
Bob:	No. I know I am certainly not 10 out of 10. I might be something like, I don't know, 7 out of 10 as a possibility.
Carol:	Do you not think it would be better than 7?
Bob:	When we talk about it things don't seem so difficult.
AJM:	What about you, Carol? How confident are you that things can move up one point?
Carol:	I want to think that things would be better before six months so I have to say more confident. I can't believe you are saying that long.
AJM:	How confident are you then? 10 out of 10?
Carol:	Yes, up one point. I would hate to think we are still here in six months time. I would like to think that things are a lot better. It's difficult to say out of 10 but I would like to think we would be up a point next week, never mind in six months. It doesn't have to be like this.

As well as identifying small achievable goals, scaling has brought out a timescale for Carol. The use of a scale for confidence has also shown the couple something of each other's view of the problem.

Miracle Question

AJM:	I would like to ask you another strange question now. I would like you to use your imagination maybe. Are you in agreement with that?
Carol:	Sounds good.

If someone says they do not want to hear your strange question, then you can say 'OK, I will ask you a different question'. Then ask the miracle question in the usual way. The interviewees will not know that this was the question that you originally intended to ask.

AJM: So ... suppose you get through today and go home to bed and go to sleep as usual ... and while you are asleep a miracle happens ... but you are asleep and so you don't know that the miracle has happened. How will you know, when you wake up in the morning, that this miracle has happened and the problem has been solved?

Bob: Well, for me I suppose I would feel that the day was less of a challenge.

AJM: Will you feel like that when you wake up?

Bob: A general feeling of more energy. I can look forward to the day rather than it being something just to get through.

AJM: If you wake up like that for the day?

Bob: It would be nicer. I have been like that. I am a morning person anyway generally and so I tend to find that time of day good.

AJM: So you would know right away that the miracle has happened?

Bob: Yes, well I think some of the things we talked about before. I think we should spend at least maybe, you know, 20 minutes or half an hour together. Just to sit and have a cup of tea together. We don't eat much breakfast but you know, we still have a bit of toast, a cup of tea. A chat that was not to do with bickering or getting at each other. If only we could feel that we had set the day off on the right foot, whereas that has not been the case. It has been the case of getting out the house as quickly as you can and then getting back as late as you can as well.

Carol: We could do that though, couldn't we? That would be good.

AJM: Carol, how would you tell that this miracle has happened? Would you know as soon as you wake up like Bob?

Carol: Yeah, it would be nice if we just woke up, turned around and had a cuddle, a kiss, good morning rather than just leap out.

AJM: So if you didn't have to just leap out of bed?

Carol: Well it would just be nice to turn around have a cuddle and then a kiss or something and said good morning and then while you are in the bathroom I will just go down and make breakfast, because that is what we always did.

AJM: Would breakfast be the same as it was then?

Carol: Yeah, and we would sit and have a chat and I would go off to work and Bob would go off to work, because we are both morning people.

Bob: Because we would both be leaving the house roughly at the same time, depending on what my shifts were of course.

Carol: But if I am not doing that now, you know, if I am not going to work. I mean I do get up, it's just that grumpy kind of carry on, whereas it would just be nice to have a cuddle first thing and just go downstairs and have each other's company.

AJM: What sort of things would you chat about then?

Carol: We usually look at the headlines. We don't sit and read the paper.

Bob: No, we don't have that long to do that kind of stuff, but usually we talk about what is going to happen at the end of the day usually. The usual things people talk about, you know, when we are going to meet up. What is going to happen in the evening?

Carol: But that would be the real miracle for me. If Bob came home, that would be the real miracle.

AJM: That would be the miracle, OK.

Carol: Then we could either go out or go to the pictures like we always used to do.

AJM: So he would come home and then you would go out again?
Carol: Possibly or we might just stay in and get a curry out and a bottle of wine or
          I would cook because I do, I do actually cook most nights. I have stopped
          doing it because he wasn't coming in, but in the main I like cooking.
AJM: So if the miracle has happened would you do the cooking in the same
          way as you do now or in a different way?
Carol: No. I would just do the same, 'cos he would just come and hover about
          and chat while I was preparing.
Bob: My miracle would be about if I came home and Carol had done something.
          If she had been out somewhere.
AJM: She had been out somewhere.
Carol: I do.
Bob: Yes, well we used to talk about things. I mean if Carol is not doing any-
          thing, if she is sitting in the house all day and she is vegetating then, it
          doesn't really give us a great deal to talk about, but when she was out at
          work.
AJM: If she was out, she would produce something to talk about?
Bob: We had more to talk about when she used to go out.
AJM: Will you be talking about what Carol does or what you do?
Bob: Both.
Carol: The miracle could happen right away because I do go out. I meet my
          friends. I do do things. It is just you never ask. You are never here.
Bob: It seems to be when I am at work, so I am not really sure and we don't
          talk about it. I don't know what you are doing half the time.
Carol: Because you are not here.
AJM: Being here … What will be different if the miracle happens?
Carol: The miracle would be if I go to work, if at the minute I am not working,
          I still go out, I go up the library. I have got a Bridge club that I go to on
          Thursday afternoon. I meet my friends at least once if not twice a week.
          I go up the job centre most days. My mum usually pops down, she has a
          keep-fit class and she pops around usually on Wednesday lunchtime and
          so I see her. I mean I do all these things; it's just that I don't have anyone
          to share them with because you are not here.
Bob: I did not really know that you are doing those things, to be honest.
Carol: Well, I have always kind of done them.
AJM: So which ones are new to you, Bob?
Carol: Probably all of them.
Bob: Well, most of them, because I go out to work and I have not been coming
          back until late.
Carol: Well, they are not new because I have always done them. It is not as if any
          of this is new.
AJM: Which ones are new to you then, Carol?
Carol: Well, meeting my friend Linda once a week, that's the only thing.
Bob: I did not realise that you are seeing them as often as you say you were.
AJM: So Carol is seeing them more often?
Bob: It's more than I was aware of anyway. Because I mean by the time I got
          back, she was in and we weren't talking about it or we would start to
          argue or whatever, so I did not really have much of any idea of the kind
          of things that she has been doing.
Carol: The only thing that I don't do now is go to that sewing class on a night.
Bob: But it's not the most exciting thing you have ever done though, is it?

Carol:	Well, I liked it. It's given us a little, that is the other thing I am thinking of, if I can't get another job.
AJM:	How come you stopped it if you liked it?
Carol:	I had done as much as I could. I had done everything in tailoring and soft furnishing. I had done the lot really over a period of three years. So, unless I go into something completely different like upholstery or something, but I don't particularly want to do that because at this stage I may be wanting to do soft work like curtains and things. If it sets off and I manage to get a business going then I might do.
AJM:	Would that be a business from home?
Carol:	Yeah, if I can't get a job.
Bob:	I did not know that you wanted to do all that kind of stuff.
Carol:	I know, but I do. When I was in the shop like I said, sometimes I had people who were asking me to make a few cushions and I got a kind of reputation there for being quite good. It is something I really like doing and if I can't get a job then one of the things I would like to do is to think about doing that a bit more. Just putting an advert in the paper would be enough, I mean there is nothing lost if I do that. I have the time in the day now; it is just whether or not I have got the bottle to do it really.
Bob:	I did not know you had that much ambition to be honest. I really didn't.
AJM:	Is there something you need to do to give you the bottle to do that?
Carol:	Well, I would like to have a bit more encouragement. I would just like to have you around.
Bob:	I have not heard you talk like that for such a long time.
Carol:	It is only since September that I have been a bit down. It's not like I have changed personality.
Bob:	It seems, Carol, that you have an interest and wanting to take it more seriously and run a business and that kind of stuff. I mean, well, I have not heard you quite talk like that before.
AJM:	You talk about encouragement from Bob then. Would there be specific things that you would want to discuss with him?
Carol:	Well, not like the financial side or anything because I could do all that. No, it's just more about wanting him to say 'Go for it', that would be really good or about what you call this miracle thing. It would be, you know, a miracle could happen, 'Go and do it', that would be really nice. Just being around so that I could say look, I am struggling with this or could you go and get a pint of milk because I have got to finish some curtains off for tomorrow morning for a customer. Anything, it's just, I really miss you being around. I feel that I have lost two of you. I lost Jane and I was prepared for that and yes, I miss her, but I miss you too and I just want you to be around more. We did loads of things and you say you are on your own and I feel I am on my own and it's not what I want.
Bob:	No, it's been empty.
Carol:	No, and we looked forward to this for so long. I admit I have been really down. I do not think I am depressed, that is why the doctor was helpful because you heard what he said, that I don't need tablets and that is what I needed to hear.

It can be helpful if the therapist looks more animated during the replies to the miracle question. However, most clients are more animated during these answers in any case, because it is a question that encourages playfulness and creativity. At other times in the session it is best to be somewhat more grave than the clients, to avoid the risk of appearing to belittle their distress. The Freudian rule that 'There are no jokes in therapy' is a reminder that it is better for the therapist to appear too stolid than too lighthearted.

AJM: Carol needs to talk to you about the soft furnishings and things and for you to hear about it?

Bob: That is not a problem. It would actually be good. I suppose it would be part of my miracle to actually see Carol with that kind of motivation again, 'cos that is something that has been missing.

AJM: You say she used to be motivated like that.

Bob: Well, she did. I mean she was out working and you know and it was more obvious that she had interests. They seem to be a bit hidden now and I don't know how that really came about but we did have holidays, we did do things together.

AJM: It has been more hidden, but it was there before?

Bob: Yes, it seems to have been hidden from me but listening to what has been said, it sounds like it has been going on, but I have not been aware of it. What she has been doing or even what kind of thoughts she has had about the future for herself.

Carol: Have you not noticed the new curtains in the lounge?

Bob: Well, I try not to. Snakes have not been my kind of fabric! [*They laugh*]

Carol: This is something we used to do a lot. We used to laugh a lot.

Bob: She used to make the most weird things.

Carol: Clothes for Jane.

Bob: That's not normal is it? Snake patterns, not really is it? I like pastel kind of things much more. I know it is a bit dull but you have always been a bit weird and wacky to be quite honest. Well, you were before.

Carol: That's the bit you fell in love with.

AJM: I think we will take a break for a few minutes now and talk to the team and then come back with some comments. Before I do that, is there anything you want to mention that we have not covered?

Bob: Nothing that I can remember.

Carol: I want to ask, I don't need to have any tablets, do I? Because this is what we came for and I don't want tablets. My doctor said I didn't need them but we have come here because …

AJM: You came here for tablets?

Carol: No, I came here because …

Bob: I thought that she needed some tablets to perk her up a bit.

AJM: OK, anything else? I will go and talk to the team.

The miracle question has lightened the atmosphere and produced topics related to private moments for the couple. Practical and achievable actions have emerged, including information from Carol about a new career. Several exceptions to the problem have also been identified. At the close of this phase of the interview a question is asked about tablets. This is a return to Bob's initial view of the required intervention which he mentioned at the start of the session. This can be viewed as a simple enquiry or as a wish for a 'miracle cure' that will resolve the problem without active behaviour change by either party.

Team Discussion

The team sympathised with Carol who had worked, dealt with finances, looked after the home and raised Jane. They identified that Bob had worked long and steadily, that his drinking was recent and that he had sought help for Carol because he was worried about her. Both had recalled past shared pleasures and had been able to identify some things that they would like to see happening in the future. They were able to come up with behavioural goals and small changes, which they could identify, as well as interesting new plans. They pointed out that the therapist had not asked the couple about who else would notice when these changes occurred. It was thought that tablets were not likely to be an essential part of recovery at this stage.

It was decided that feedback should focus on future positive ideas and on the shared elements of their relationship. A response to their question about tablets was included, avoiding specific advice about taking them or not.

Feedback

AJM: There is a lot of information that you have told us. [Acknowledging the problem] We can see that it has been difficult for both of you for at least the last five months and you have both felt quite isolated. [Compliments] You have come together today in spite of it being a struggle. You both worked hard in the session and it seems to us that you both want things to be better so they are as good as they used to be. Carol, you are ambitious, you have a lot of ideas for the future. Bob, you are being encouraging and positive and you are both coming up with ideas for change, talking and walking together, going on holiday, having breakfast together. Depending on how things go, you may still want to think about tablets, but in that case you need to talk to the doctor again. [Advice] In the meantime the team would like you to go and try out some of these things that you have come up with and come back and tell us how it goes.

If you think that another meeting will be useful, how soon would you like us to meet again?

Subsequent Progress

The couple chose to have a further appointment five weeks later. They had done a number of things which they had discussed in the session. At short notice they had gone away together for a weekend, visiting Jane in the process but enjoying time together as well. Carol had put time into exploring the possibilities of working from home, but had not committed herself to this option. They made another appointment for four weeks later but Carol telephoned on the day to say that they were 'doing well' and did not want to attend or to make another appointment. She stated that Bob was spending more time at home instead of in the pub. They returned a follow-up questionnaire one year later which recorded that they had achieved their goals in therapy and that no new problems had arisen for either of them since then.

Conclusion

The session reported above displays many of the features normally encountered in a first session and shows the process of language matching in action throughout. Work with couples includes making sure that both partners remain engaged with the conversation and that each point of view is explored.

Key Points

- Empathy and establishing collaboration.
- Avoid engaging with negative affects and attitudes where possible.
- The therapist is responsible for maintaining the focus and direction of the interview.
- Remain alert for strengths and resources during the interview which can be used later in the feedback.
- Remain alert also for safety issues or other problems which may need to be addressed, for example medication use, alcohol misuse.
- Reflections from the team are most helpful if they are immediately available; supervision serves a similar function but usually occurs after the event.

Note

I offer my thanks to the colleagues and others who helped with these sessions and with their subsequent preparation for publication.

4

Ethical Issues in Therapy

Contents

- General ethical principles
- Ethical codes for the practitioner in the UK
- UKASFP draft code of ethics
- Other ethical issues
- Ethics in supervision
- Ethical issues specific to solution-focused brief therapy
- Conclusion

In this chapter we examine some of the ethical issues in psychotherapy and counselling and how these relate to solution-focused therapy in particular.

General Ethical Principles

Everyone concerned with health and welfare is required to behave in an ethical fashion as defined by their peers and society at large. The rules vary from culture to culture but all cultures have accepted standards for healers and care-givers. In parts of India it is considered advisable to consult an astrologer before any major decision. However, in Western Europe the advice of the astrologer would not be seen as an important issue. Some hospices which provide terminal care have a strong religious commitment. They may be reluctant to prescribe adequate doses of pain-relieving drugs on the grounds that pain is a test of faith. This is an ethical issue for the workers. Also, how does it affect a hospice resident who belongs to another faith? These are cultural issues and therefore responsive to cultural change. A cultural change may also have occurred in the world of Western psychotherapy, where the predominant paradigm of psychodynamic ideas is now challenged by other approaches to 'talking therapy'.

Ethics consists of moral principles applied for the benefit of a social group. Thus moral conduct by a practitioner equates with the ethical practice of their profession. That ethical practice then meets with the standards set by society for that profession.

The earliest references to ethics in health care come from the Ancient Greek and Roman writings of over 2,000 years ago. The original rule for doctors in the time of Hippocrates was *Primum non nocere*: first do no harm. In other words, the safety of the patient was the prime concern of the physician. Providing treatment and relief of distress was a secondary requirement.

Ethics in Psychotherapy

The situation for psychotherapy is rather different. Many support systems, including religions and other interventions, have been used for comfort down the centuries. Psychotherapy can be viewed as a development of such support systems. It is a part of the social nature of human beings to give the credit for their survival to agencies other than themselves, which makes it difficult to tell which support systems are most effective. One supportive and confiding relationship has been shown to be a predictor for psychological health (Bowlby, 1969, 1973, 1980; Brown and Harris, 1978).

There is a lack of definite information about what will help or harm in psychological terms, although we know that most techniques work for a significant percentage of clients. We know that some therapists are better than others. We also know that common factors are a large part of successful outcomes. Because scientific information is lacking, individual experience is privileged over hard data. In reality, we cannot be sure that it was therapy and not non-specific factors or the resilience of the client which led to success.

However, the balance for practitioners must lie with reducing the risk of harm caused by inappropriate actions. Therapists wish to be healers and helpers, but there are many sources of psychological damage that are not easy to repair. These include childhood sexual abuse, inappropriate dependence, traumatic life stress and false memories implanted by well-meaning therapists. The specifics of ethical practice are considered below but 'First do no harm' is central to them all.

The majority of therapies are the subject of honest belief by their practitioners, which has been shown to increase the chance of a good outcome (see Wampold, 2001 and Lambert, 2004 on therapist allegiance). The ethical difficulty is that such allegiance makes the disputes ideological rather than evidence-based. In the physical sciences many specialists can completely disagree with one another and calmly debate the evidence for their views. Only in the field of psychotherapy can one see placid and respectable individuals flatly criticise one another's views in public without advancing any evidence to support their case. Hence, a sound ethical framework is essential in order to prevent harm to our clients through well-intended enthusiasm.

Many of the relevant issues are covered in detail by Bond (2000). He proposes that our ethical framework is derived from at least six sources: our personal values; the values expressed in the model of therapy used; those of the employing agency; the codes of our parent profession or discipline; those of moral philosophy as expressed within our culture; and the legal framework prescribed by the society in which we live. For example, he identifies that in the UK there is no legal duty to breach confidentiality in the attempt to prevent a suicide, whereas in the USA such a legal duty does exist. However, confidentiality may be breached if the worker believes that a suicide attempt is a real possibility. With children, vulnerable adults and the elderly, the question of mental capacity may also apply (Mental Capacity Act 2005).

Ethical Codes for the Practitioner in the UK

The Health Professions Council (HPC) regulate the titles and standards of a number of health professions in the UK (see HPC, 2008). Their ethical code is designed to cover all the professions for which they are or will become responsible. They regulate psychologists and art, music and drama therapists, and are expected to be given responsibility for regulating counsellors and psychotherapists in the near future. The exact definition of 'counsellor' and 'psychotherapist' is not yet resolved.

The first code of ethics for counsellors was put forward by the British Association for Counselling and Psychotherapy (BACP) (see BACP, 2006). There are several groups of counselling and psychotherapy organisations within the UK, but the United Kingdom Council for Psychotherapy (UKCP) and the BACP have the largest numbers of members. Other organisations include the British Psychological Society, the British Confederation of Psychotherapists and the British Association of Psychotherapists. (For codes of ethics see BACP, 2006; UKCP, 2005)

The United Kingdom Association for Solution-focused Practice (UKASFP) has used the Health Professions Council (HPC) Code of Ethics as the basis for its draft Code of Ethics.

UKASFP Draft Code of Ethics

As a solution focused practitioner, you must protect the health and wellbeing of people who use or need your services in every circumstance.

Everyone applying to join UKASFP must confirm that they have read, and agree to keep to, the standards explained in this document. Also, every member must be familiar with the standards, and must make sure that they keep to them.

The Standards of Conduct, Performance and Ethics

This document explains the standards of conduct, performance and ethics that all members must keep to. We also expect anyone who wants to join the Association to have kept to these standards. They are the basis against which we will assess complaints made against a registered member of UKASFP, and we can use the standards to help us decide whether to allow a prospective member to join. We might take action against you if you do not keep to the standards set out in this statement.

Your main responsibilities are summarised below, grouped into the categories of conduct, performance and ethics. Please remember that this is not a complete list of all the issues that can arise in relation to your conduct, performance and ethics.

In the standards below, the word 'clients' is used to signify clients, patients, users, carers, family members, work colleagues or other members of the public.

You must always keep high standards of conduct. You must always:

1   act in the best interests of your clients;

　　You are personally responsible for making sure that you promote and protect the best interests of the people you care for. You must not exploit relationships with clients, allow your views on their sex, age, colour, race, disability, sexuality, social or economic status, lifestyle, culture or religious beliefs to affect the way you treat them. You must not do anything, or allow anything to be done, that you have good reason to believe will put the health or safety of a patient, client or user in danger. This includes both your own actions and those of others.

　　The safety of patients, clients and users must come before any personal and professional loyalties at all times. As soon as you become aware of any situation that puts a patient, client or user at risk, you should discuss the matter with a senior professional colleague.

2   respect the confidentiality of your clients;

　　You must only use information about a client:

　　to continue to care for that person; or

　　for purposes where that person has given you specific permission to use the information.

3   maintain high standards of personal conduct;
     If you are convicted of a serious criminal offence we may remove you from the register.
4   provide any important information about conduct, competence or health.
     You must tell us information relating to your own personal and professional conduct, as well as that relating to other members, and cooperate in any investigations. You must always keep high standards of performance. You must always:
5   keep your professional knowledge and skills up to date;
6   act within the limits of your knowledge, skills and experience and, if necessary, refer on to another professional;
7   maintain proper and effective communications with clients and other professionals;
8   effectively supervise tasks you have asked others to carry out for you;
9   get informed consent as and when necessary;
     You must explain to the client what you are proposing to do, and any alternatives.
10   keep accurate client records;
11   keep within health and safety guidelines as appropriate to your working environment;
12   limit your work or stop practising if your performance or judgement is affected by your health.
     Finally, you must always keep high standards of ethics. You must always:
13   carry out your duties in a professional and ethical way;
14   behave with integrity and honesty;
15   follow our guidelines for how you advertise your services;
     Any advertising must be accurate, and you may not claim to provide better services than others unless you can prove this to be true.

The BACP and UKCP ethical codes are likely to be subsumed within the HPC guidelines in the near future. The BACP emphasises personal qualities and the diverse nature of our multi-cultural society. The UKCP system is more prescriptive. Its effect is close to that of the HPC code. Detailed accounts of the UKCP and BACP codes may be found on their websites.

Other Ethical Issues

Lambert (2004) discusses ethical issues in psychotherapy research. He agrees that value choices are unavoidable in research and in the examination of change in humans. Research often focuses on single disorders, which means that the conclusions are less applicable to everyday practice. Yet if the researchers are challenged on this point it often becomes clear that the diagnostic categories are not as rigid as had been claimed. Many of the problems inherent in such research are overcome by scientific rigour, peer review and further studies. But this is a slow and approximate mechanism. Meanwhile, personal careers and the rapid electronic dissemination of information move quickly.

Lambert, like McKeel (1999), questions the ethical standing of including a 'no-treatment' condition in comparative studies (Lambert et al., 2004). If we know that a treatment is potentially effective, can we justify withholding it because society will benefit from the rigour of the research process? Waiting-list controls and trials in comparison with standard treatments are commonly used to address these concerns.

Sue Walrond-Skinner (1986) gives a wider overview of ethical issues within the psychotherapies. Many of her topics are covered within the Codes of Ethics described above, but some are not. For example, she points out that the training of therapists has to include clinical practice, which means exposing clients to inexperienced therapists. Society will benefit from therapists who have had training, but the individual client may not benefit as much from seeing a trainee instead of a qualified therapist. One strength of live supervision in family therapy and brief therapy is that the clients are shielded from errors by trainees because there are experienced therapists also taking part.

A central element of psychodynamic training is the need for personal therapy for therapists. This is expensive for the trainee in money and emotional energy, and has not been shown to correlate with becoming a better therapist. McAskill's review (1988) concluded that damage to self or to relationships occurs with up to 10 per cent of trainees during personal therapy. It has also been suggested that trainees are less effective as therapists while undergoing personal work (Strupp, 1958; Garfield and Bergin, 1971).

Walrond-Skinner comments that sexual exploitation by the therapist is always wrong, but that non-sexual touching can be acceptable as a part of normal therapist–client interaction. Some therapies use touch as a formal part of their treatment technique. It can be hard to distinguish between these elements of touch, especially when clients are distressed or have experienced inappropriate touching or exploitation in the past.

An American study of sexual exploitation of clients reported abuse by 7.1 per cent of male psychiatrists and 3.1 per cent of female psychiatrists. These figures are likely to be an underestimate. Other studies suggest higher rates of abuse with therapists who are not medically qualified, possibly because of the ethical aspects of the medical role in society (Gartrell et al., 1986; Beutler et al., 1994). A study of psychotherapists in the USA estimated that sexual contact occurred between 11 per cent of male therapists and their clients and between 2–3 per cent of female therapists and their clients (Pope and Bouhoutsos, 1986). The complaint of sexual exploitation may not be made until many years later (Bond, 2000). This undesirable aspect of therapy may be less likely when brief approaches are used.

The possible influence of third parties is also considered by Walrond-Skinner. Sometimes therapists are acting on behalf of third parties in treating children or those subject to legal powers. Therapists can find themselves reporting to courts or to funding agencies about their clients and being put under pressure to shape their conclusions in one way or another. Many solution-focused therapists complete such reports in consultation with clients in the hope that being collaborative will reduce the effect of external pressures.

Ethics in Supervision

Supervision itself is not a widely tested concept. Almost all practitioners report the value of supervision and/or consultation with a senior colleague. However, evidence for this is not extensive. Triantafillou (1997; see Chapter 6) records better outcomes in residential care when solution-focused supervision is compared with supervision as usual. Steinhelber et al. (1984) found no connection between supervision and client outcome as such. They showed that outcome results were better when supervisors worked with therapists who had a similar therapeutic orientation. Harkness (1997) compared two supervision models: skill-building or empathy-focused. Both appeared to be equally effective for patient outcomes, although trainees preferred the skill-building model. Nonetheless, some form of supervision is a common part of everyday practice around the world, and is specifically required by most codes of ethics, as seen above.

Thomas (1996) has written extensively on the role of supervision in solution-focused therapy and elsewhere. In his view, the supervisor role begins with a clear contract about responsibility. Naturally, this differs if the supervisee is a trainee within an agency or if the supervisee is an independent practitioner coming as an outside professional. When Thomas has serious concerns about unethical or dangerous behaviour he recommends posing the question as a dilemma and discussing it openly with the supervisee. He seeks to maximise the choices for all parties in the situation while accepting that in the end the supervisor must act according to his own conscience and best judgement.

In my own experience, with any therapy, the context of supervision and the contract with the supervisee needs to be clear and explicit. There may be times when the supervisor has to say for legal or ethical reasons that the supervisee *must* do something. Otherwise the role of the supervisor becomes professionally ineffective. For example, a trainee may offer to meet a client away from the therapy room for a specific purpose connected with the therapy. The supervisor can comment on possible problems with this but may allow the trainee to make the decision. However, if the trainee uncovers current and active danger to the client or another person, then the supervisor needs to be able to insist that confidentiality may be breached in order to increase the safety of the individual concerned. In most jurisdictions, confidentiality can be set aside if a child is in immediate danger of physical or sexual abuse. It may fall to the supervisor to require the trainee to act accordingly. If the supervisee is not able to agree with these requirements, then sometimes the supervision contract has to be terminated. In this case consideration has to be given to informing the parent organisation or the professional body of the supervisee.

Tohn and Oshlag (1996) discuss their work with mandated clients. They remind us that some client goals may not be ethical, such as a wish to carry out rapes more effectively. In other circumstances goals may be negotiated, including freedom from legal pressure, provided that the path to that freedom is based on an end to offending.

However, it might be that there are some clients with whom any particular therapist cannot work. In that case it is ethical to end the relationship, making arrangements for the client to be dealt with elsewhere. Humans instantly have a liking for 10 per cent of people that they meet and have an instinctive dislike of another 10 per cent. Relationships with the remaining 80 per cent of humanity depend on the circumstances and the willingness of the individuals to work on and to develop relationships. This means that there are some relationships which will never succeed, no matter how much effort is put into it. It is important to recognise this situation and to deal with it appropriately.

O'Connell (2005) states plainly that it is unethical to be in practice as a counsellor without supervision. Like Frank Thomas, he uses supervision to build competence and expertise in the supervisee or trainee.

Ethical Issues Specific to Solution-Focused Brief Therapy

Cade and O'Hanlon (1993) comment on the ethical position of the 'non-directive therapist'. Following Goffman (1956), Haley (1976) and Watzlawick et al. (1974), they assert that all communication, including therapy, is intended to produce a response in the other party. It is thus always 'manipulative' or 'directive'. If this is accepted, then it is important to acknowledge this effect and to seek to use it in ways that are constructive, or at least non-harmful to our clients.

Brief therapy is sometimes challenged by psychodynamic therapists because of their understanding of concepts such as 'flight into health' and 'symptom substitution'. The concept of 'flight into health' was applied to explain cases in which recovery occurred before the therapist had completed the work that they considered necessary. It was suggested that this was a type of 'manic defence' in which unjustified elation was summoned by the unconscious to defend itself against psychodynamic intrusion (Rycroft, 1972). It could be equally useful to view 'flight into health' as evidence that brief treatment by the therapist had been sufficient to meet the client's needs. The error would then lie with the therapist privileging their theory instead of the client's experience. It was further suggested that insufficient exploration would lead to symptoms being replaced sooner or later by further symptoms or dysfunction: 'symptom substitution' (see Walrond-Skinner, 1986).

In practice, neither concept has been verified by studies of brief psychodynamic therapy, nor by studies of behavioural and cognitive approaches, nor of systemic family therapy. Within solution-focused research, specific enquiry about the development of new symptoms has been made by Burr (1993), de Shazer (1985, 1991), de Shazer et al. (1986) and Macdonald (1994a, 1997, 2005). New symptoms did not appear in statistically significant numbers in any of these studies. The follow-up to the large Finnish study by Knekt and Linforss (2004) has shown continued benefit from all the therapies so far studied. Equally, even lengthy psychodynamic treatment (16 years) has not successfully resolved the problems faced by some clients (Wallerstein, 1986). The large study summarised by Wallerstein would probably not receive ethical approval now, yet it has added an enormous amount to our knowledge of the processes of long-term therapy.

In spite of this lack of evidence, some therapists will state that solution-focused brief therapy is unethical 'because you must explore the deeper meaning of the symptom'. Against this view, most clients appear pleased not to be asked to take part in painful discussions about past unhappy experiences. There are many people who deal successfully with their past experiences and lead satisfactory lives without ever seeing therapists. There are others who develop what appear to be false memories on the basis of conversations with therapists who insist that 'something caused this'. Not everyone who has their psychological defences dismantled by psychoanalysis finds that they are better off as a result. Sometimes psychological defences have a benefit for the client, and no amount of insight and empathic support can replace them.

Behavioural and postmodern therapists make the counter-charge that therapies which address goals not chosen by the client, or in which goals are considered altogether irrelevant, are themselves unethical. Goals may change during therapy, or clients themselves may have the strength to pursue goals regardless of what the therapist offers. However, few taxi-drivers will earn a living if they say 'Let's just move through the traffic for a while and see where we end up'.

Cognitive-behavioural therapists and doctors challenge the ethics of solution-focused practice from the 'expert' position, asking how clients can be trusted to find solutions for themselves. Yet most problems in life are solved without therapists and often without advice other than one's own experience. They also ask how it can be ethical not to tell clients what to do when the therapist clearly knows the right thing to do. There are several objections to this in practice. Drugs and cognitive-behavioural therapy, like other therapies, both have an average 70 per cent success rate, so that there is a one-in-three chance that the advice is wrong for this client at this time. Many clients do not follow the advice given, although they may be too tactful to say so. So good advice is wasted unless the client genuinely wants advice. There are many situations where advice that will work for the therapist will not work for the client.

Solution-focused workers will give advice on the few occasions when they know what is likely to help. An example may be the information that modern methods of toilet training are rarely effective before a child is over 12 months old. This may correct a pattern of faulty parenting, or it may not. Toilet training itself occurs at widely different ages in different cultures, so that this advice is only relevant in certain contexts. Sometimes the collaborative solution-focused approach means that the client will take advice, but often it is no more successful than with any other approach.

Mandated clients and offenders may find that they can work with solution-focused brief therapy (see Chapter 5), perhaps because it is collaborative and does not require them to reveal private matters. Most other psychotherapies do not succeed well with these groups. In England the Home Office decided that a specific cognitive-behavioural therapy package for anger management was to be given to all relevant offenders by the Probation Service. The probation staff were not allowed to use another model even if they preferred it, and offenders had no choice about the treatment offered. This expensive initiative has had little benefit so far. Is this also an ethical issue?

Conclusion

This short discussion has looked at the ethical limits for psychotherapy in general and at the role of solution-focused therapy within these limits. Ethics are derived from expected standards within society and are modified as a result of changes in accepted morality and developments in science. Solution-focused therapy may itself be such a development. In the UK, over-arching standards of practice are being developed for all talking therapies by the Health Professions Council. The case study in the previous chapter demonstrates that ethical practice has some bearing on every step of the process.

Key Points

- Ethics apply to individual behaviour but are derived from the standards of the social group.
- There are differences in emphasis even between leading organisations within one country.

- The Health Professions Council is seeking to rationalise some of these disparate views.
- Ethical issues form a background to a large proportion of counselling and psychotherapy.
- Supervisors must be aware of ethical issues and convey them appropriately to supervisees, if necessary through formal agreements.
- Specific ethical challenges have been made to all directive therapies and to solution-focused therapy in particular.

The Historical Roots of Solution-Focused Brief Therapy

Contents

- Concepts of mental activity prior to Freud
- Psychodynamic theories
- Behaviour therapies
- Systems theory
- Brief therapies
- Conclusion

Exponents of postmodern brief therapies including solution-focused brief therapy sometimes suggest that these therapies have very different assumptions from other past and present approaches. This chapter seeks to place solution-focused ideas in the context of their historical development and describes their relationship to other current approaches. It is based both on experience as a practitioner and on the relevant literature.

Concepts of Mental Activity Prior to Freud

Freud's descriptions of mental mechanisms are often seen as the beginning of psychotherapy as a discipline. However, many of the concepts had been identified prior to Freud's publications. For example, in 1759 the Irish author Lawrence Sterne wrote in his famous novel *Tristram Shandy*: 'My father ... was a great MOTIVE-MONGER, and consequently a very dangerous person for a man to sit by, either laughing or crying – for he generally knew your motive for doing both much better than you knew it yourself.'

William James, writing on religious experience in 1902, refers to 'concealed mental processes' (James, 1988[1902]).

In his masterwork *In Search Of Lost Time* (1922, vol. IV, p. 28), Marcel Proust wrote: 'the specific for curing an unfortunate event (and three events out of four are unfortunate) is a decision; for it has the effect, by a sudden reversal of our thoughts, of interrupting the flow of those that come from the past event ... and breaking it with a counter-flow of thoughts from the outside, from the future.' Compare this with Steve de Shazer (1985, p. 7): 'All that is necessary is that the person involved in a troublesome situation does something different.'

In Great Britain in the nineteenth century mental disorder was regarded as largely genetic in origin. The treatment consisted of asylum care, sedation and keeping the patients occupied. The occupation provided was usually productive work, such as hat-making or agriculture, whose profits supported the asylum. A report from the Cumberland and Westmorland Lunatic Asylum in Carlisle shows that of 1,537 admissions between 1882–92, 29 per cent died of diagnosed physical illness, showing that the asylums also provided care for chronic and terminal diseases. However, 62 per cent of the admissions were discharged improved or recovered. This would be an acceptable success rate for many mental illnesses today (Macdonald, 2000). On average there were 600 residents with a total of 53 attendants for 24-hour care. These staffing levels are low by current British standards.

For continental Europe in the nineteenth century, mental disorder was seen as a form of disease, to be managed by neurologists. Franz Mesmer developed his theories and treatments while regarding patients as objects upon whom the physician would display his skill. His ideas were eventually rejected by the scientific establishment, partly because he often demonstrated his treatments on the same well-practised patients who travelled with him. It is likely that he was inducing trance states in these patients, in all likelihood both producing and relieving symptoms.

Psychodynamic Theories

Freud was a neurologist and a skilled clinical observer. From 1895 he began to publish material on the value of making explicit information of which the patient was not conscious or aware. He showed that it was not necessary for the patient to be in a trance for this purpose. His skills as a communicator and author brought his ideas to the scientific and public communities, where they are still major influences today.

Initially, psychoanalysis was brief, being about six months in duration. The training consisted of a personal analysis, which was similarly brief. Training and therapeutic analyses were often performed by a close colleague or even a member of your family. Later it came to be believed that a personal analysis also removed unconscious failings and 'blind spots' on the part of the therapist, so that nowadays training requires a personal analysis as well as academic seminars and supervised clinical experience.

Analysis for training or otherwise will last three to four years in most cases. A good report on the progress of the training analysis is necessary in order to complete the qualification process. Many schools of therapy derived from psychodynamic ideas still require therapists to undergo a personal experience of therapy. This undoubtedly enlarges knowledge of the process but there is no research evidence to support it as a necessary part of training. The other major approaches to therapy, such as behavioural and systemic paradigms, have never seen personal therapy as necessary or relevant for training.

Single-session therapy by Freud in his private analytic practice has been described by Wells and Gianetti (1990).

Friends of Freud developed his ideas and their dissemination. Splits with his colleagues such as Jung and Ferenczi arose when Freud disagreed with their individual elaborations of his theories. The overall development and dissemination of psychodynamic ideas was rapid in the early twentieth century, although British psychiatry did not accept these ideas until later. The translation in Freud's work of 'Angst' to 'stress' instead of 'fear' confused the issue somewhat. Freud meant 'fear or anxiety' as an individual's response to difficulty. He did not mean 'stress' as the word is used in physics, in the sense of change under load. This mistranslation changed the emphasis of therapy from personal internal experience to a concern with external events such as the relationship with the therapist.

As a result of World War I the British were forced to recognise that stress could induce mental disorder. The best of the country had been sent to war, yet their good genetic backgrounds did not protect them from the horrors of trench warfare. The life expectancy of a junior officer in the British Army at the front line in 1916–17 has been estimated as two weeks. The anthropologist and psychoanalyst W.H.R. Rivers (1917) was a leader in promoting the use of psychodynamic treatments for the disorder known as 'shell shock'. This was attributed to proximity to high explosive blasts. However, it appears to have been a variety of disorders, including simple exhaustion, grief, combat fatigue, depression, anxiety and post-traumatic stress. By contrast, some others advocated extreme approaches, such as using electric shocks and heavy medication. The provision of pensions for those suffering from shell shock may have contributed to prolonged symptomatology in some individuals. Shephard (2000) gives a trained historian's account of the history of psychiatry in modern warfare. However, his sources on leucotomy are historically incomplete. He records that leucotomy ceased in Britain in the early 1950s. In fact, the practice was used as recently as 1975, when a formal investigation into its effectiveness by the Medical Research Council was stopped due to public rejection of the practice.

By the end of the war the literary establishment had drawn Freudian ideas into art and literature across the developed world. The stigma of mental disorder might have been reduced by this widespread shift in attitude towards mental processes. However, an epidemic of an illness called *encephalitis lethargica* affected much of Europe in the 1920s (Von Economo, 1931). This disorder is presumed to have had a viral origin. The disorder sometimes left patients with extensive brain injuries and poor impulse control. Some individuals were extremely dangerous, and in Britain a few spectacular murders led to a public rejection of all mental illness. The specialist hospitals were moved out of towns and given farms to provide food and occupation. Attendants were provided with housing on the hospital site and were discouraged from living elsewhere. There was little effective change in these attitudes until the advent of the National Health Service (NHS) in 1948, when the asylums passed from the control of town councils into the care of the health services. This was followed by significant increases in funding and in public accountability. On the credit side, the first child guidance clinic in the UK opened in London in 1935.

During the 1920s and 1930s, many British and American analysts developed psychodynamic theory further. The British object-relations school expanded with the work of Melanie Klein on infant development and the roles of envy, hate, gratitude and reparation. In the USA, Alfred Adler drew attention to the importance of social roles and the equality of the sexes. He highlighted the wish for power and for positive experiences as being common human phenomena. Interpersonal analysts such as Rank, Sullivan and Horney focused on the development of the ego. Although the psychodrama of Moreno included the choice of a goal by the client, the underlying model remained aligned with psychodynamic theories of causation (Holmes and Karp, 1991). Since training in psychoanalysis had been restricted to medical practitioners in many countries, the medical model remained influential. Some psychoanalysts obtained medical qualifications solely in order to be allowed to practise analysis.

Like previous wars, World War II produced numerous emotional casualties. This led to major developments in group therapy in Britain because of the number of casualties and the small number of experienced psychotherapists available. The Army's assumption that soldiers do everything in groups has also been described as a relevant factor.

Talking treatment expanded dramatically in the USA from 1954 because changes to legislation meant that the costs of mental health treatment became refundable through health insurance. This forward-looking change led to the acknowledgement of much distress. Psychodynamic theory gained influence as the best available theory to explain emotions and their connection with mental processes.

In the excitement, the failure of psychodynamic theory to explain the behaviour of large groups passed unnoticed. War and persecution were neglected in favour of examining the internal world of the individual. Bruno Bettelheim, a psychoanalyst in the USA who had survived the concentration camps, wrote 'many people have enemies who wish them evil; it was the indifference of all those others who should have come to their aid which was so finally destructive to Jewish hopes' (1979, p. 211). In other words, the crucial element was the reaction from their social context. Yet it was many years before these words were linked to the interactions between people which occur in the therapy room. The focus of therapy continued to be the relationship with the therapist, as if the therapist was the centre of the patient's world. Events in the external world were considered secondary to the work in the therapy room. This emphasis on one-to-one relating might have some advantages but it has delayed our understanding of human interactions.

The psychodynamic (not psychoanalytic) view is that expressing emotions (catharsis) undergoing 'corrective emotional experience' and developing insight will bring relief. But the work of Bushman et al. (1999) suggests that catharsis makes people more aggressive, not less so. Aggression is not decreased if it is a success; it is repeated.

The appearance of reliable antipsychotic drugs (chlorpromazine, 1952) and antidepressants (monoamine oxidase inhibitors, 1957; imipramine, 1958) strengthened the medical model within psychiatry in the developed world. However, the resulting improvements in outcomes aided moves towards community care and the wider application of mental health techniques to the public in general.

So we see that the Freudian influence continued into the 1960s. Valuable features drawn from psychodynamic psychotherapy which still apply in solution-focused work are the attention to the client's words, respect for the client's views and no pressure on the client to be different.

Rogers' client-centred therapy moved from theories about mental processes towards an emphasis on the interaction in the consulting room. Rogers believed that clients could solve the problem themselves if the therapist provided a non-directive relationship with the right qualities of empathy, warmth and genuineness. Not all clients found this useful, and it was difficult to keep therapy to an acceptable length. Studies in brief therapy and elsewhere have suggested that clients expect task-setting or advice from therapists. The lack of this element in Rogerian therapy may have diminished its effectiveness. However, Roger's confidence in the client's own resources has re-emerged in solution-focused therapy.

Behaviour Therapies

We now turn to the other major source of therapeutic approaches in the twentieth century: the behaviour therapies. The Russian scientist I.P. Pavlov began his work in the late nineteenth century. He demonstrated stimulus-response conditioning in dogs. This is usually summarised thus: ringing a bell when food was presented led to salivation when the bell was rung in the absence of food. However, Pavlov's own writings (1926) are a model of scientific clarity and reveal more complex material. There is a misunderstanding about Pavlov's work. Writing in the Russian language he talked of 'conditional' reflexes, that is, reflexes which occurred after certain previous conditions had been experienced. In translation this became 'conditioned' reflexes, implying that the reflexes were induced or inserted by the experimenter (see http//:en.wikipedia.org/wiki/Ivan_Pavlov). This moved the focus of interest towards control by the experimenter and away from the innate abilities of the animal and from the context in which the reflexes were induced. This led behaviourism to be interpreted as a form of didactic process, and less attention was given to the responses of the subject of the experiments.

Pavlov's own writings demonstrate his attention to the varying abilities of his subjects. Note that statistical tests could not be applied because, instead of the group studies which would be expected in the present day, Pavlov tested one dog at a time. Some dogs conditioned successfully; some dogs needed constant retraining; some never learned, becoming aggressive or immobile. Perhaps these latter dogs had personality disorder, or were not clever enough to learn, or were born anarchists. When Pavlov's laboratories were flooded by bad weather some dogs forgot everything that they had learned. The significance of this for human behaviour is unknown. (The meaning of the term 'flooding' in modern behavioural treatment is different. It refers to exposure to your fear repeatedly until you stop being afraid. Its effectiveness is probably modified by personality and relationship factors in the therapeutic process.)

The American psychologist B.F. Skinner extended Pavlov's work on stimulus and response in the early twentieth century. Psychology at this time was about measuring and matching: Binet developed tests to classify children on entry to the schools of Paris in 1905, at the request of the civil authorities. In the USA, teams were asked to develop intelligence tests for adults in order to assess some of the millions of immigrants coming through Ellis Island in the hope of living in the country. Some of the original ideas of Binet in France and Wechsler in the USA are still in use today.

By the 1960s, many psychologists had added behaviour therapy skills to their existing repertoire. This change brought a variety of new treatments and increased the total amount of therapy time available to the public. The use of goals and of baseline measurements required in behaviour therapy has been usefully inherited by brief therapy.

From the 1960s Beck (1967) in the USA and Marks (1987) in the UK refined the practice of cognitive-behaviour therapy (CBT) for depression and obsessive-compulsive disorder. Attempts to modify the cognitive elements associated with specific behaviours became part of the treatment process. In the 1980s, cognitive-behavioural methods gradually supplanted psychodynamic therapy as the most commonly used psychological treatment within British psychiatry. The case for CBT in depression has been challenged by Wampold et al. (2002). Nevertheless, it has now been widely applied to a variety of other mental health problems, including personality change. The evidence base for these uses is less certain. CBT is no longer brief; treatments may require 16–24 sessions over a year or more. The leading behaviourist Emmelkamp (1994) is of the opinion that there is no useful difference between CBT and behaviour modification.

Cognitive-analytic therapy (CAT) was developed by the psychoanalyst Anthony Ryle (1990). The work focuses on identifying repetitive mistakes in behaviour and relationships, which are held to have been learned through unsatisfactory experiences in the past. The client keeps a diary of these mistakes and seeks to change them directly, while also working with the therapist to develop an understanding of how these patterns have arisen. It is believed that this understanding facilitates changes in day-to-day behaviour. This approach has been proposed as a treatment for borderline personality disorder (Ryle, 1997). It is said to be similar to CBT as regards length of treatment. CAT retains the assumption of expert knowledge on the part of the therapist, which is common to both psychodynamic and cognitive-behavioural paradigms.

Dialectical behaviour therapy is a version of CBT for borderline personality disorder. It includes noting the client's perception of the therapist (Linehan, 1993). The use of this model has been extended to other mental health problems without supporting research. Although the published work on the use of dialectical behaviour therapy is small, it has been adopted by the NHS as a workable and important treatment, often funded when others are not. This is reminiscent of the way in which the political influence of Freudian ideas extended well ahead of their research base.

CBT identified the importance of client thoughts and perceptions, features it shares with solution-focused therapy. It retains the role of the therapist as expert advisor to the client, who is assumed to lack the resources to manage their condition.

Systems Theory

Elsewhere the cybernetic revolution led to new ideas about processes themselves and the way in which living systems interact. The work of Geoffrey

Bateson, the social anthropologist (Bateson et al., 1956), played a large part in the transfer of these ideas to the human sciences. The Mental Research Institute in California, the innovative family therapists of the Milan group in Italy and many talented lesser figures linked these ideas with therapy. An essential feature of systems thinking as applied to the field of therapy is that behaviour and cognition occur within cultures and contexts. They are reinforced or extinguished by the responses of other beings within our context.

While systemic ideas flourished in the therapy field, the skills of observing behaviour in individuals and groups drawn from behaviourist and mathematical models led to deductions about social systems based on animal observations.

Examples include the work of Hinde (1989) on the relational aspects of mother–infant interaction in monkeys and the observations of Goodall (1990) on social relationships within clans of chimpanzees. The psychoanalyst John Bowlby rephrased psychoanalytic ideas in terms of social attachments (Bowlby, 1969, 1973, 1980). His great insight was to assume that fears and attachments had meaning and value and were not simply irrational phenomena. He found much support for his hypothesis in ethology and the many new studies of survival-based behaviour in primates and other animals. He drew attention to the advantages of mutual protection, mature dependence and altruism for social animals such as human beings. Many of these psychodynamic insights have now been supported by systemic theory and studies on the neurobiology of human infants.

Among brief therapists there is debate about whether solution-focused brief therapy is or is not a systemic therapy. Solution-focused brief therapy does share the systemic view that any interaction will affect all parts of the system or social group. Each client can only change themselves, but such changes will also affect others. Acting 'as if' change has already happened will produce changes in the systems of which the client is part. At a practical level, taking a break during sessions and having live supervision from behind a one-way screen are common elements of solution-focused therapy, which have their origin in systemic practice.

Brief Therapies

In the field of brief therapy, Dr Milton Erickson was a major influence through his clinical skill in hypnosis (Haley, 1973) and his innovative approaches to behaviour change. Erickson left no formal accounts of his methods, but others have studied his clinical work in detail. His focus on 'utilization' led him to start with whatever the client presented. He stated that change, not understanding, is the pre-eminent goal and this has had a great influence on the postmodern therapies. The seminal work on lunatic asylums and other 'total institutions' by the sociologist Erving Goffman (1968) is well known. He was the first to use the term 'strategic' in the sense of actions taken to influence the other (1956). He drew on interactions seen in marketing and advertising as well as on his knowledge of mental disorder and sociological enquiry.

Many well-known names are associated with the Mental Research Institute in Palo Alto, California, and with the development of strategic therapy: Don Jackson, Paul Watzlawick, John Weakland, Jay Haley (Watzlawick et al., 1974; Fisch et al., 1982). Watzlawick et al. explicitly identify the ineffectiveness of logical thought as a tool for solving problems in the sphere of human emotion and interaction.

In my view, strategic therapy identified several key elements for solution-focused brief therapy:

• a non-expert stance;
• the emphasis on the client's language;
• the requirement that the number of sessions is kept to the minimum;
• the value of making changes slowly; and
• the recognition that the problem and the solution are not connected.

In hypnotherapy and neurolinguistic programming, creative visualisation is used to generate new ideas and to reduce anxiety (Bandler and Grinder, 1979; Cade and O'Hanlon, 1993). The 'miracle question' commonly used in solution-focused brief therapy often stimulates creativity and the visualisation of preferred future events. In everyday practice, there are similarities between creative visualisation, the Ericksonian 'letter from yourself in the future' technique (Dolan, 2000), the miracle question of solution-focused therapy and 'thickening the counterplot' as used in narrative therapy (see below).

New ideas peculiar to solution-focused brief therapy itself include a faith in people's abilities, resources and motivation; and a lack of a formal theory of change. The focus is on the client, not on the expert knowledge of the therapist.

Ben Furman is a leading solution-focused therapist and psychiatrist from Finland. He and his colleague Tapani Ahola have developed their own range of skills around 'solution talk' (1992). These have been applied within industry and in public service broadcasting. Their training programme has led to national accreditation of solution-focused therapy from the Finnish government. The techniques are largely solution-focused but also draw on narrative influences and the personal insights of the authors.

The leading narrative therapists of the southern hemisphere (White and Epston, 1990) described the formation of new stories and the concepts of reauthoring and 'thickening the counterplot'. To an outsider these phenomena seem to occur in both narrative and solution-focused brief therapy, although they are taught and marketed as different approaches. White and

Epston also discussed the concept of 'therapy as text', but they derive this from sources other than Wittgenstein and de Shazer. Narrative therapists explicitly address political aspects of the human condition. This is seen as inappropriate by solution-focused therapists unless the client specifically identifies a wish to address these issues.

The 'afterconversations' and reflecting teams devised by T. Andersen (1995) are similarly very close in concept to solution-focused work and to narrative approaches even though they were developed independently. Milner and O'Byrne (1998) discuss some of these overlaps in more detail.

Just to complicate matters as the therapeutic relationship becomes ever more central, Sapolsky (2002) suggests that among baboons, friendships between individuals are at least as significant as social hierarchies. Furthermore, baboons appear able to identify which group members are probable descendants. They offer more support to those who are likely to carry their genes. This suggests a far greater degree of long-term knowledge than had been expected. If a single act of intercourse two years ago can affect the behaviour of a male baboon towards a member of the next generation, what assumptions affect humans of which we are not aware?

Conclusion

Many elements of solution-focused brief therapy can be found in historical predecessors and that every style of therapy has useful ideas or skills that are incorporated into postmodern practice. Freud, Pavlov, Erickson and the Mental Research Institute have all played their part in identifying the core skills of solution-focused approaches. The skill is to retain what is effective in any model while removing the unnecessary elements. As this becomes clear to us, we are presented with Wampold and Seligman, changing yet again our perspective on the important aspects of therapy. Their work points to the many forms of talking treatment which may be equally effective, and to the fact that much of the benefit arises from therapist and client variables rather than the model of therapy employed.

From 1986, the new elements within solution-focused brief therapy introduced by the Milwaukee team led the way to further changes in therapy methodology. Knowledge about how change is viewed by individuals has been advanced. The expansion and development of these ideas has had a huge effect on therapy. The issues have spread beyond therapy to management science, anthropology and philosophy. Parallel concepts from linguistics and narrative therapy are helping to sustain the change. The language of solution-focused therapy is now often seen in the teaching materials used by therapists from other models of behaviour change.

The history of science suggests that complex ideas will be reviewed about every 60 years. There will then be a reformulation or a rejection of many of the complexities. It may be that we are at such a stage in the development of psychological therapies. Nevertheless, we need to be aware of the roots of our practice in order to retain the best of our history and in order to avoid employing ideas that have already been tried and found wanting.

Key Points

- Many aspects of mental activity had been studied prior to Freud's writings.
- Psychodynamic psychotherapy has contributed attention to the client's words, respect for the client's views and no pressure on the client to be different.
- Roger's confidence in the client's own abilities has re-emerged in solution focused therapy.
- Goals and baseline measurements are linked with behaviour therapy.
- Cognitive-behavioural therapy also highlights client thoughts and perceptions.
- Systemic elements include acting 'as if' change has already happened in order to produce changes in systems.
- Strategic therapy identified key elements of brief therapy: a non-expert stance; emphasis on the client's language; the minimum of sessions necessary; the value of making changes slowly; and the recognition that the problem and the solution are not connected.
- New ideas peculiar to solution-focused brief therapy itself include a faith in people's abilities, resources and motivation and the absence of a formal theory of change.

6

The Research and Evidence Base for Solution-Focused Therapy

Contents

- Process research in psychotherapy
- Process research in solution-focused therapy
- Meta-analyses
- Systematic reviews
- Randomised controlled studies of outcome in solution-focused therapy
- Comparison studies of outcome in solution-focused brief therapy
- Effectiveness studies in solution-focused brief therapy
- The effect of solution-focused therapy on therapists
- Future developments
- Conclusion

Solution-focused therapy had an evidence base of six evaluation studies in 1994, which has increased now to 97 relevant studies, including two meta-analyses and three systematic reviews. This is better than many earlier psychotherapies can show. This chapter assesses the current state of psychotherapy research and then examines the available information about solution-focused therapy in particular.

From the outset, the development of solution-focused brief therapy by the Milwaukee team was research-based, in the sense of being driven by feedback from clients as to which elements of therapy were effective in increasing goal attainment. This differs from many styles of therapy in which therapy methods have been derived from theoretical postulates about human behaviour and how to influence it. The focus is on the client, not on the expert knowledge of the therapist. As discussed, Steve de

Shazer (1994) made the distinction between 'text-focused' reading, in which the text or conversation is the primary source of information, and 'reader-focused' reading, in which the reader's internal information is continuously matched against the content and meaning of the text and conversation. He drew the parallel between therapy methods that concentrate on what the client brings as opposed to the alternative applied in traditional therapies in which the reader/therapist has special knowledge and only needs enough from the clients to make a fit with the preconceived ideas and plans of the therapist. An extreme example can be taken from early psychoanalytic work, in which reports by clients about incest were assumed to be fantasy or wish-fulfilment, because that was the official view of the trainers. It would be rare nowadays for any therapist to make this assumption without considering the possibility that the client was reporting actual events.

This concept of therapy as text-focused links well with Wittgenstein's view of language as the essential tool for thought. The lack of technical language in solution-focused brief therapy is both a consequence of this view of therapy and an asset in communicating with clients.

Scientific validation of any therapy must rely on formal evaluation. It is necessary to decide which evaluation studies should be included. For outcome studies the criteria here are that they should have been published in a durable form following peer review and that they should include some form of post-therapy follow-up data. Many psychotherapy studies record outcome at the end of therapy, at which time there may be 'honeymoon effects' for both therapist and client. Also, unless their organisation insists, few therapists will discharge a client at a time when things are going badly.

The literature is now very extensive, a Google search in English producing some 800–1,200 new references every year. At the time of writing (2010) there were 97 relevant studies, two meta-analyses, and 17 randomised controlled trials showing benefit from solution-focused approaches with nine showing benefit over existing methods. Of 34 comparison studies, 26 favour the solution-focused arm of the study. Effectiveness data are also available from some 4,000 cases with a success rate exceeding 60 per cent, requiring an average of three to five sessions of therapy time. This body of research is better than many other psychotherapies can show. The overall effectiveness of psychotherapy has been shown to be 60–70 per cent, regardless of diagnostic categories, with higher levels of success being found for specialist teams or programmes (Wampold, 2001; Seligman, 1995).

The solution-focused model is approved by the USA Federal Government. It has been accepted as a valid treatment approach by the State of Washington and the State of Oregon. Approval from the State of Texas is being sought.

Finland has a government-approved accreditation programme. Canada has a registration body for practitioners and therapists.

Process Research in Psychotherapy

Detailed information is now available for most major forms of psychotherapy. The role of common factors across different therapy models is being increasingly highlighted. Some of the main findings are summarised below.

The *Consumer Reports* study (Seligman, 1995) obtained self-report data from 2,900 therapy clients. This was the biggest follow-up study of psychotherapy ever undertaken. The study found that psychotherapy works but that there was no link between problem type and which therapy was helpful; that clients who make active choices about their therapy do better; and that exercising choice and control are beneficial for clients but will hamper randomised trials. There are echoes of solution-focused brief therapy in these conclusions. The study found that 52 per cent of therapies were completed after six months and 64 per cent by 12 months. The report does not link this to the number of sessions of treatment received. Restrictions on the client's choice of therapist or on the length of treatment reduced the effectiveness of therapy.

The randomised controlled study reported by Knekt and Lindfors (2004), comparing solution-focused and short-term psychodynamic therapy, is described below. Note here that the average length of solution-focused therapy in this study was 7.5 months for 10 sessions as against 5.7 months for 15 sessions of psychodynamic therapy, so that both might be considered 'brief' therapies but still required six months of activity.

Howard et al. (1986) identify a dose-related effect in psychotherapy, but studies of solution-focused brief therapy do not support this. Most brief therapy clients are discharged as soon as they feel able to continue on their own. Studies of psychotherapy in general have not yet been successful in defining the relative contributions of face-to-face therapy time, the duration of therapy and the effects of external life events and the passage of time.

A well-reasoned paper by Mathers in 1974 suggested that identity change takes up to 18 months to consolidate but actually happens in three months or less. He based this view on his experience as a psychotherapist and on observation of military personnel who had experienced a wide variety of life events. He suggested that this rule for change over time applies both after life events and in psychodynamic therapy. This idea has considerable implications for both brief therapists and for those who undertake long-term work.

A concept paper by Masserman in 1972 is of interest. Jules Masserman was both a psychoanalyst and a specialist in behaviour modification. He proposed that the benefit of all types of psychotherapy is the reduction of uncertainty, whatever the method of therapy employed. Once uncertainty is at a manageable level, then the client's anxiety becomes tolerable and they feel able to function without the therapist. One can conceptualise solution-focused therapy and other brief therapies as looking at the minimum necessary input to reduce uncertainty down to the level at which a client can function independently once more.

Hubble et al. (1999) described in detail many of the common factors likely to be affecting therapy outcome. At that time interest was directed at Lambert's (1992) 'educated guess' that technique accounts for 15 per cent of effectiveness, hope and expectancy for 15 per cent, relationship factors for 30 per cent, and client and extratherapeutic factors for the remaining 40 per cent. *The Heroic Client* by Duncan and Miller (2000) highlights the client factors in some detail. It also discusses some of the general factors that may be relevant, in particular the role of therapist and process variables, which may not be related to the particular model of therapy in use.

The major meta-analysis of psychotherapy research conducted by Wampold (2001) has emphasised the role of common factors in the practice of psychotherapy. He concentrated his enquiry on studies in which there were direct comparisons between different models. He concluded that the absolute efficacy of psychotherapy is 13 per cent. Within that 13 per cent, specific factors account for at most 8 per cent; and client factors account for 22 per cent, including the client's assessment of the therapeutic alliance and the client's liking for the model offered. Outcomes are better for clients if the therapist has allegiance to a model (any model). General and external factors such as placebo effect account for up to 70 per cent of the variance in outcome.

Wampold suggested that some therapists are more effective than others but that the way to find such a therapist is by reputation, not by any specific training or experience. If correct, his conclusions contradict existing beliefs about matching treatment to diagnosis and employing manualised treatments. The lack of a link between diagnosis and response to treatment is an issue currently challenging the 'Evidence-based Practice' movement in the USA and elsewhere (Wampold and Bhati, 2004). These issues present a challenge to existing training institutions and structures that compete with each other to have the 'best' model. Wampold challenges the use of randomised controlled trials as a means of assessing psychotherapies on the grounds that these are designed to fit the 'medical model'. He states that the base assumptions ignore variables such as different therapist skills and personalities. The medical model assumes that therapists are interchangeable and that exposure to one treatment does not affect subsequent responses to another. These assumptions are unlikely to be true of psychotherapy.

Other studies have shown that for all models, central issues for effective therapy include client–therapist collaboration in a therapeutic alliance with an emphasis on clear goals. The therapist must keep the focus on life problems and core relationships. Clients expect therapy to be brief: about five sessions lasting around half an hour each (Garfield, 1986).

In Scotland, Rothwell (2005) asked the question 'How brief is solution-focused brief therapy?' A comparative study using pseudo-randomisation identified 41 solution-focused clients and 119 who received cognitive-behavioural therapy. The solution-focused group had an average of two sessions while the other averaged five sessions. There was no difference in the outcome between groups on the therapist's global assessment of function rating (GAF) from DSM-IV (APA, 1994) .

Lambert (2004, p. 10) has said that 'Almost all therapies that are studied ... are brief, lasting less than 20 sessions.' If this is the current trend, then long-term therapies are becoming of less significance for training and practice.

A new tool of enormous value to psychotherapy research is the micro-analysis of conversations. Studies in numerous countries are pursuing this work. One of the best-known workers in the solution-focused arena is Janet Bavelas and her team (Tomori and Bavelas, 2007; other publications in press). Word-by-word analysis of therapy sessions shows clear differences between styles of therapy and individual practitioners; it shows the accepted form of interviews and identifies the responses made to each style of questioning.

Process Research in Solution-Focused Therapy

Jay McKeel published an extensive review of process research in solution-focused brief therapy in 1996. He concludes that solution-focused talk increases changes and encourages the completing of therapy. Pre-treatment changes are common and premature termination is less common if the therapists talk about the pre-treatment changes (Allgood et al., 1995; Johnson et al., 1998). The miracle question leads to goal setting and optimistic attitudes. Exceptions and scaling questions are often used and lead to more talk on these topics. Clients value the solution-focused emphasis on strengths, compliments and 'what works' as well as the atmosphere of the therapy session (Metcalf et al., 1996).

McKeel agrees that the solution-focused brief therapy model must have been followed appropriately during the research. He asks whether only comparison studies should be acceptable as outcome research and if so, are no-treatment comparison groups necessary, valid or ethical? He proposes 'dismantling' studies in which one or more elements of therapy are different between the groups studied, or where therapist characteristics are different between the groups. The outcome measures will thus identify features that are necessary or sufficient for treatment success. Another option is to study two groups, both of which receive routine treatment for their condition but where one group receives solution-focused therapy in addition. He comments that multiple measures are important in presenting solution-focused therapy to various potential consumers. Therapists may be convinced by certain measures while third-party payers, relatives or clients themselves may value different measures. Objective measures are acceptable to the scientific community and are helpful in comparing different treatment approaches.

Scaling by clients has been shown to be as reliable as testing using objective measures in five existing studies and other work. DeJong and Hopwood (1996) examined 141 cases after therapy had ended and found that scaling and client feedback were usually in agreement. Dahl et al. (2000) examined the results of 69 elderly clients. Scaling by the clients and the GAF usually matched. Nelson and Kelley (2001) treated a group of five couples with marital problems. Eight reported improvement on standard tests of marital function and for seven clients improvement on scaling was associated with this. In the UK, Wiseman (2003) offered a single solution-focused session to 40 self-harm cases. The client's scaling at six month follow-up correlated with a lack of repeat self-harm in 78 per cent of cases. In Gostautas et al. (2005), investigators found that scaling by adolescents correlated well with the test battery.

In Carlisle we studied nine cases using the GAF and the OQ45 symptom/ function questionnaire (Lambert, 1998), which was designed specifically to measure psychotherapy outcome. At the end of therapy, scaling predicted the OQ45 score in seven and the GAF score in nine. Seven cases traced after one year showed correlations in the predicted direction between scaling and the other measures.

The use of a post-therapy enquiry is reported in Shilts et al. (1997). The clients experienced the therapists as listening to their story. They reported that they found the questions helpful in promoting self-confidence and encouraging them to make changes. The researchers found the clients' replies useful and now regard this post-therapy enquiry as part of their therapy practice, because they can modify subsequent sessions in the light of the clients' reactions. Jay McKeel's colleagues at Bowie Child and Family Services (1999) use a similar question set after all sessions.

The Lonnen team in Sweden (Knutsson et al., 1998) hired a researcher from another style of brief therapy to interview clients after therapy was completed. The researcher was experienced in Tom Andersen's reflecting team approach to family therapy (Andersen, 1991). The client responses to his enquiries were supportive of the solution-focused approach. Clients preferred questions to statements. They preferred the questions to continue even if someone was crying because it helped them to move on. They found the scaling questions more useful than the miracle question. Many found the break helpful. They thought that the team should intervene or comment, otherwise 'Why have a team?' (This work is available on the author's website and on the European Brief Therapy Association website at www. ebta.nu)

Mark Beyebach and his colleagues at the Universidad Pontifica in Salamanca have carried out a number of detailed and rigorous studies on brief therapy (1996, 1997, 2000). They have used objective measures, translating them into Spanish and revalidating them where necessary.

The Salamanca team found that 'internal locus of control' in clients was positively linked with compliance with tasks and with a threefold increase in successful outcomes for therapy (Beyebach et al., 1996). However, task compliance was not directly associated with good outcome. Useful pre-treatment changes were reported more often by clients with belief in their own efficacy and with internal locus of control. Such pre-treatment changes were associated with a fourfold increase in successful outcomes. Clients who expected themselves to be successful had clear goals and were seeking to make changes to their situations. Clear goals predicted a twofold increase in success. The team suggest that therapy might be modified according to locus of control and expectancy measures to build on these associations. They suggest that helping clients to develop a sense of control over their lives is one of the tasks of therapy.

Their 1997 data show that exchanges between therapist and client reflecting neither 'one-up' nor 'one-down' relating were associated with continuing to attend therapy. This confirms findings from studies of other brief therapies (Koss and Shiang, 1994). Competitive symmetrical escalation between therapist and client was associated with dropout from therapy. Responses fitting the client's last statement were more common in cases with a good outcome. The pattern of communication between therapist and client changed after a break was taken. Outcomes suffered when the therapist sought to control the pattern of the whole session.

A much-quoted paper by Adams et al. (1991) describes three groups of 20 families each. One group received the Formula First Session Task (FFST) and a solution-focused second session followed by problem-focused therapy; another group the FFST and problem-focused therapy thereafter; the third group received a problem-focused task and then problem-focused therapy. The FFST is: 'Between now and the next time we meet, I would like you to observe, so that you can describe it to me, what happens in your family/life/marriage/relationship that you want to continue to have happen.' Compliance with tasks, clarity of goals and improvement in the problem were better in FFST groups at the second session but outcomes were equal for all groups at session 10.

Littrell et al. (1995) allocated high school students to one of three treatment groups for a single session of therapy. Of a total of 61 students, 19 received a session focusing on the problem and ending with a task, 20 received a session about the problem without a task, and 22 received a solution-focused session ending with a task. Sixty-nine per cent were better at six weeks' follow-up in all groups, but the solution-focused sessions were all shorter than in the other groups.

Working with a rural community in Dumfries, Scotland, our team made a trial of proceeding directly to therapy questions without asking for any information about 'the problem'. Our outcome results for this group in terms of goal achievement at one-year follow-up were the same as for our overall population. However, the comments about the therapy experience were more critical: 'The team had their own agenda', 'We got better but the team were not interested'. We concluded that we had failed to join appropriately with the attenders. We returned to spending a few minutes defining the problem in terms of name, frequency and duration before proceeding. Critical feedback then diminished while outcomes remained the same.

Bowles et al. (2001) examined the effect of training on nurses' communication skills. Sixteen student nurses received training and 10 were followed up after six months on six items. All the items shifted in the desired direction but the differences did not reach statistical significance. Qualitative data are reported in this study also: staff reported increased self-confidence and less work-related tension.

Following the work of Bowles in the UK, Australia and Canada have examined the effects of solution-focused training on nurses' communication. In the UK, Hosany et al. (2007) provided two-day training for 36 mental health nurses working in two acute admission units. At follow-up after three months there was a significant increase in the use of solution-focused questions.

Nurses in two Australian emergency departments completed questionnaires before and after participating in solution-focused nurse training focused on working with complex clients who self-harm. A comparison group of nurses also completed questionnaires. Results indicated some benefits of the intervention. There were improvements in participants' perception that nursing is strengths oriented and in nurses' satisfaction with their skills. There were no significant improvements in nurses' reports of their professional self-concept (McAllister et al., 2008).

The Canadian experience, reported by McGilton et al. (2006), was a 10-week follow-up of solution-focused communication enhancement training. Twenty-one nurses and 16 patients provided data. Nurses felt closer to patients and had higher job satisfaction at a statistically significant level.

Dr Ronald Warner of Canada has presented a number of studies of training effects in solution-focused work (2000). His measures form a useful way of thinking about progress, by analysing sections of an audio or video tape of an interview and looking for the specific solution-focused elements. The students scale the rapport within the interview as they perceive it in super-vision reviews. They are asked to identify points for further improvement in their skills and to identify relevant references in the literature for this purpose. This form of structured review can be used as a part of continuous assessment.

In summary, process research is beginning to show us which elements of therapy are effective and for which clients. The outline that emerges is similar to that now being discerned in studies of other psychotherapies. The important difference for solution-focused therapy is that many non-essential elements within therapy have already been discarded.

Meta-Analyses

Two meta-analyses of solution-focused therapy have been carried out. The forthcoming research handbook by Franklin et al. (2011) will include the findings from both. That of Stams et al. (2006) has been published in Dutch. They selected 21 studies comprising a total of 1,421 clients. They examined client characteristics, the type of problem, the characteristics of the intervention, the form of the study and factors that might affect publication bias.

The authors calculated Cohen's d (a Cohen's d of 0.80 means a large effect; d = 0.50 means a moderate effect; and d = 0.20 means a small effect). The mean effect of solution-focused therapy on reduction of problems was d = 0.37, which implies a small to moderate positive effect. This effect was not better compared to the 'treatment as usual' control group, though the effect was better than the 'no-treatment' condition (d = 0.57).

The meta-analysis showed that solution-focused therapy had more effect on behavioural problems (d = 0.61) than on marital, psychiatric and 'other' problems (respectively, d = 0.55, 0.48 and 0.22). The meta-analysis showed that adults profited more from solution-focused therapy than children, and that clients in residential settings profited more than clients treated in non-residential settings. The effect of studies with a control group was much smaller than the effect of studies without a control group (respectively, d = 0.25 and 0.84). Recent studies showed the strongest effects.

The authors, clearly adherents of solution-focused approaches, are dis-appointed by the somewhat meagre results. In the discussion they try to explain the fact that solution-focused therapy does no better than 'treat-ment as usual' by the hypothesis that all forms of therapy are equally effective and that common factors determine the effect of a therapy. The authors concluded that solution-focused therapy satisfies 'the clients need for autonomy' more than other treatments and is shorter, 'Therefore it's reasonable to consider this form of therapy when it's tuned to the client and his problems' (Stams et al., 2006, p. 81).

The meta-analysis by Kim (2008) examined 22 studies using three categories based on the outcome problem each study targeted. The three categories were externalising behaviour problems, internalising behaviour problems, and family and relationship problems. A large number of other factors were also examined. The study found that solution-focused brief therapy demonstrated small but positive treatment effects in favour of solution-focused approaches. Cohen's d produced an overall weighted mean effect size estimate of 0.11 for externalising behaviour problems, 0.26 for internalising problem behaviours, and 0.26 for family and relationship problems. Only the magnitude of the effect for internalising behaviour problems was statistically significant at the $p<0.05$ level, thereby indicating that the treatment effect for the solution-focused group was different than the treatment effect for the control group. This meta-analysis places solution-focused therapy as being as good as 'treatment as usual', that is, equivalent to other therapies. Like Stams et al., Kim found the greatest effectiveness for personal behaviour change.

Kim's work shows that an average of 6.5 sessions was required across the included studies to produce these effects. The average number of sessions in the Dutch publication is not given. Neither author has highlighted the point that solution-focused therapy is shown to be as good as other treatments in spite of requiring less therapist time. On the basis of the effectiveness demonstrated by different studies, Kim suggests that competence in solution-focused therapy requires in excess of 20 hours' training (Kim, 2006). This is still much less than that required by other models of therapy, but the finding is important for future planning and accreditation.

The significance of these two meta-analyses is greater because they used very different methods to identify and include studies. Only eight studies appear in both, so a wide variety of work has been examined by these authors.

Systematic Reviews

The first systematic review of solution-focused therapy was published by Gingerich and Eisengart (2000). For their purposes, outcome studies must formally refer to solution-focused brief therapy in the text and include some form of comparison. However, they will accept case–control studies in which there is no separate comparison population and studies in which outcome is measured at the time of discharge from therapy. They do not see peer review as a necessary condition for inclusion and they include studies such as doctoral dissertations, which are not easily accessible to the general reader. Using these criteria they identify 15 outcome studies, of which they found five to be strong studies, four to be moderately strong and six to be poor. They concluded that there was preliminary evidence for the effectiveness of solution-focused therapy. By 2001 they had updated this study, finding seven strong studies, five moderate and six poor. There was statistically significant improvement in 10 studies and of the 11 studies that compared solution-focused therapy with other treatments, seven found solution-focused therapy to be the better treatment (updated version at www.gingerich.net). A further update is in preparation.

Corcoran and Pillai carried out a systematic review of the research on solution-focused therapy in 2007. On the basis of statistics, design, follow-up and numbers, they included 10 quasi-experimental studies, all in English, only two of which were follow-up studies. By their criteria they found a moderate or high effect size in four studies. They ask 'Are qualified workers better than students?'

In 2009 Kim and Franklin reported an extension of Kim (2008) examining seven studies of solution-focused therapy in school settings. This review suggests that solution-focused therapy may be effectively applied with at-risk students in a school setting, specifically helping to reduce the intensity of negative feelings and to manage conduct problems and externalising behavioural problems. Age ranges for applications in schools appeared flexible, from 10 years to older children and adolescents.

Randomised Controlled Studies of Outcome in Solution-Focused Brief Therapy

There have been 17 randomised controlled studies of solution-focused brief therapy reported in the literature.

Two randomised controlled trials of solution-focused brief therapy are reported by Lindforss and Magnusson (1997). They took their samples from those entering a Swedish prison for recurrent offenders. The base condition was being an imprisoned recurrent offender and the dependent variable was the addition of solution-focused therapy. In the pilot study prisoners were allocated in turn to experimental or control conditions before being offered therapy. The experimental study was randomised more precisely because both experimental and control groups were made up of prisoners who had already agreed to have treatment if offered it. The prisoners made their own choice of problem for therapy. The therapists were independent of the prison administration. Reoffending rates and details of subsequent offences were used as the follow-up measures.

In the pilot study 14 of 21 (66 per cent) experimental and 19 of 21 (90 per cent) controls reoffended at 20 months. One prisoner in the control group died of drug-related causes. In the main study with 30 experimental and 29 controls over a 16-month follow-up, 18 (60 per cent) in the experimental group reoffended and 25 (86 per cent) in the control group. There were more drug offences and more total offences in the control group. Three prisoners in the control group died and none died in the experimental group. The prisoners received an average of five treatment sessions. There were no significant demographic differences between the groups. Lindforss and Magnusson estimated that over €291,000 were saved (nominally) by reduced reoffending.

The study is elegant and statistically significant. At the beginning neither the prisoners nor the prison staff expected any changes. All the prisoners saw themselves as 'born unlucky' and therefore did not object if they found themselves allocated to the control condition. It is also interesting that in spite of the extensive provision made in Sweden to separate children and young people from bad circumstances, all the prisoners had retained active and recent contact with family members. Many of the families were valuable resources for the prisoners in developing solutions to their problems.

The Helsinki Psychotherapy Study Group have conducted a very large randomised trial of four psychotherapies (Knekt and Lindfors, 2004; Knekt et al., 2008). The study was a randomised comparison study of solution-focused therapy, short-term psychodynamic therapy, long-term psychodynamic therapy and psychoanalysis. Ninety-three received solution-focused therapy against 98 receiving short-term psychodynamic psychotherapy for problems exceeding one year in duration. A wide range of social and health measures were used as well as measures to ensure treatment integrity. The average for solution-focused therapy was 10 sessions over 7.5 months, and for short-term psychodynamic therapy was 15 sessions over 5.7 months, so both were 'brief' therapies. Solution-focused therapy produced 43 per cent (mood) and 26 per cent (anxiety) recovery at seven months, maintained at 12 months. Short-term psychodynamic therapy produced recovery in 43 per cent (mood) and 35 per cent (anxiety). There was therefore no significant difference in therapy outcome.

Some of the additional measures suggested that solution-focused therapy was effective more quickly in depression and that short-term psychotherapy produced changes on some measures of 'personality disorder'. This was based on personality disorder as diagnosed by the therapist, but the formal measures of personality used did not support this. It may be that this represents differences in diagnostic practice for the two schools of therapy rather than a difference in effect for the two therapies. Measures of socio-economic status showed no apparent social class difference for outcomes. No figures for partial recovery have been published. The authors are concerned that for both therapies a reduction in symptoms was not accompanied by major change in the social and work measures. Similar results were found in the long-term group. At three years follow-up gains were maintained only in the long-term psychotherapy group. This is not surprising, given that many things can happen to people in three years. Constant support may or may not be desired by people but is expensive. Short-term therapies were followed by more healthy lifestyle changes. Unpublished reports from the Helsinki Group are that one of the solution-focused group has been rehospitalised as against five from the short-term and six from the long-term psychotherapy groups. The psychoanalysis comparison data are not yet published.

Zhang et al. (2010) carried out a randomised study of patients with schizophrenia in China. A solution-focused health education programme for 58 patients produced significantly better (p>0.05) social support and coping skills than routine health education for 56 controls.

Another precise study using a randomised controlled design was conducted by Cockburn et al. (1997), who compared two approaches to rehabilitation following orthopaedic treatment for injuries sustained at work. Twenty-five experimental clients were offered six solution-focused sessions while 23 controls received the standard rehabilitation package. When reviewed after 60 days, 68 per cent of the experimental group had returned to work within seven days compared with 4 per cent of the controls.

From Norway, Nystuen and Hagen (2006) report on a solution-focused intervention for sick-listed employees with psychological problems or muscle skeletal pain. This was a randomised controlled trial of long-term sickness. Fifty-three subjects received eight sessions of group treatment and there were 50 controls. At one-year follow-up there was no significant difference in return to work but mental health scores significantly improved. The authors question their sample size and the measures chosen.

Smock et al. (2008) have conducted a trial of solution-focused group therapy for level 1 substance abusers. Twenty-seven experimental subjects were randomised to six-weekly groups, while 29 controls received the six-weekly Hazelden group programme. Nineteen experimentals and 19 controls completed the study. At post-test there was significant improvement in depression and symptom distress but dependence scores remained unchanged.

Froeschle et al. (2007) examined the efficacy of a systematic substance abuse programme for adolescent females. Thirty-two subjects received a package of 16 weekly solution-focused therapy group sessions, plus action learning and regular mentoring. There were 33 controls. Using a pre-test-post-test design, the study found that drug use, attitudes to use, knowledge of drugs, home and school behaviour all improved significantly.

From Texas comes a randomised study of adolescent mothers (Harris and Franklin, 2009). There were 33 mothers in the experimental group and 40 comparison mothers. The solution-focused Taking Charge group programme was added to the usual school routine. They found significant post-test improvement in attendance, grades, social problem solving and coping. Less drop-out occurred in the Taking Charge group: 3 per cent versus 20 per cent. (Two smaller studies (n=46, n=23) replicate these findings).

For Korean 15–18-year-olds on probation, Ko et al. (2003) report a randomised trial of group counselling. Thirty received the intervention of six weekly sessions while 30 controls received no treatment. Better problem coping was reported in those who received the intervention.

Again in Korea, Shin (2009) carried out a similar randomised study of 20 adolescents on probation who received six weekly group sessions and 20 controls who received 'as and when' support. At the end of the programme there was reduced aggression and increased social adjustment in the experimental group.

With the support of the European Brief Therapy Association annual research grant, Karin Wallgren Thorslund conducted a randomised study of group therapy for patients on long-term sick leave (2007). There were 15 experimental and 15 control subjects, who had been off work for 1–5 months. After eight sessions there was an increased return to work (60 per cent vs 13 per cent), and psychological health improved at three-month follow-up.

A study carried out by Wilmshurst in 2002 in Texas compared two treatments for youths with emotional and behavioural disorders. Clients were randomly allocated to treatment for 12 weeks. Twenty-seven attended a five-days per week residential programme based on solution-focused methods, with 26 hours of family contact in addition. The other 38 clients received a community-based cognitive-behavioural therapy (CBT) programme and 48 hours of family contact. At one-year follow-up, total behaviour was improved in both groups. Attention deficit hyperactivity disorder (ADHD) behaviours had improved in 63 per cent of those who received CBT and 22 per cent of those in the solution-focused group. Grouped scores for anxiety had reduced by 24 per cent with CBT and 3 per cent with solution-focused work, while grouped scores for depression had reduced by 26 per cent with CBT and 11 per cent with solution-focused intervention. The conclusions from this study are equivocal because there were numerous differences between the treatment packages, so that solution-focused therapy was only one of the variables tested. The author suggested that the difference may lie in the amount of family contact in the two groups. She also suggested that the findings support other studies which indicate that residential care is not the best option for troubled youth.

Daki and Savage (2010) looked at the effect of five solution-focused groups for seven children with academic and emotional difficulties. Seven controls received academic support instead. They found a significantly larger effect size on 26/38 measures in the experimental group and only 10/38 for controls.

Wake et al. (2009) report a large study of overweight children in Australia. In a sample of 258 children, solution-focused health education produced no changes in Body Mass Index, nutrition or activity. This contradicts other health education studies in developed countries. Too few sessions attended or ineffective screening programmes are proposed by the authors as an explanation.

Nine of these randomised studies demonstrate greater effectiveness against 'treatment as usual' (Lindforss and Magnusson (two studies); Zhang et al.; Cockburn et al.; Froeschle et al.; Harris and Franklin; Ko et al.; Shin; Thorslund) or equivalent results to those achieved by short-term psychotherapy (Knekt and Lindfors); the Hazelden programme for substance misuse; and a CBT-based programme (Wilmshurst).

Comparison Studies of Outcome in Solution-Focused Therapy

There are 34 published comparison studies of outcome in solution-focused therapy, of which 26 show good or better results for solution-focused approaches. Thirty-one studies are reviewed here.

In Korea, Chung and Yang (2004) examined the effects of solution-focused group counselling programme for the families with schizophrenic patients. Forty-eight schizophrenic patients within 56 families were studied: 24 patients and 28 families each in experimental and control groups. Eight group sessions were provided for the experimental families. There was a significant reduction in family burden and expressed emotion in the experimental group.

In a short but intriguing paper from the USA, Eakes et al. (1997) studied experimental and control groups, each made up of five clients with chronic schizophrenia, and their families. The study followed the solution-focused therapy model but also used a reflecting team (Andersen, 1991). In the data comparison, for the experimental group the Family Environment Scale showed a significant increase in 'expressiveness' and 'active-recreational orientation' and a decrease in 'incongruence'. Controls showed a significant increase in 'moral-religious emphasis'.

A significant study has been carried out (again supported through the European Brief Therapy Association) by Plamen Panayotov and his colleagues in Bulgaria. Fifty-one patients suffering from schizophrenia received treatment as usual and also solution-focused therapy with goals chosen by the individuals. The outcome measure was days of medication compliance, with each person acting as their own control: compliance was 244 days on average before therapy, which increased to 827 days after therapy. Seventy-six per cent were still taking their prescribed medication at the end of the study. This study will be published in 2011 in the forthcoming American research handbook by Franklin et al.

A large but little-known British study by Forrester et al. (2009) examined an intensive family preservation service for families affected by parental substance misuse. This took the form of motivational interviewing and solution-focused work for 279 children compared with treatment as usual for 89. At follow-up 3.5 years later, 40 per cent of each group had been in care but for less time and with cost saving for the intervention group.

The project by Franklin et al. (2007) examined a programme based on the remarkable Gonzalo Garza Public Alternative School in Austin, Texas. The intention was to reduce dropout from high school and to retrieve the child's studies. Forty-six children in the experimental group earned significantly more credits and more credits per time spent than 39 comparison students even with lower attendance rates. There was an 81 per cent graduation rate for the experimental group against 90 per cent for the comparison group after correcting for differences between the policies in the different schools.

Another study by Franklin et al. (2008) examined 30 children from School A who received 5–7 solution-focused groups and 29 controls from School B. At one-month follow-up of 43 children, teachers reported that externalised and internalised behaviours were significantly improved, while students reported externalised behaviours to be significantly improved.

Newsome (2004) examined solution-focused groups for with at-risk junior high school students. Twenty-six in the experimental group and 26 controls had poor grades and attendance. A group programme for the experimental students produced improved grades significantly in comparison with the controls when tested after the group programme. (Quoted as 'promising treatment' by the USA Office of Juvenile Justice and Delinquency Prevention: www.dsgonline.com/mpg2.5/TitleV_MPG_Table_Ind_Rec.asp?ID=712)

Gostautas et al. from Lithuania (2005) reported a study comparing the results of solution-focused therapy by experienced therapists with a group of adolescents from foster care 'family' units and others from outpatient health services. There were 81 in the experimental group, of whom 44 were in foster care and 37 were attending health care institutions. A comparison group of 52 matched for age, gender and psychosocial adjustment completed the same test measures. All completed further measures 1–4 weeks after completing 2–5 sessions of treatment (average 3.42 sessions). Grouped data are reported: there was a significant difference on all measures for the experimental group; the therapists rated 82 per cent much improved. Client scaling scores were in keeping with the standard instruments.

LaFountain and Garner (1996) published a comparison study between 27 solution-focused counsellors who saw 176 students and a control group of 30 non-solution-focused counsellors who saw 135 students. The experimental students improved significantly on three out of eight measures compared with the controls. Eighty-one per cent of the experimental group achieved their goals, but no data are given for the control students. There was less exhaustion and depersonalisation in solution-focused counsellors after one year compared with the control counsellors.

Lambert et al. (1998) reported a treatment comparison study using the OQ45, a self-report questionnaire from the USA devised specifically to measure changes resulting from psychotherapy. It measures symptoms, relationships and social functioning. Twenty-two cases treated with solution-focused therapy (from the full series of 38 cases published in Johnson and Shaha, 1996) were compared with 45 who received psychodynamic psychotherapy at a university public mental health centre. Both methods achieved 46 per cent recovery; solution-focused therapy by the third session and the mental health centre by session 26. The solution-focused therapist was an experienced therapist in private practice; the university therapists were a more diverse group. The clients were from separate populations who were included in what were essentially two separate outcome studies. There is no information on whether therapy gains were sustained.

Lamprecht et al. (2007) followed a group of 40 first-time self-harming patients after a single solution-focused session. Only two (6.25 per cent) had harmed themselves again compared with 40 (13.2 per cent) of 302 untreated cases. (This study updates Wiseman, 2003.)

The comparison study by Littrell et al. (1995) is described earlier in this chapter.

As the world becomes more crowded, raising children becomes more expensive and families therefore place their hopes on a smaller number of children. At the same time, resources for helping troubled children are never enough to meet local needs. So cost-efficient interventions are valuable and several interesting studies from around the world are described.

A comparison study by Corcoran (2006) dealt with 239 children with behaviour problems. Eighty-three received the group intervention and 156 'treatment as usual'. The intervention group showed better treatment engagement but there were no outcome differences.

In Norway, Kvarme et al. (2010) studied a group programme for schoolchildren. There were 55 girls in the experimental group and 26 boys; the control group numbers were 44 and 20 respectively. There was an increase in self-efficacy on standard measures at post-test for girls and at three-month follow-up for boys and girls, with a slight improvement for controls also at three months.

Nowicka et al. have reported two studies (2007, 2008) with obese children. In 2007, 54 obese children, aged 6–17 years, were referred to an outpatient obesity clinic. The families received solution-focused family therapy provided by a multidisciplinary team. There were significant improvements in weight loss, self-esteem and family climate. The 2008 study followed up 49 who received a Family Weight School group and 17 no-treatment controls. At one year the experimental group with moderate obesity had significant weight loss. Reinehr et al. (2010) in Germany have followed up their cohort of 663 obese children for 5 years, finding the greatest benefit for younger children (the Obeldicks programme).

Seidel and Hedley (2008) used solution-focused brief therapy with older adults in Mexico. Ten in the experimental group received three sessions and there were 10 controls. Various outcome measures were used. They found significant improvement on the OQ45 for the treatment group.

In 2006 Perkins reported on single-session therapy for children and adolescents with mental health problems. They had the option of additional sessions if required. After four weeks severity was improved in 74.3 per cent versus 42.5 per cent of controls, and frequency of symptoms in 71.45 per cent versus 48.3 per cent respectively. A follow-up study at 18 months (Perkins and Scarlett, 2008) traced 91 of 152 children: 60.5 per cent had received only one session and 9.7 per cent had received five or more. For any length of therapy, there was no increase in frequency or severity of symptoms at follow-up.

Springer et al. (2000) studied the effects of a solution-focused mutual aid group for Hispanic children of incarcerated parents. Five schoolchildren were offered six sessions of group treatment using solution-focused, interactional and mutual aid approaches. There were five waiting list controls. The main finding was of a possibly significant increase in self-esteem in the experimental group.

In 2004 Stith et al. described a substantial study of treatment of intimate partner violence within intact couple relationships. Fourteen of 20 couples who were seen together and 16 of 22 couples who were seen in multi-couple groups completed the programme. Nine couples who refused treatment formed the comparison group. The female partners were contacted six months later. Recidivism had occurred for 43 per cent of the individual treatment couples and 25 per cent of the multi-group couples. There was further violence for 67 per cent of the comparison couples. Two years later, for those couples traced the figures for recidivism were 0 per cent (individual), 13 per cent (multi-group) and 50 per cent in the comparison group. The authors suggest that the multi-group format produced more benefit because the secret of domestic violence became public and because the participants recognised that others were struggling with the same problem. They point out that their group was drawn only from mild-to-moderate violence couples. They believe that their results support the case for conjoint therapy for such couples.

Another comparison study, this one from the field of developmental delay, has been reported by Stoddart et al. (2001). Sixteen of their 19 clients completed eight sessions of treatment and were followed up after six months. The comparison group came from the clinic's existing long-term psychotherapy programme. Scaling techniques had to be modified for some of the clients, either using shorter scales or simple drawings. There was a better outcome if the clients had fewer problems and less developmental delay. Having real-life goals and being self-referred also predicted success, supporting Seligman's findings about client choice and control as being important to therapy outcome. In the brief therapy group, caregivers and therapists became more confident about clients' abilities to manage situations. Solution-focused therapy covered an average of 118 days whereas the long-term comparison group remained in contact with the service for an average of 372 days. Client satisfaction was similar for both groups but brief therapy clients would have liked more sessions.

In Finland, Peter Sundmann (1997) studied the effects of basic training in solution-focused ideas for nine social workers. Eleven controls worked as usual. Session tapes and questionnaires were analysed after six months. In all, 382 clients were seen, of whom 199 (52 per cent) replied. More positive statements, more goal focus and more shared views were found in the experimental group.

A paper by Triantafillou (1997) reports that four sessions of solution-focused supervision were provided for the staff of an adolescent residential unit. The supervision model had four elements: establishing an atmosphere of competence; searching for client-based solutions; feedback to the supervisee; and the EARS process (Berg and Reuss, 1995) to identify positives to seek prior to next session. The staff's clients were compared with those of other staff who received 'standard' supervision. At 16 weeks' follow-up, the five clients of the solution-focused group had 66 per cent less incidents and the use of medication to control behaviour had decreased. The seven clients in the control group had 10 per cent less incidents and the use of medication had increased.

A court initiative in Hawaii 'Pono Kaulike' (Walker and Hayashi, 2009) aims at reducing violence through restorative justice and solution-focused approaches. In a 4-year pilot programme, of 59 eligible offenders 41 received the intervention, of whom 38 were evaluated along with 21 controls. Ten of 38 (26 per cent) reoffended compared with 12 (57 per cent) controls; this difference is significant. A follow-up after two years (Walker and Greening, 2010) found that 16 of 23 (70 per cent) had not reoffended. The State three-year recidivism rate is 54.7 per cent, suggesting that the intervention may make a difference.

In Newcastle-upon-Tyne, John Wheeler (1995), a social worker in a public child and family clinic, carried out a three-month follow-up of 34 solution-focused therapy referrals and 39 routine referrals who had been traced after three months. In the solution-focused group 23 (68 per cent) were satisfied versus 17 (44 per cent) of the routine care group. Other clinic resources were required by four (12 per cent) of the solution-focused therapy clients versus 12 (31 per cent) of the routine care group.

In China, Yang et al. (2005) found a significant difference in improvement for therapy combined with paroxetine in the treatment of obsessive-compulsive disorder. After 6–8 solution-focused sessions, 83.3 per cent of 30 experimental patients were improved as against 60 per cent of 30 controls (who received medication but no therapy) at two-week follow-up.

A study by Zimmerman et al. (1996) used standard measures to assess change in 30 clients who received six solution-focused sessions directed at managing adolescent offspring successfully. Twelve controls received no therapy. (The controls received a similar treatment package after the research project was completed.) There was improvement for the treated group on the Parenting Skills Inventory but no change on the Family Strengths Assessment. The authors suggested that the latter may not be a suitable instrument for this type of study.

With another set of co-workers Zimmerman (1997) carried out couples group therapy. Six groups were held at weekly intervals. There were 23 experimental clients and 13 no-treatment controls. Several relationship measures improved in the experimental group.

In summary, the majority of the comparison studies reported here show solution-focused therapy to be better than treatment as usual. LaFountain found less exhaustion in the counsellors and Wheeler found less use of other resources by the clients. Forrester found reduced length of stay and expenditure for the treated group. Two studies (Lambert, Littrell) show results as good as the alternative treatment but requiring less therapist time. Zimmerman (two studies) shows advantages over no-treatment groups and the results of Springer et al. are equivocal.

Effectiveness Studies in Solution-Focused Brief Therapy

Seligman (1995) makes a valuable distinction between efficacy studies, 'this treatment works', and effectiveness studies, 'this treatment helped my client'. In Seligman's view, most comparison studies are efficacy studies, whereas naturalistic studies are generally trials of effectiveness. He suggests that effectiveness studies are more relevant to therapists than 'gold standard' controlled trials in rigid experimental conditions. The studies described below are naturalistic 'effectiveness' evaluations. A selection of the 41 published studies are reviewed here, looking at a variety of different problems and approaches.

Mental Health

There are a number of studies on the use of solution-focused therapy in mental health settings. Most of these are with outpatient populations. Authors report that the diagnosis or type of problem is not correlated significantly with outcome. There is little information provided in the published work about the actual diagnoses allocated. Either information on past health and treatment is not available in the settings where research occurs, or it is not routinely collected by solution-focused therapists, following their view that the road leading to the problem is not relevant to the question of how to solve it.

Darmody and Adams (2003) reported a project with several experienced teams in the UK. Clients' goals and the Coping Resources Inventory (CRI) score were recorded initially. The CRI is a 60-item self-report measure designed in the USA that records perceived strengths and resources. Comments from therapist and client about the sessions and another CRI score were collected at the fourth or last session, whichever came first. The CRI was repeated three months after therapy had ended. They collected full data on 20 cases with a three-month follow-up. Overall change was not significant. Intrapersonal problems did better than symptom-based problems. Clients saw conversation about the past as more important than did therapists.

The Salamanca group have published extensively in Spanish on outcome in solution-focused therapy. For example, Beyebach et al. (1996) followed up 39 mental health outpatients. Eighty per cent achieved their goals after an average of five sessions, with a mean of 33 minutes per session. Agreeing concrete goals and identifying pre-treatment change were significantly associated with good outcomes.

A telephone follow-up study was reported by the same group (Perez Grande, 1991). Eighty-one of 97 cases were traced 6–35 months after therapy was finished. One-quarter of the cases were children, and therapy lasted an average of five sessions. At the end of therapy 71 per cent reported improvement but 13 per cent reported relapse at follow-up. Other problems had improved by the time of follow-up in 38 per cent of cases. More clients dropped out of therapy if the problem was longstanding.

Another Spanish publication (Beyebach et al., 2000) reports a similar telephone follow-up of 83 cases, about a year after therapy. Eighty-two per cent were satisfied with the effect of their therapy. Therapy required an average of 4.7 sessions and outcomes did not differ between trainees and expert therapists, although there were fewer dropouts when the therapist was experienced. There was a better outcome for 'individual' problems such as anxiety, depression or addictions than for relationship conflicts. This is the first time that any study of solution-focused therapy has shown a difference in outcome on the basis of problem type.

A number of follow-up studies have come from the Brief Family Therapy Center in Milwaukee, Wisconsin. De Shazer (1985) carried out a telephone enquiry six months after discharge. Twenty-three (82 per cent) of 28 cases had improved; 25 had solved other problems. Treatments averaged five sessions. A further telephone follow-up by de Shazer et al. (1986) successfully traced 25 per cent of 1,600 cases seen over a five-year period. Seventy-two per cent reported improvement, having had an average of six therapy sessions each. De Shazer (1991) reported a further study of 29 cases. Twenty-three (80 per cent) reported that they had either resolved their original difficulty, or made significant progress towards resolving it. At 18 months the success rate was 86 per cent; 67 per cent reported other improvements also. An average of 4.6 sessions was required. Those who attended for more than four sessions were more likely to achieve their goals.

DeJong and Hopwood in Milwaukee (1996) published a telephone follow-up of 141 cases at eight months (on average) after discharge. Fifty per cent were under 19-years-old and 93 per cent were under 45-years-old; clients received an average of 2.9 sessions. Goals were achieved by 45 per cent, and 32 per cent made some progress towards their goals. There were equal outcomes by age, gender, race and economic status. An immediate post-therapy measure of change in scaling scores for 136 subjects had been collected: 25 per cent made significant progress; 49 per cent moderate progress; and 26 per cent no progress (Berg and DeJong, 1996). These findings in combination suggest that progress continues after therapy attendance has ceased. They have also reviewed their data to include DSM-IV (APA, 1994) diagnoses for all cases (DeJong and Berg, 2001). This review does not show any link between DSM-IV diagnosis and response to therapy.

Paul Hanton's (2008) study of Beck Depression Inventory (BDI) scores in seven depressed adults found an average of 55.12 per cent improvement on the BDI score. Relationship, future focus and compliments were identified by patients as most useful; break and feedback were thought least useful.

Lee et al. (2001) carried out a pilot study of solution-focused therapy in the treatment of depression. Ten clients were seen for a set of six sessions. Various pre- and post-treatment measures were used. Nine clients were traced for follow-up six months later, of whom eight had improved on all measures.

In the UK the first published data came from the Brief Therapy Practice in London. George et al. (1999) carried out a telephone follow-up six months after the end of therapy. Forty-one (66 per cent) of the 62 traced were satisfied with the results of therapy.

Three studies of brief therapy teams in the UK have been published by Macdonald (1994a, 1997, 2005). In each study a goal achievement questionnaire was completed by clients and their family doctors one year after therapy had ceased. The time period was chosen on the grounds that any sooner might tap into a 'honeymoon effect' related to ending therapy, while a longer follow-up period would allow the occurrence of new life events which would obscure any specific effects of therapy. 'Good outcome' means that either attenders themselves reported that the problem was better or the family doctor reported that the problem was better if information from the attenders was not available. Responses from attenders were preferred in all cases if there was a choice. There was no significant difference overall between outcomes reported by patients and those reported by family doctors. In the small number of cases in which the reports from attenders and family doctors differed, there was no significant link with any other variable measured.

In the first study of 41 cases an average of 3.7 sessions was required and 29 (70 per cent) clients had improved. Those with problems lasting more than three years did less well. The second study traced 36 clients, of whom 23 (64 per cent) had improved; other problems had also been solved in 10 clients who had a good outcome and in two cases who had not achieved their main goal. Clients used an average of 3.4 sessions. Again there were similar outcomes for all socio-economic classes and longstanding problems did less well. In 2005 a further 41 cases were reported. Here, 31 (76 per cent) reported a good outcome, with an overall average of 5.02 sessions, 20 per cent attending only one session.

Combining the results from all three studies, 170 referrals had been received of whom 136 attended and 118 were traced. Good outcome was reported by 83 clients (70 per cent) with a mean of 4.03 sessions per case; 25 per cent required only one session.

Of those who responded to these questions, 31 of 53 'good outcome' cases reported solving other problems in addition, as opposed to five out of 15 'others' (not significant: chi-squared 0.42, df 1). Further professional help had been sought by 20 out of 54 'good outcome' cases as against nine out of 17 'others' (not significant: chi-squared 0.775, df 1). No new problems had arisen for 38 out of 53 with a good outcome, while 11 out of 17 'others' had new problems. This difference is significant (chi-squared 5.8, df 2, p<0.02, confidence interval 0.129 to 0.179). Taken together, these observations may imply that successful problem solving improves one's ability to solve other problems or that the energy released by solving a problem is then available to address other problems.

Longstanding problems (over three years duration) predicted less improvement. In all three studies there are no significant differences in outcome between socio-economic groups (see Table 6.1). This is an important finding because all other psychotherapies are more effective for those from higher socio-economic and educational groups.

There is, thus, evidence that brief therapy should be attempted even in longstanding cases because there are no known predictors for success or

TABLE 6.1 *Pooled data: socioeconomic classes, 1989 to 2002*

Social class	I	II	IIIN	IIIM	IV	V
Northwest England*	6%	30.2%	23.1%	21.1%	14.6%	4.4%
All samples	16 (13.56%)	16 (13.56%)	15 (12.71%)	21 (17.80%)	36 (30.51%)	14 (11.86%)
'Good outcome'	12	13	9	15	23	11
'Others'	4	3	6	6	13	3

*Office of National Statistics (2001)
Note: No significant difference between groups by Mann-Whitney U test or chi-square test for trends.

failure in solution-focused therapy. For example, one of our first referrals was a middle-aged woman who had had panic attacks for four years for no apparent reason. She had previously received many drugs and had undergone several admissions to hospital. After two sessions her symptoms had disappeared and had not recurred at follow-up or when the family were seen for unconnected reasons five years later.

An encouraging example was that of a young woman who had developed compulsive handwashing after the birth of her baby some months before. Her problem was resolved after three interviews attended by herself, her husband and their baby. At follow-up she revealed the resolution of additional problems, including checking behaviour and various rituals. When first seen therefore a DSM-IV diagnosis of obsessive-compulsive disorder would have been justified. Such a diagnosis would normally have led to a gloomy prognosis and a multiplicity of treatment attempts instead of the rapid improvement that she achieved.

The diagnoses resembled those seen at routine psychiatric outpatient clinics in the UK, except that acute psychotic episodes were referred elsewhere. In the total sample three patients had diagnoses of long-term psychosis. Relatively few drug and alcohol problems were seen because there were separate specialist services for these referrals. In our joint experience clients with major personality disorders respond no better to solution-focused work than to any other approach.

In one case the individual attender disliked his only session intensely and said so. Nevertheless, he and his doctor both agreed that the problem had been solved and the desired goal achieved. In another case the family doctor had seen a middle-aged housewife for half an hour every week for 10 years. He referred her urgently because one day she said that she would kill herself within the month if nothing changed in her life. She and her husband were seen for three sessions over three months by our team. They reported at follow-up one year later that the problem was solved and that she had started a college course. Despite this, the family doctor was dissatisfied with the outcome of therapy because she still came to see him every week.

There are no detailed studies of solution-focused therapy in mental health inpatient units. However, Vaughn et al. (1996) describe changes in practice in their Denver, Colorado psychiatric hospital. Prior to the introduction of solution-focused therapy throughout the treatment programme, 688 cases had an average length of stay of 20.2 days; after solution-focused therapy was introduced, the length of stay for a subsequent 675 cases fell to an average of 6.6 days. Some patients had been sufficiently disturbed to have begun their stay in the locked ward area. The nursing staff involved are said to experience greater satisfaction in their relationships with clients and with other health care systems since the change was made (Vaughn et al., 1995).

Children

In Germany, Burr (1993) published the results from 55 children and young people seen at a children's clinic. They were followed up 6–12 months after the end of treatment. Thirty-four were traced, of whom 26 (77 per cent) were improved. Four sessions was the average; new problems were reported by four cases who had improved and four who had not. Burr comments on the economic value of a therapy which can be conducted by a single therapist.

Guy Shennan (2003) has published an account of an Early Response project in Leicester. This was funded from the voluntary sector in order to support the local Children and Adolescent Mental Health Service. The team of volunteers (with professional supervisors) saw families from the local area. They were all seen within 14 days; the initial limit of three sessions proved unnecessary because with no session limit the average was 2.7 sessions per family. A telephone follow-up six to nine months after contact managed to trace 40 of 72 parents. Of these, 62.5 per cent reported that the problems were improved and 75 per cent reported that their coping ability had improved.

Lee (1997) reports a six-month telephone follow-up of 59 North American families using independent raters. The children were all outpatients with a wide variety of problems. Improvement was described by 64.9 per cent: goal achieved 54.4 per cent; part of goal achieved by 10.5 per cent. On average 5.5 sessions were needed. There was no difference in outcome if only one parent attended with the child.

In a counselling study from the midwest of the USA, Cruz and Littrell (1998) reviewed 16 high school students two weeks after two sessions of therapy. Ten had achieved 54.7 per cent of their various goals. Some students would have liked additional sessions. Another study by Thompson and Littrell (2000) used a similar design with 12 students. Ten of the 12 had achieved 100 per cent of their goals two weeks later.

Franklin et al. (2001) investigated seven schoolchildren with learning problems (from a total of 19). Objective measures were collected for one month prior to therapy as a baseline and then repeated during therapy (an average of seven sessions). They were followed up after one month. There was some improvement in all, and six of seven were regarded as recovered.

A similar project is reported by Conoley et al. (2003). Solution-focused family therapy with three aggressive and oppositional-acting children used a treatment manual and objective measures. The children received an average of 4.6 sessions and were reviewed after three months. All three families were satisfied with the result. The researchers highlight the need for rapid results with such children because of resource pressures and the risk of the behaviours becoming persistent.

In an interesting study of solution-focused group work with children, Newsome (2004) provided eight group sessions for 26 pre-teenage children. Results found improved social skills at six weeks' follow-up if they had attended at least five of the sessions. Classroom behaviour and homework completion had also improved.

A different approach was used by Morrison et al. (1993). They applied solution-focused questioning within a systemic approach to school behaviour problems. Several school staff and the families were invited to each meeting. Thirty children with school problems were managed, six of whom had special educational needs. Sessions varied from one to seven according to need. Twenty-three (78 per cent) improved with this approach while the other seven had later relapses into further difficult behaviour. Again, the attendance of only one parent did not affect outcome.

Young has reported two studies of anti-bullying interventions (1998; Young and Holdorf, 2003). In the 1998 cohort, bullying stopped in 47 of 50 cases. Forty (80 per cent) stopped at once and the remainder stopped within five weeks. No problems became worse. The 2003 study reported individual work with students. There were 92 cases but 26 single-session cases were excluded from the analysis; one-quarter came from primary schools; 85 (92 per cent) were successful with an average of 3.4 sessions.

Another use of solution-focused therapy with students is reported by Ziffer et al. (2007). School counsellors conducted groups (8 sessions each) for parents, older and younger children. All had improved at six-month follow-up interviews.

Alcohol

Substance misuse attracts a lot of concern and is an expensive social issue. There are good studies now showing that solution-focused therapy can play a useful role in addressing such issues. The comparison studies by Froeschle et al. (2007), Smock et al. (2008), Forrester et al. (2009) and Li et al. (2007) are described above.

The specialist alcohol service in Bruges, Belgium has used solution-focused therapy for over 10 years. The programme consists of inpatient treatment to a maximum of three weeks and then outpatient care, largely carried out by nursing staff. Dr Luc Isebaert and Steve de Shazer have published a formal follow-up study from the Bruges clinic (de Shazer and Isebaert, 2003). The study took the form of a telephone follow-up, including information from a relative, of 131 alcoholics four years after an episode of inpatient care. Of these, 118 were contacted; a further nine had died of alcohol-related causes. The results show that 100 (84 per cent) were abstinent (60) or had successfully controlled their drinking (40).

Another four-year telephone follow-up of 72 alcoholics after outpatient treatment showed that of 59 (82 per cent) contacted, 36 were abstinent and 23 were successfully controlled. The clients chose at the start to aim for abstinence or controlled drinking, but this was not linked to their eventual outcome category. Neither was there any link between any of the data collected initially and the final outcome. It appears that the only relevant variable was therapy. Again, in these studies all socio-economic classes did equally well (Isebaert, 1997).

The work by Li et al. (2007) compared styles of group therapy for couples with substance abuse issues. Of 27 couples, 20 completed the programmes: multiple couples group 13/15; individual couples group 7/12. There were no significant differences between group results. At six months 80 per cent (43) were traced: 46 per cent (20) were 'a great deal better' and 49 per cent (21) found that therapy had 'helped somewhat'.

However, the results must be seen in context: it is known that 25 per cent of problem drinkers will resolve their problems without treatment and that a further 25 per cent will benefit from any treatment at all.

Violence

The results below and those of Lindforss and Magnusson (1997) are important because offenders often fail to respond to traditional psychotherapies.

The Plumas County Mental Health Center in California has remarkable results with its domestic violence programme. The court gives offenders the choice of gaol or attendance at the programme, for which they must pay. The treatment is a standard package of eight solution-focused groups run by two therapists. The clients must choose a goal linked to some relationship issue – not necessarily violence – by the third session. The remaining sessions are spent working on this goal. The results are collated by an independent researcher (Lee et al., 1997).

In one study (Sciotto, California) of 117 clients treated between 1993 and 1997, the package was completed by 88 offenders. Only 7 per cent (6 clients) had reoffended by 1997. In the second study (Plumas, California), carried out between 1994 and 1996, 34 clients completed seven of eight standard sessions. Three per cent (1 client) had reoffended by the end of the study period.

The same group have now published a description of their programme, including useful material on working with groups in a solution-focused way and on working with potentially violent clients (Lee et al., 2003). In 2007 they reported follow-up results for their programme between 1996–2004. They had treated 127 offenders and traced 88 (70 male) for follow-up; 92.8 per cent had completed seven of eight sessions and were held to have completed treatment. The cumulative recidivism rate was 10.3 per cent, which is considerably better than other recognised programmes aimed at domestic violence. Agreed goals and specific goals predicted more confidence and less recidivism. Overall, they found that brain injury predicted recidivism but that having been abused in childhood did not.

Judith Milner is a therapist and trainer in the UK with a wide experience of forensic and probation work with perpetrators of violence and sexual abuse of various ages. She uses solution-focused methods and narrative work. She reports that finding tiny exceptions to violent behaviour forms a useful starting point in many cases. She employs the 'Signs of Safety' approach (Turnell and Edwards, 1999) when assessing risks. For those who are reluctant to acknowledge responsibility, she asks 'How can you make yourself safe from allegations that you have done such things?' Her 2003 paper recounts the outcome for 23 domestic violence perpetrators who received treatment from her. Twenty were male and three female; they received an average of five sessions of individual or family work and were followed up for 18 months. Nineteen (95 per cent) did not reoffend during the follow-up period (Milner and Jessop, 2003).

Milner and Singleton (2008) have wide experience of domestic and sexual violence interventions. In 2008 they reported a cohort of cases of domestic violence with both male and female perpetrators. Sixty-eight referrals (16 female) took part in an average of 4.3 sessions and 50 completed the programme. They had not reoffended, according to multiple sources, at a minimum 3.5-year follow-up, resulting in a 73 per cent good outcome.

An examination of a solution-based counselling service at a domestic violence shelter by McNamara et al. (2007) found significant improvement on clinical measures of life functioning as well as coping ability along with a sense of being helped and satisfied with the social work services received.

Gambling

Problem gambling is an atypical disorder because the 'problem' consists not of gambling, but of continuing to gamble when losing. Successful gamblers do not present for treatment so that their strategies for 'managing the problem of losing' may merit further enquiry. However, the issue of problem gambling is one of concern to governments and social agencies across the world. A high degree of social and family disruption can occur, while the income generated may not remain in the locality that provides the casino.

A study by Mintoft et al. (2005) examined the effect of a package of measures for clients for whom gambling was a problem. The first session provided motivational interviewing and cognitive-behavioural techniques. Thereafter, the clients received up to 16 weeks of solution-focused therapy and a self-completion booklet about goals and exceptions. The 23 clients were compared with 62 who refused further treatment and with national statistics. Eleven clients who completed the programme showed improvement on all measures, but the numbers were too small for statistical analysis. No data on number of sessions or partial completers are given in this publication.

Golf

For those who work with sports enthusiasts, Bell et al. (2009) tried out guided imagery to decrease putting yips. This is a feared disability in golfers. The small sample of three players showed improvement at three weeks after a five-session intervention. The method is described in detail in the paper. It is of interest because the solution-focused dialogue takes place in the subject's mind, following a sequence of instructions from the therapist. So matching language and the response of the therapist do not influence the process in the ways which we usually expect.

In summary, these studies of effectiveness are comparable with normal day-to-day practice for therapists from many countries and across a wide variety of problems and client groups. They provide information on a total of over 4,000 clients with follow-up ranging from two weeks to four. Therapy success rates vary from 60–90 per cent, with better success rates for specialist teams.

The Effect of Solution-Focused Therapy on Therapists

Solution-focused therapists seem to fare better than therapists who use other methods. Some such therapists say that there is a 'secret society of skilled clients' who make surprising and rapid changes with a minimum of therapist help. 'Burnout' among solution-focused therapists may be less, thus preserving valuable resources for the community. LaFountain and Garner (1986) and Vaughn et al. (1995) make comment on this issue. Two attempted studies of therapists using anthropological and sociological questionnaires have sought to explore these issues. Unfortunately there were not enough replies for statistical analysis so the results remain unproven. The responses to Tomasz Switek (Poland) and Alison Johnson (California) suggested that solution-focused therapists are happier and use solution-focused thinking in their everyday lives. Professor Michael Houseman and Marika Moisseeff (Paris) found suggestions that solution-focused therapists wanted less training because they were comfortable using only solution-focused brief therapy.

Future Developments

Caroline Klingenstierna of Stockholm has carried out a randomised controlled study of solution-focused groups for returning the unemployed to work. The study was funded by the local authority responsible for welfare payments to the unemployed. There were 15 clients in each group who had been on sick leave for more than six months. The experimental group made a faster return to actively seeking work and showed less distress symptoms than the control group. There were no significant differences between the groups after five months of follow-up.

Many therapists are not natural researchers, having different skills and interests. This hampers all psychotherapy research and makes it difficult to establish the differences and similarities between various types of psychological treatments. The European Brief Therapy Association research project team has agreed that solution-focused brief therapy, as defined for editorial purposes in research publications, must include: goals, exceptions, pre-treatment changes, clients' resources, miracle question, scaling, compliments and tasks. Return visits must begin with 'What is better?' or a similar question. This is seen as a minimum guide because every therapist uses their own existing interactional skills and other knowledge in addition to the basic solution-focused model. Supervisors will be able to confirm that the manual is being followed correctly during the therapy (manual and protocol available www.ebta.nu and www.solutionsdoc.co.uk). The Solution-Focused Brief Therapy Association in North America (SFBTA) are extending this manual.

Practical Exercises

Suppose that research into solution-focused brief therapy has produced absolute
  proof that it is useful to the population with whom you work.

Think or discuss in small groups for a few minutes: What difference will this make
  to you and your colleagues from next Monday?
How will this new research affect your colleagues in the organisation?
How will this affect those who do not use solution-focused approaches?

Conclusion

Of the 97 relevant studies, nine of 17 randomised controlled trials show
benefit from solution-focused approaches over existing methods. Of
34 comparison studies, 26 favour the solution-focused arm of the study.
Effectiveness data are also available from more than 4,000 cases with a success rate exceeding 60 per cent, requiring an average of three to five sessions
of therapy time. In addition, there are over 100 small published studies
which have not been discussed here. Solution-focused therapy is a realistic
and practical approach to many problems in mental health and elsewhere.
The model is cost-efficient and training is straightforward. There is evidence
for the benefits of clinical supervision and an increasing body of published
work which supports the model.

Outcome and process studies on solution-focused therapy have come
from many parts of the world. The total amount of available research knowledge compares favourably with that of many other psychological therapies.
The worldwide efficacy of psychotherapy exceeds 60 per cent, although
the exact figure quoted depends on a number of variables (Lambert, 2004).
Higher levels of success are found for specialist teams or programmes. Thus,
solution-focused therapy can claim to be the equal of other psychotherapies, while also taking less time and resources for treatment, reducing the
strain placed on therapists and providing help for a number of groups
and clients who have previously found it hard to obtain useful help from
psychological therapies.

Further research may help to reduce the number of clients who do not
benefit from the solution-focused approach. If 60–90 per cent of clients
worldwide will benefit from solution-focused approaches, then we still
have more to learn about how to help the remainder. Teams who focus on
special topics such as alcoholism or violence report higher success rates.
Perhaps we need to isolate some specific features of solution-focused

therapy that apply to specific categories of problem or client. Or perhaps the client who does not respond to solution-focused brief therapy is in need of referral for more specialist therapies, such as cognitive-behavioural therapy or psychodynamic work.

Research into psychological therapies has expanded greatly in the last three decades. Postmodern approaches generally have simpler theories of change than do traditional therapies. An interesting consequence of these processes has been that the boundary between 'counselling' and 'psychotherapy' or 'therapy' has become blurred. Follow-up studies show that talking treatments are equally effective, regardless of model or diagnosis. Some problem-specific elements have been identified, but most treatments appear to exert effect through general or non-specific factors. Similarly, the amount of training needed to be an effective counsellor or an effective psychotherapist seems to be less different than had been believed. This arises partly because the emphasis on bringing about change through common factors (cf. Rogers, Chapter 5) has reduced the need for trainees to learn and manipulate complex theoretical issues and constructs. Cost-efficiency considerations along with social and technological changes may make therapy by telephone or via the Internet the preferred approach for the future. Solution-focused therapy is well suited to such developments.

Key Points

- All psychotherapies show equivalent levels of effectiveness.
- Brief therapy is the usual model, intended or not.
- Nine of 17 randomised controlled studies show solution-focused therapy to be better than 'treatment as usual'.
- Twenty-six of 34 comparison studies show benefit from solution-focused therapy.
- Other studies show results similar to other therapies after a modest number of sessions and brief training courses.
- Meta-analyses support the above findings.
- Several studies demonstrate that solution-focused therapy is effective for offenders and other hard-to-treat clients.
- Socio-economic status does not affect response to treatment, in contrast to all other psychotherapies.
- There are numerous future directions and projects within the solution-focused community.

Note

For the interested reader, there have been several special issues of journals on solution-focused therapy:

Journal of Family Therapy (UK) (1997), 19: 117–232.
Contemporary Family Therapy (USA) (1997), 19: 1–144.
Journal of Systemic Therapies (1999), 18: 1–88 and (2000), 19: 1–13.
Journal of Family Psychotherapy (2005), 16:1/2 (Education and Training in Solution-focused Brief Therapy; published simultaneously in book form; Ed. Nelson, T.).

7

Applying Solution-Focused Brief Therapy within Mental Health Services

Contents

- The 'medical model'
- Urgent assessment
- Self-harm enquiry
- Preventing suicide using a solution-focused approach
- Scheduled assessments
- Specific conditions
- Domestic violence
- Sexual abuse of adults
- Sexual abuse and child protection
- Other mental disorders
- Conclusion

This chapter begins by examining the 'medical model' of health care. The application of solution-focused ideas to the assessment of a variety of common disorders and their management will then be considered. For the most part these conditions are managed outside hospital. The subsequent chapter will examine severe mental illness and its management with medication and access to hospital facilities. Both these chapters are based on my own clinical experience as a practising psychiatrist as well as on research into the psychotherapies and into mental health care. Support for the approach can be found in Bakker et al. (2010).

The 'Medical Model'

The 'medical model' is a basic paradigm in health care. It is also used as the title of a specific sociological view of illness care. It assumes that there is a cause: name the cause and you have a 'diagnosis', which leads to a treatment and hopefully to a cure. The model could equally well be called the 'mechanical' model since the same process of fault identification is also applied to cars and domestic appliances. This model supports the predominance of doctors in mental health care but is not always a useful framework for managing mental health problems. In daily practice much of the help comes from a team and is not intentionally directed by the doctor. For example, a psychologist may receive the referral from the doctor but recommend hypnosis, a treatment resource helpful to the client but unintended by the doctor.

Longstanding or recurrent disorder does not fit the medical model. As a result, management of such disorders is sometimes imperfect. For example, neurosurgeons perform amazing feats of skill in intervening to prevent death. Sadly, some patients are left with brain damage and major residual disability. Neurosurgeons are rarely involved with care for these patients, who pass to underfunded community or mental health facilities. Whether due to past trauma or current causes, mental illness is often longstanding or recurrent. How well it fits the medical model is debated. The public know what they mean by 'disorder of health' and are concerned to obtain helpful resources, not to discuss models of care.

Mental disorder was specifically recognised prior to the Middle Ages in Europe. We know this because medieval laws existed to manage the property of the mentally incompetent (Roffe and Roffe, 1995). These laws distinguished between those born incompetent and those who become incompetent during life. However, not doctors but religion or restraint were considered the correct resource to apply to such individuals.

The accepted approach to mental disorder is affected by cultural and social issues as well as scientific or medical ones. For example, native healers are considered more reliable than Western medicine in many areas of Africa. They are also cheaper and usually more accessible, so the medical model is only invoked late in the process (Swartz, 1998). The same applies in India (Bagadia et al., 1979).

The impact of cultural values is also shown by the differential use of legal powers in modern practice. Germany is reluctant to coerce individuals and detains far fewer people for mental disorder than does the UK. Conversely, Switzerland detains five times as many persons as the UK, 'failure to look after yourself adequately' being grounds for detention under Swiss law (Reicher-Rossler and Rossler, 1993). India detains no-one, perhaps because extended families are expected to care for the disabled or perhaps because the country has few beds (2.5:100,000, Patel and Saxena, 2003; UK 44:100, 000, www.performance.doh.gov.uk/hospitalactivity/data_requests/).

The provision of high-security places for the mentally ill varies from country to country. England has 2.9 places per 100,000 population, Sweden has 11.36 per 100,000 while Portugal and Israel have none. It is unlikely that the population of any one of these countries is very different from any other, so this again is a cultural and social decision.

In practice it is the public themselves who make the decision that a behaviour amounts to 'mental disorder'. My occupational therapist colleague Chris Morgan (1982, personal communication) has suggested that the defining characteristic is relevance: the behaviour may be normal but if the context is wrong, then 'mental disorder' will be invoked. The public then turn to professionals expecting the disorder to be classified (diagnosed) and managed. Both clients and others will accept very wide variations in what is done and offered. Note, for example, the discrepancy between public and professional views about what psychotherapy will be like (Garfield and Bergin, 1986) and about the value and risks of antidepressants.

Studies in the UK and Australia (e.g. Jorm et al., 1997: 85 per cent response from 2,031 Australians sampled) have shown that the public believe that counselling and vitamins are the optimal treatments for depression and that antidepressants are addictive. There is a body of scientific evidence against both of these ideas but continued public education has not altered them. The international controversy about Attention Deficit Hyperactivity Disorder (ADHD) and its treatment is another example of public concern leading to professional debate. As far as the public are concerned, the least acceptable response from a mental health professional is to say: 'This problem is not a matter for our service.'

As far as mental disorder is concerned, there is one significant problem linked to the medical model discourse. Some physical health problems have no cure or treatment, and the public recognise this. In the latter half of the 20th century it has not been acceptable to say that a mental disorder has no cure or treatment. This may arise from care providers wishing to maximise their market or from a belief among the public that these disorders are actually not 'medical' in the same sense as physical ailments. As a result the need for resources for mental distress is constantly growing, while many professionals feel overwhelmed and unable to meet the demands placed on them. The pharmaceutical companies are aware of this expanding demand for resources.

That mental disorders are actually not 'medical' in the same sense as physical ailments may well be true. Internationally, schizophrenia affects about 4 in 1,000 of the population and manic-depressive/bipolar/affective disorder affects 1 in 100 (Gelder et al., 1996). However, every individual country also has many other cases of major disorder which vary from one country to another. A mental health professional who only talks to clients with schizophrenia or affective disorder by the international definitions, will have a small caseload, will find that treatment does not require the full use of his or her training, and will not be well thought of in his catchment area.

The open dialogue approach in Western Finland (Seikkula et al., 2003) adopts a different view of psychosis and the incidence of diagnosed schizophrenia falls (33:100,000 to 7:100,000, Aaltonen, 1997; Seikkula et al., 2000). Dingleton Hospital in Scotland was run on therapeutic community lines in the 1960s and achieved similar successes (Jones, 1968).

There are some common factors between the medical model and the solution-focused model. The medical model is essentially a pattern recognition exercise. A musician can hear a few bars, recognise the piece and predict the whole composition, perhaps for hours ahead. A gardener can see an anonymous green shoot in their garden and say, 'In two weeks that will be a [specific] plant and it will need some time if it is going to be the right shape.' In medicine this is done by listening to clients, looking for exceptions, and recognising that problems and solutions may appear different. (Ambrose Bierce (1971[1911]) suggested that swallowing tablets was like throwing stones in one neighbourhood to kill a dog in another part of town.) But medicine has an expert knowledge mindset; it is based on action by the medical authority and for good reasons it is linked to the fastest possible change or repair. In these qualities it differs from solution-focused thinking.

It has been suggested that multinational pharmaceutical corporations support the medical model discourse by seeking to ratify new diagnoses to enable niche marketing of available drugs, while neglecting research into rare but proven conditions because the profit margins will be lower. However, the same companies have developed drugs to treat a wide variety of diseases to the benefit of many patients. Similar marketing behaviours can be seen in the arena of psychological treatments where there is competition for trainees and for academic influence.

Urgent Assessment

Referrals for urgent assessment follow a number of routes, with the need as perceived by the referrer being the major determinant, modified by local service provision as understood by the referrer. In psychiatric practice with adults, behaviour giving rise to public concern usually passes directly to legal or medical services for social control. This is the common pathway for mania, psychosis (whether drug-induced or not) and occasionally for acute self-endangering behaviour.

The assessment of self-harm can be done through simple questions in ascending order of concern or through a variety of indirect strength-building ideas as described below. Unless the person has definite depressive symptoms, they are encouraged to pursue social and solution-focused approaches for a few days before considering medication. Similarly, their doctors are asked to review them after a few days, before commencing medication. There are risks associated with putting powerful medications into the hands of those who are thinking of harming themselves.

Self-Harm Enquiry

Self-harm and suicide are not confined to the mentally ill members of society. Literary references to suicide are commonplace. At least 10 per cent of suicides (Gelder et al., 1996) occur in people who are not apparently mentally ill but who find that their lives are intolerable, often through physical illness or other distress. People have leapt from burning buildings, choosing to die from the fall rather than by fire. In philosophical terms this is a rational choice, not a sign of mental illness.

Within mental health services, self-harm or suicide can occur due to impaired judgement brought on by mental illness. Self-harm can be considered when someone perceives a situation to be unresolvable by other means. Sometimes they seek to press someone else to make changes; in other cases they simply seek to escape from what appears to be intolerable stress. Within the mental health services, deliberate self-harm and suicide are everyday topics. Because of the high stakes involved, the workers have to decide quickly and accurately whether someone's judgement is intact and what level of risk is involved. Many people will change their minds quite soon about their impulse to die, but in the meantime they may need help and support to reduce the chances of actions that are dangerous or fatal. It is known that for many completed suicides, anger and the perception that one is alienated from all support and help are the final triggers for the fatal act (Morgan and Priest, 1984). Relationships with workers and others are therefore an important part of both assessment and intervention.

As a result of these factors, the issue of self-harm and suicide is anxiety-provoking for those who work in helping agencies, however experienced they may be. The stakes are high, the clients may have difficulty in assessing their situation, time is often short and the decisions require complex social and clinical discriminations. Building a good relationship with the client at the same time is also important. It is therefore helpful to be able to call upon suitable tools and question sets. It is best to address the situation, even briefly, as soon as it arises in the conversation. This shows the client that the therapist has confidence in their own skills and is not afraid to discuss difficult topics. As the worker, it is difficult to carry on with other enquiries if it is constantly in mind that it may not be safe for the client to leave the room.

The first set of questions is designed not to conflict with solution-focused thinking while quickly forming a judgement about the safety of the client. The questions are ordered in terms of increasing concern, so it may not be necessary to ask them all. Once safety issues are clear, the solution-focused interview can continue. Equally, if the client is significantly unsafe, this may take priority over continuing the therapy dialogue. As well as giving information, asking these questions will focus the client on the real and final nature of their potential actions. This will sometimes change their intentions. The questions will also clarify whether someone intends to die, or whether their self-harm has other purposes, for example as a way of relieving emotional tension. Callcott (2003) suggests that suicidal acts are a means to an end, not an end in themselves.

Self-Harm Enquiry: Key Questions

If reference is made to self-harm and you decide further enquiry is needed, don't show fear of the worst scenario.

How long have you been thinking of self-harm?
Do you think about it often?
Have you thought of what you might do to harm yourself? Such as take pills? Cut yourself? Jump off a high place? Hang yourself?
Have you harmed yourself before?
Have you made preparations (e.g. collecting pills or buying hoses or ropes)?
Have you made a will?
Have you life insurance? If so, have you checked if it will be paid if you kill yourself?
Have you left instructions about the kind of funeral you want?
Who will miss you most? Your family? Your friends? Your pets?
Are there elderly or sick people in your family? Who will die first, you or one of them?
Will you leave a note to tell others what was wrong or what they should have done to help? If so, is there a chance of saying these things and getting listened to without having to die?

When finished always ask: 'Have you told others about this before? How did they react? Do you need to say more about it just now?'

Asking if the client has told others, helps to provide information about their relationships with others and the role of selfharm conversations in these relationships. It may identify whether this is a new issue for the client or if this situation has arisen before. Asking if they need to say more 'just now' allows either party to return to the topic later if necessary.

A French colleague, Pascal Soubeyrand of Lyon, a psychologist and former mental health nurse, suggests the additional question: 'Why is it important to die now rather than later?' He believes that because one's feelings vary naturally, any postponement will hopefully move away from self-harming actions.

Preventing Suicide Using a Solution-Focused Approach

John Henden has made a study of solution-focused approaches to suicide prevention for many years. He published an account of his work (Henden, 2005) and has made his techniques widely available because he believes that anything that might prevent a suicide is desirable.

His team within the Somerset Mental Health Service has developed specific question sets for urgent referrals when suicide is thought to be an issue. First they ask questions such as:

- When everything comes at once, sometimes it can seem to get on top of one.
- How far is all this getting you down right now?
- How often recently have you felt that you are getting to the end of your tether/unable to cope with any more?
- How close do you feel, right now, to ending your life?
- On a scale of 1–10, where 1 is 'not at all well' and 10 is 'very well', how do you feel that you are doing at the moment?

After any one of these, they ask: 'If you decided to go ahead with the last resort option, what method would you use (i.e. pills, rope, razor blades, vacuum cleaner tube, firearms etc? How prepared are you should you decide?' The responses identify those who are seriously intent on taking their lives, who will often provide detailed descriptions of methods and times. However, if not serious they will quickly backtrack such as 'I'm not that desperate yet!' or 'I would upset too many people'. The most useful predictor of risk in Henden's experience was the interviewer's own 'gut feeling' described on a scale from 1 ('highly suicidal') to 10 ('not at all suicidal').

If there is reason for concern about potential suicide, a further set of questions is used:

1 Tell me about a time in the last week when you felt least suicidal.
2 Before you were feeling as you do now, what did you do in the day that interested you?
3 What has stopped you taking your life up to this point?

4

    A On a scale of 1–10, where 1 stands for very suicidal and 10 for not at all suicidal, how suicidal do you feel right now?

    B On a scale of 1–10, where 1 stands for very suicidal and 10 stands for not at all suicidal, how suicidal were you before you decided to seek help?

    C What would you be doing/thinking about/feeling to be another half point higher?

5   What have you done in the last week/couple of weeks that has made a difference to this terrible situation you are in?

6   On a scale of 1–10, how determined are you to give other options (other than suicide) a try first?

7   What would have to happen here today, in this session, for you to think it was worthwhile coming?

8   Graveside scenario: Just suppose you decided to take this last resort option before considering all the other possibilities. You are in the grave but your spirit is hovering 3 metres above looking down on the assembled crowd below.

    A Who is there?

    B Who is most upset?

    C What advice would they have liked to have given you before you took the 'last resort' option?

    D What would you be thinking of in terms of other options you could have tried first?

    E Who would throw some soil in first? What might they be thinking as the soil hits the lid?

    F As the guests walk away from the graveside/crematorium, who might say what to whom about how you might have sorted things differently?

9   The miracle question.

10 When was the last time (before this current time in your life) that you thought of ending it all?

11 What did you do then that made a difference and enabled you to pull yourself back?

12 Suicide is the last resort as we know: what other ways have you tried so far to crack this problem?

John Henden has also developed other techniques for use with clients who are considering self-harm (2008). These are based on tools used by Yvonne Dolan (1991) for work with adult survivors of sexual abuse.

Deathbed Scenario

Let us suppose for one minute that you decided not to go for this option and you lived to a ripe old age (say 70, 80 or 90). You are looking back on your life as a person who survived this dark period and lived a purposeful, meaningful life. What would your life have been like?

What sort of things would you have done?
What people would you have known and met?
What new places might you have visited?
What sorts of holidays would you have had?
What other challenges in life might you have had to resolve?
How would you have allocated your time in retirement?
Where might you have seen the best sunrises and sunsets?

Wise Old You

Just suppose you decided not to go ahead with this last resort option and you are much older and wiser than you are now. What advice would you give to yourself now, to solve this problem/get through this time of difficulty?

Both the 'Deathbed Scenario' and 'Wise Old You' can bring out considerable and unexpected resources from the clients. The process of describing the events often lifts mood and generates new and hopeful possibilities. There is much additional material in Henden's book (2008), including a valuable chapter on relationship-building 'Suicide encounters: the crucial first ten minutes'.

From Canada, Heather Fiske has published a valuable text on conversations about suicide (Fiske, 2008). The book includes useful data about crisis cards for clients to carry and information about involving parents and others in teamwork to support the client. There is a good framework for beginners on differentiating self-mutilating behaviour from true suicidal intent. Several good transcripts are presented showing conversations with angry or despairing people.

Callcott (2003) is the manager of a self-harm assessment team in Gateshead. His service deals with clients who have already made an attempt to harm themselves. He suggests that suicidal acts are intended to achieve something, perhaps to stop something happening to them, to bring a loved one back, to obtain support or to punish someone. The assessment session may be the only session, so it is important to achieve as much as possible. The team's goals are to establish a helping relationship, to identify any need for psychiatric treatment, to assess safety and to have a conversation that in itself may be useful.

The Gateshead self-harm team use solution-focused questions to find strengths and exceptions and to assess safety. Scaling questions are used as above to identify the client's self-rating for safety and how they have managed such situations in the past. They use Sharry's (2002) scale from 1–10: 'How confident are you that you can get through the day/the weekend without harming yourself? What would increase that by one point?' They also use the interview to take stock of the effect of the event itself: 'After this event are you more or less likely to harm yourself again? Are there things that you are thinking now that had not occurred to you before the overdose? Is it possible that some good might come of this? If you look back in six months and see that this turned out for the best, what will you be doing then?'

Many of the techniques for addressing self-harm and plans for suicide can also be used or adapted for crisis resolution.

In acute loss and bereavement, the response to the miracle question will direct you either to crisis intervention or to future-building questions. Once their miracle no longer includes the return of the lost person, then questions aimed at eliciting preferred futures can be used.

Scheduled Assessments

In the outpatient or ambulatory service there are a variety of presentations, but the urgency is less. For example, clients will be referred with psychosis-like symptoms such as hearing voices or self-harming behaviour.

The usual opening words are 'You have been sent here because X wants ...' or (slightly better) 'What's the problem?' Opening the consultation by asking 'What do you want to get out of being here?' immediately sets a new context. It is necessary to collect the information required by the agency and to do any necessary paperwork. Postmodern workers often find this awkward, but most clients are realistic about it. They politely make it clear that they expect some redundant questioning from every agency. Thoroughness in record-keeping may be seen as evidence of competence, which is one variable that many clients regard as important. (The other key variable is warmth, although this is not reliably identified by clients.)

It is usually preferable to carry out agency data collection first. Possible compliments and resources can be noted as well as useful information about problems and exceptions and the social context of the client's life. Using their language and tracking their concerns throughout will help to build a collaborative relationship, followed by moving on to scaling and the miracle question, based on the information already collected.

It is good practice to invite clients to bring anyone whom they think will be helpful when they come to the first visit. They can be useful resources for the client and can provide additional information. A partner's facial expression will be enough to reveal if the client's version of events is not the same as that accepted by others. In legal matters the consent of family members may be specifically required.

Burns (2005) reports an exercise devised by Steve de Shazer as a response to questioners who have asked 'Surely you cannot use solution-focused brief therapy with [diagnosis]?' He asked participants to role-play the relevant diagnostic category while being interviewed in a solution-focused way. It soon became clear to questioners that the method can be applied readily because the questions are not derived from the diagnosis or from over-arching ideas about mental health. Rather they derive from a pattern of interviewing related to finding solutions as a general activity.

Specific Conditions

Anxiety

The assessment of generalised anxiety follows the usual solution-focused lines. Many such clients have experienced previous episodes and will have ideas about how to manage relapses. Most anxiety disorders benefit more from psychological therapies than from medication. There is a risk of prolonged dependence on medication unless other approaches are also used. Some therapists (Dolan and others) use solution-focused therapy for post-traumatic stress disorders, sometimes in combination with Ericksonian hypnotherapy or eye movement desensitisation and reprocessing (EMDR) (Shapiro, 2001). John Henden has published a wide variety of techniques for dealing with post-traumatic stress disorder, which he retitles more positively as Combat Operational Stress Reaction (COSR) (Henden, 2011).

Acute trauma such as bereavement or examination stress may benefit from a hypnotic to improve sleep and hence daytime functioning. Sedative antidepressants may improve sleep and reduce daytime anxieties, if cognitive function is not a primary concern. If the client is going to undertake childcare alone or work with machinery, then this option may be unsuitable. Benzodiazepine drugs should be avoided: the risks include dependence, disinhibition and impairment of cognitive function. Benzodiazepine drugs can also delay the processing of affective experience and thus the process of adjusting to loss can be prolonged. So the cost of less emotional distress now is a longer period of emotional distress overall. This is a difficult judgement to make in a crisis situation. Clients and their families may benefit from a discussion of these issues before a prescription is given. To manage an acute family crisis it may be most effective to offer medication to the person who is the boss in the family or the one who is most noisy and demanding, who may not be the identified patient.

Potentially useful medications for anxiety include buspirone. This is not addictive and has few side-effects so that a maximum dose can be tested out quickly. The mono-amine-oxidase inhibitor phenelzine can be useful for phobias and generalised anxiety, although doses are often higher than for antidepressant use. Some antidepressants have anxiety-reducing properties. They can be useful because dose tolerance and dependence do not occur, although withdrawal needs to be undertaken cautiously when the time comes.

Other than for short-term use in acute situations, hypnotics are best avoided. Dependency and tolerance are both risks, as well as nocturnal unsteadiness in the elderly. Simple sleep disturbance can be managed by sleep hygiene or solution-focused management. Failing that, many people will accept the plan of taking a hypnotic on alternate nights, so that one waking night is followed by a reliable sleep. Naturally, having had one disturbed night means that sleep is more likely on the second night, apart from any direct effect of the medication. Over-the-counter antihistamines are available in the UK as sleeping tablets. They are effective for occasional use, although tolerance and night-time confusion can occur. After being told of this option, a surprising number of clients will come back to their doctor saying 'I'm not paying that much just to sleep!'. In depression an antidepressant that improves sleep (as most do) is a safer option and leads to a simpler medication regime. For those few people who require hypnotics every night, a useful regime is to rotate a benzodiazepine, chloral hydrate and an antihistamine in succession so that tolerance to any one preparation does not arise.

Panic attacks are often due to habitual chronic or acute-on-chronic over-breathing. A trial of hyperventilation will confirm the diagnosis by reproducing the initial symptoms. Regular practice of slow breathing will produce substantial improvement without the need for medication, solution-focused work or a psychiatric label (Lum, 1981; Clark et al., 1985; Macdonald, 2004). A detailed analysis of this issue and an instruction sheet for clients is found in Appendix II.

Compulsive Disorders

Compulsive disorders are believed to be an aspect of anxiety disorders. Obsessive-compulsive disorder is regarded by conventional psychiatry as a difficult and intractable disorder requiring lengthy treatment. In my experience it responds well and quickly to solution-focused therapy, sometimes in combination with clomipramine or high-dose fluoxetine, both of which are antidepressants with specific benefits in some cases of obsessive-compulsive disorder. The solution-focused approach follows the usual pattern. Clients are usually advised to continue existing medication and to ask their doctor about an increase of medication if it is not at the maximum recommended in the formulary. If they are on no medication and solution-focused therapy is not effective within five sessions, then the possibility of medication in addition can be considered.

Substance Misuse

Solution-focused therapy is helpful to many who abuse substances. The misuse of alcohol is a major worldwide problem. Few cultures anywhere in the world have failed to produce alcohol of some kind, unless there is a major local alternative. Coca leaf was preferred in South America and cannabis in parts of Asia, in both cases because a directly usable form grew freely in the area. Some ethnic groups lack the genes to produce the enzyme alcohol dehydrogenase, which metabolises alcohol in the body. They can only tolerate lower doses of alcohol and so their traditional drinks are lower in potency than the equivalent from other countries. However, problems of misuse can still occur. Countries with a religious proscription of alcohol often use cannabis instead. The intoxication produced is reported to be more short-lived and to cause less long-term damage. These countries do not report a higher incidence of schizophrenia, thus challenging current research in Western countries, which suggests that cannabis is a causative agent in vulnerable individuals (Macdonald, 2006a).

The alcohol intake admitted to by most people is usually 50 per cent or more below the true amount. Countries in which alcohol is consumed in small doses on a regular social basis see problems linked to damaged physical health and cognition in middle age. In the UK the common presentation is of loss-of-control drinking, often at a younger age. They usually present with social problems including arrests, violence, motoring offences, poor work performance and resistant depression. Employers et al. often collude with the individual, which delays access to treatment. Repeated amnesic episodes and isolated epileptic fits suggest excessive use. Many types of interventions are effective, but there is an average of five relapses before recovery. Abstinence may not be a useful goal, but at least six weeks of abstinence is advisable before the client attempts to return to controlled drinking.

Many studies have shown that for alcohol problems, brief interventions are the most effective choice (Hester and Miller, 1995; Cuijpers et al., 2004). The exceptions are those who have short-term memory impairment due to alcohol-related thiamine deficiency. Such clients show stereotyped habits and have difficulty in visualising new futures. Blood tests will show thiamine deficiency. High dose parenteral thiamine brings about improvement in cognitive function in about two-thirds of such cases. People's ability to think abstractly and to envisage new futures increases, although not all will then decide to reduce their drinking (see Macdonald, 1994b; Cook and Thomson, 1997). The current UK recommendations are 1,250–3,500 mg total dose of parenteral thiamine, usually by the intramuscular route to reduce anaphylactic reactions. Oral thiamine 300 mg daily has been suggested as an alternative but is not adequately absorbed (Taylor et al., 2009).

Cerebellar degeneration leading to ataxia and alcoholic peripheral nerve disease may also respond to the restoration of thiamine stores, but benefit is less predictable.

As most alcoholics have only come for treatment as a last resort when faced with an ultimatum from their partners, employer or doctor, they may find miracles impossible to consider at a first session. It may be the third session before they can look as far ahead. On the other hand, it has been pointed out that almost everyone who comes to therapy is under duress in some way. The pressure may come from themselves or others, but no-one comes to therapy for the pleasure of the experience. Everyone comes because some kind of change is necessary or is threatening to occur.

For withdrawal from heroin there are substitute drugs available such as methadone, buprenorphine and codeine. All of these can readily be used in combination with solution-focused approaches to reduction of drug use and to relapse prevention. Many users of substances use more than one drug, so that work is often needed to reduce the use of drugs for which substitutes are unavailable or inappropriate. Heroin users are particularly at risk of changing to alcohol misuse. This is cheaper for them but perhaps more dangerous in the long run. Alcohol is easily accessible in many parts of the world, so the temptation to misuse it is easy to gratify.

Those who are using amphetamine-based recreational drugs may develop voice, hearing and persecutory fears. Five per cent of the population will develop symptoms from only one dose but prolonged or heavy dosage will produce these symptoms in most users. It appears that these effects become more persistent with continued use and that, as with alcohol, the effects will become permanent in some. Low doses of antipsychotic medication appear to reduce the symptoms but only single-case reports have been published (Brimstedt, 2002). Users of amphetamine-based drugs and solvents may develop diffuse cognitive impairment, which may be irreversible. A decreased ability in abstract thinking and therefore envisaging possible futures is common; their responses to the miracle question are appropriate but limited. I have personally seen numerous young men whose measurable IQ has fallen more than one standard deviation. No sign of intellectual recovery has emerged after they have ceased substance misuse. Koumtsidis et al. (2006) report that a man who had abused MDMA ('ecstasy') heavily was unable to carry out common tasks and had experienced no recovery of his intellectual abilities seven years later.

Substance misuse problems often respond well to solution-focused therapy, perhaps because it is perceived as less coercive than other models. Many substance misusers in the UK are young people whose backgrounds have been neglectful or damaging. As a result they lack literacy and verbal skills, although their lifestyle has made them astute at self-protection. For them substance misuse offers rapid gratification which does not require intellectual effort or stable relationships. The relative simplicity of the solution-focused approach and its emphasis on small practical steps taken at their own pace makes it suitable for such clients.

Eating Disorders

Eating disorders will often respond well to solution-focused ideas (Jacob, 2001). Bulimia also responds to cognitive-behavioural therapy and to biofeedback, but fewer sessions are usually required if a solution-focused approach is used. In bulimia this can usefully be combined with high-dose fluoxetine, which reduces carbohydrate craving and thus makes it easier to reduce binging behaviour.

Jacob finds the stages defined by Prochaska and DiClemente (1994) useful in judging intervention with eating disorders. Solution-focused questions quickly uncover whether a client is ready for anything beyond information (pre-contemplation). Relapse prevention in the maintenance stage is a useful conversation, although there is less published work on this aspect in the solution-focused literature. Eating disorders and substance misuse often benefit from some attention to this aspect. Jacob describes the HALT technique: to stall a binge when the first impulse occurs by asking 'Am I Hungry?'; 'Am I Angry?'; 'Am I Lonely?'; 'Am I Tired?' In each case a mindful response to the actual need can avoid the need to binge. Appropriate eating when hungry, using ways of coping with anger, making contact with others or yourself or arranging a rest or a change of activity can all help to change patterns of dealing with emotional discomfort.

The antidepressant fluoxetine is sought by those with anorexia nervosa because it reduces the desire for carbohydrates: it should not be prescribed for them because although it may reduce binging it also makes weight loss easier. In most cases the emotional apathy and cognitive slowing seen in anorexia are due to malnutrition and not depression (Kingston et al., 1996; Macdonald, 1995; Kumar and Clark, 2002). These have been recognised as a consequence of ascetic religious practice since 2500 BC (Suzuki, 1970). Emotional responses become blunted below 1,500 calories daily, whatever the cause of the restriction. Limiting calorie intake is a traditional method of controlling subject populations and the residents of institutions.

In anorexia nervosa it is best to avoid complex conversation and to pursue feeding with a normal diet until emotions reappear. Jacob suggests that therapy be suspended if the patient reaches the point of hospital admission under legal powers. Initially, emotions are simple expressions of sadness or anger, as the ability to feel emotion returns. Then more complex emotions arise and some degree of conversation can be helpful, moving later to formal solution-focused work if necessary. Families need to be advised of this sequence and encouraged to focus on brief positive comments instead of complex or critical advice. Small doses of chlorpromazine help initially as it is an anti-emetic and encourages weight gain. Large doses of medication and over-enthusiastic refeeding carry physical risks for the client. Strict behaviour modification and restriction are not thought helpful, but it is wise to have someone sitting with the client for one hour after meals to discourage immediate vomiting. A Body Mass Index (weight kg/height m squared) of 13 or less allows legal detention in the UK. Whether detained or not, bed rest is advised until their weight passes this level because of the risk of cardiac arrest due to biochemical imbalance. Above this weight their activity is unrestricted as long as weight gain continues. Any subsequent weight loss leads to 24 hours in bed before returning to activity. Many clients manage their own problems adequately once refeeding has restored their cognitive abilities, but some benefit from further solution-focused work. Autonomy and self-esteem are important for older teenagers, so individual sessions may suit their needs best. Younger teenagers do better with family therapy. Adults with eating disorder may favour individual or couples work depending on their circumstances.

Personality Disorders

The topic of personality disorder has been contentious within psychiatry and psychology for many years. There is a vast literature on the topic which can be examined by the interested reader. It is relevant here because certain clients present to mental health services but do not seem to benefit from the same treatments and approaches as do others. A great deal of therapeutic time and effort can be devoted to these clients with no benefit or with clear lack of benefit. A brief comment on the issue is therefore relevant.

Personality traits are normally distributed in the community in the same way as intellectual ability. It is feasible to identify individuals who show extremes of any trait, for example people who are more or less sociable. A combination of extreme personality traits can be regarded as amounting to a syndrome of 'personality disorder'. However, it may not be useful to call these mathematical and social extremes 'disorder' solely on the basis of being more or less frequent in their occurrence. Perhaps we should talk of 'personality disability' or 'personalities with special needs'. Enduring maladaptive traits can lead to a diagnosis of 'personality disorder' but some of these traits lead to success in politics, business or warfare. Some military heroes, and Winston Churchill himself, were not highly regarded by their peers until the right context arose in which their energy and recklessness were effective.

For a contrasting view, in high-security hospitals there are individuals who have committed criminal acts and who are clearly unlike most people in normal society. However, they show no evidence of illness. They are impulsive, form intense but short-lived relationships or none at all and are lacking in social anxiety. As a result, their actions are not affected by concern for others. Some are active or aggressive while others are passive. The latter can display extreme hostility when roused. Forensic psychiatrists regard this group of criminals as having 'personality disorders'. From their perspective, it is suggested that those in the community who exhibit lesser versions of the same behaviours are incomplete or milder forms of the same disorder.

Studies of 'nature or nurture' have not resolved these problems of definition and none of the many classification schemes developed have proved universally acceptable. The *International Classification of Diseases* (ICD-10) (WHO, 1994) is the standard for Europe and has the merit that it is descriptive with a minimum of assumptions about causation. In everyday clinical practice, such clients may be helped by crisis support techniques, occasionally by medication and by avoiding the inappropriate use of treatments and medications if there is no benefit. Many such clients find life easier as they enter their fourth decade of life, which supports a number of theories about physical and social maturation as the origin of their behaviours.

Many solution-focused practitioners find that they become reluctant to diagnose personality disorder. Many clients appear unusual but prove to be able to function well and competently once their immediate problems are resolved. This raises the possibility that contact with ineffective services generates a story about the untreatability of 'personality disorder'. It also supports the common experience of solution-focused therapists – that it is better to focus on the client and the problem now, rather than to be guided by the previous history of the client. In some clients, their behaviours are a consequence of past experiences such as childhood sexual abuse or other major traumas. Although they may appear to have persistent maladaptive traits, many will use and benefit from solution-focused and other approaches. However, some clients with major personality disorder do not find solution-focused work any more helpful than any other approach, or may only be able to use it in combination with other medical and social interventions. It can be useful for crisis management in such clients when the goals are necessarily limited and for the short term.

Domestic Violence

After centuries of tacit acceptance, domestic violence is now recognised as a major problem and a serious cause of direct and indirect harm to all members of families. Its management has features in common with anger management and in work with offenders. The most important step is to be aware of the possibility and to ask relevant questions when indicated.

The following questions need not all be asked, provided that the therapist is satisfied that they have an accurate assessment of the safety issues. In couples' work it is important to ensure that both partners feel safe before continuing the interview. Some agencies are wholly opposed to couples work, but over 80 per cent of couples make at least one attempt to live together again after a violent incident. It is therefore necessary to deliver services that will make this safer and perhaps make it a step forward for all concerned. Eve Lipchik (Lipchik and Kubicki, 1996) has a special interest in couples work in this field. She sees each partner separately before negotiating the treatment contract to make sure that safety plans are in place. The act of asking questions about the possibility of domestic violence shows the therapist's willingness to address it and makes it an open topic for discussion. This in itself can reduce the risks (see Stith et al., 2004).

As an example, a well-educated farmer complaining of depression was seen with his wife. He described several previous episodes, in each of which a key symptom was that he would kick his wife every morning. He and his wife seemed surprised that this led to questions about other violence and possible police involvement. Kicking his wife stopped immediately after the first interview, although it was some time before his depression responded to treatment.

Violence/Abuse

Make sure you know in concrete terms what clients mean by key words such as 'depression', 'fights' or 'abuse'. Take their account seriously.

If necessary, ask specific closed questions (examples below) to obtain details, stopping once you are receiving 'no' responses. You are seeking the minimum necessary information for risk assessment and further action. You have a duty to know and to comply with your local/organisational policies for any child who is in immediate danger.

Fight means with words? Or physically?
He hits you? Once or more? Slap or punch? With a weapon or object?
He kicks you? He jumps or kneels on you? He chokes you? Do you pass out?
Have others seen this happen?
Have you had injuries from this? Have you needed to see the doctor or go to hospital/ casualty?
Have the police been involved? Have charges been made in court?
Do you fight back? **(If 'yes', repeat above questions about details of attack and consequences.)**
Are others hit? The children? Have social workers been involved?

These questions will assist the process of deciding with the clients if action is needed and how urgently, and whether other agencies such as the police or Women's Refuge need to be involved.

Sexual Abuse of Adults

In a similar fashion, any reference to past or present sexual abuse in an interview justifies some further enquiry. It is known that much sexual abuse goes unreported, being kept secret by victims for many different reasons. It is unlikely that clients mention it by chance or accident. It is also known that abuse can persist from generation to generation, so that a report of past abuse may reveal continuing risk to children now. Therefore, if abuse is mentioned, then it is important to obtain enough details to know what further steps are needed. It is important to take the allegations seriously and to obtain enough information to decide how to proceed. This may be the first disclosure of the abuse. It is important not to appear rejecting or disinterested because an unhelpful response may cause the client to withdraw and a chance to help will be lost.

The following list of questions is designed to avoid prompting the client, so as to avoid claims that the memories are false or prompted by the therapist. It is important not to prompt the client because subsequent police interviews may be affected if prosecution becomes a possibility.

Sexual Abuse (adults)

What age were you? From what age until what?

Who? A family member? A close relative? A friend? A stranger? More than one abuser? Who?

Showing things to you? Touching you? Touching what with what?

Painful? Something put inside you? What? Into what?

Did you tell anyone? Why not? What reaction did you get? Who knew or knows? Were others also treated in this way?

Were you physically hurt also? Tied up? Made to wear special clothes? Rituals/satanists?

When finished always ask: Have you told others about this before? Do you need to say more about it just now?

Most clients asked these questions report that they are relieved to be taken seriously, that they prefer to be asked practical questions of this type and that they believe that the therapist has shown competence in dealing with the topic.

Solution-focused brief therapy is a useful method of working with adult survivors of sexual abuse. Yvonne Dolan is a solution-focused therapist whose books describe her own approach to this demanding work (1991, 2000). She originated the concept of the sequence from 'Victim' to 'Survivor' to 'Authentic Self'. This was based on the finding that disclosure and dealing with the past still leaves clients unprepared for leading their lives in the future. Yvonne Dolan is an Ericksonian hypnotherapist who believes in the Ericksonian Utilization approach, in which every aspect of the client's behaviour, past life, talents and relationships is valuable in generating a more fulfilling and pleasant future. She offers techniques drawn from this model to assist her clients in dealing with flashbacks and in controlling anxiety and distress, which may occur during the process of therapy.

Some clients experience true post-traumatic stress phenomena, such as recurrent vivid flashbacks, which have no identifiable triggers. These clients may benefit from Eye Movement Desensitisation and Reprocessing (EMDR) (Zabukovec et al., 2000; Shapiro, 2001) or similar techniques, which modify the emotional response to flashbacks directly, provided the therapist has appropriate training and experience in these methods. These models can usefully be combined with solution-focused therapy.

Sexual abuse by a close family member and associated threats or promises may damage or distort relationships in later life. Statements by the abuser such as 'This means you are special in the family' or 'This is really a sign of my affection', can produce mixed feelings in a child who expects close family members to be truthful and to mean them well. Equally, threats such as 'It will kill your mother if she finds out' or 'You will be taken away if you tell anyone', can have repercussions long after the abuser has gone. More extreme threats to the child and those dear to them, including pets, are not uncommon and have a correspondingly greater effect. In comparison, sexual assaults by strangers, however dreadful they may be, are often single incidents and may not damage relationship capacity in the same way.

Another aspect of sexual abuse within the family is that whoever reveals it is often scapegoated or ostracised by other family members; for example, 'He did that to me and I never told; why did you make a fuss?', 'He would soon have moved on to your sister and left you alone if you had kept quiet'. This can split and damage families and relationships, so this aspect also needs to be addressed in therapy. On the other hand, there are the heroic stories of abuse victims described by Allan Wade (1997) and reported in Yvonne Dolan's work.

Sexual Abuse and Child Protection

When a child or young teenager appears to be disclosing past or present sexual abuse, it is necessary to be cautious because of the risks of misunderstanding the child's statements or accidentally planting ideas through inappropriate use of leading questions. It is often possible to obtain the necessary minimum information (see below). If there is clearly something to investigate, then specialist agencies can be involved to take the matter further. The risk to the child and perhaps other children is commonly more immediate than when adults report sexual abuse experiences, which are often in the past.

Sexual Abuse (children)

If a child discloses/alleges something:

Open questions: Tell me more about …; Explain …; Describe … Who was it?
Do not ask any other questions.
Record their words with time, date and action taken.
Discuss with children's services duty team.

In interviews with children or adolescents it is particularly important to be aware of local policies on the management of such disclosures. There may be specialist interviewers available or specific procedures to be followed.

The 'Signs of Safety' Approach

The 'Signs of Safety' approach was devised by Andrew Turnell and Steve Edwards (1999). It is a method of assessment and management for child protection issues. Andrew Turnell is a family therapist and Steve Edwards is a social worker. They developed the approach when working with isolated Aboriginal communities in Western Australia. For historical reasons removal of children from Aboriginal families in Australia is generally unacceptable. It was therefore necessary to devise a collaborative approach which would identify risk while also developing good solutions for the child and family. Because of resource issues this had to begin at the first contact.

The approach involves a scale from 0–10 for safety, based on the presence of factors increasing risk and of factors increasing safety. There is a further 0–10 scale to identify how seriously the agency involved will rate the case.

Goals are defined for the agency, for the family and for small steps, which will show immediate progress.

The method has been found useful in several countries. It has been adopted by a number of Social Service departments in the UK as the basis of their whole Child Protection strategy. Hogg and Wheeler (2004) give a good account of the effects of introducing solution-focused practice into child protection teams within social work.

Two recent English reviews of practice (Gardner, 2008; DSCF, 2009) suggest that the Signs of Safety approach is the one approach that incorporates a strengths base alongside an exploration of danger and risk.

Gardner's research focuses on working with neglect and emotional harm and states that:

> In England some children's departments are adopting this [Signs of Safety] approach to improve decision making in child protection. Police, Social Care with adults and children and Children's Guardians thought it especially useful with neglect because: parents say they are clearer about what is expected of them and receive more relevant support; the approach is open and encourages transparent decision making; the professionals had to be specific about their concerns for the child's safety and this encouraged better presentation of evidence; the degree of protective elements of actual or apprehended risks could be set out visually on a scale, easier for all to understand than lengthy reports; once set out, the risks did not have to continually be revisited; the group could acknowledge strengths and meetings could focus on how to achieve safety. (2008, p. 78)

Family Preservation Projects

Insoo Kim Berg has worked with several county- and state-wide Child Protection services in the USA. An account of the approach she developed is given in Berg (1991). These projects have made significant differences to the delivery of such services. A number of Social Services departments in the UK are exploring the use of similar teams and concepts within their child protection services.

One Social Services department in the North of England has recently introduced a Family Regeneration Project based on principles outlined by Berg and then further developed by a Family Regeneration Team in Michigan. They have six workers, who carry two cases each for a period of six weeks. They receive referrals from other departments within Social Services for the area. If the case is accepted, then they begin contact on the same day and are available 24-hours a day.

The project was evaluated after one year: 32 families including 92 children had been accepted and managed. The majority of referrals were for child neglect and in the hope of avoiding care proceedings. No child was received into care while in contact with the Family Regeneration Team.

After return to more traditional social service teams, care proceedings were commenced for 10 families (31.2 per cent), leading to 12 children from three families being placed under care orders at home. A further 23 children from nine families were removed from home for a period. In an attempt to improve this outcome, the handover of care packages from the Family Regeneration Team to their successor teams has been improved. Following the success demonstrated by this small team, the Directors are considering moving the whole Social Services Department to a solution-focused model.

Other Mental Disorders

Those with long-term problems also find solution-focused brief therapy helpful. This can include disability linked to mental illness, acquired brain injury and learning disability. It is useful to aim for small steps, focusing on daily living skills. It is best for the therapist to use simple, clear language and to persist with the programme over long periods. Clients appear able to benefit from solution-focused ideas even if they cannot recall the specific details. They sometimes benefit from advice along the lines of behavioural therapy in order to break goals down into small achievable steps.

Elderly patients with dementia respond well to solution-focused tracking of their language once their attention span and memory is too short to allow more complex conversations. They appear to recognise that attempts are being made to establish contact with them through language and thus become more compliant. Carers find solution-focused approaches helpful in managing the situations with which they are confronted when relatives have stable or advancing brain disorders. Sometimes significant improvement in mental functioning is revealed once specific problems are resolved (Iveson, 1993, 2002). This may be due to a general reduction in anxiety or to some other mechanism. Seidel and Hedley (2008) and Dahl et al. (2000) have published outcome studies on work with the elderly. Janes and Trickey (2005) give a brief but vivid account of the use of solution-focused approaches in planning for discharge in an older adult psychiatric day hospital.

Vicky Bliss, a psychologist in the North of England, has extensive experience in the use of solution-focused approaches with Asperger's syndrome and high-functioning autism. The Missing Link Support Service (www.missinglinksupportservice.co.uk) that she heads includes counsellors who have themselves been service users with these conditions. Bliss focuses on finding competence, coping skills, exceptions and resources (Bliss and Edmonds, 2007). Tilsen et al. (2005) give an interesting account of narrative therapy for a boy with Asperger's syndrome.

Conclusion

Mental health problems are often seen as intractable. Solution-focused brief therapy offers benefits within mental health care because it is rapidly effective, cost-efficient and liked by users. Benefits will often extend into other areas of the sufferer's life. It is easy to learn the basics of the approach and it can be applied in a wide variety of situations, reducing the need for other skills. It is easy to record clearly for administrative purposes, and care plans are easy to pass to colleagues within the team. Team and multi-disciplinary meetings are shorter and more effective once a solution-focused framework is adopted.

Key Points

- The 'medical model' has disadvantages as well as advantages for mental health care.
- Self-harm and safety assessment can be quickly and reliably assessed using solution-focused ideas.
- Domestic violence can be assessed and addressed with a solution-focused model.
- Anxiety and compulsive disorders need appropriate assessment but can often be managed with less therapist time.
- Substance misuse and eating disorders often respond well to solution-focused therapy as a part of a package of measures.
- Personality disorder is less common than has been suggested; many clients find solution-focused ideas helpful.
- Sexual abuse in adults and children can benefit from solution-focused approaches, including child protection services which include these approaches.
- Asperger's syndrome, dementia and acquired brain injury may all benefit from solution-focused approaches and conversations.

Solution-Focused Approaches to Severe Mental Illness

Contents

- General issues in relation to prescribing
- Using medication in combination with solution-focused thinking
- Feedback
- Affective disorders
- Psychosis
- Management of the acutely disturbed inpatient
- Medication in the inpatient setting
- Continuing inpatient care
- Solution-focused work within the mental health structure: common problems
- The wider hospital system
- Conclusion

Solution-focused approaches and active solution-focused therapy can be used with severe mental illness and long-term disability. This is a particular advantage because most other therapies are not considered appropriate in such circumstances. Cognitive-behavioural therapy is often proposed for severe mental illness but is rarely provided during the acute phase. Severe mental illness often requires the use of hospital care and medication in combination with psychological approaches. The management of both acute and long-term disorders can be enhanced by the use of solution-focused conversations and approaches. Antidepressants, antipsychotics and hypnotics will be considered independently and in relation to specific diagnostic categories.

General Issues in Relation to Prescribing

It has been suggested that giving clients medication will reduce their motivation to take action towards helping themselves (Thase and Jindal, 2004). Beyebach et al. (1996) found that those with internal locus of control, who believe that their own actions influence their situation, report more pre-session changes, have clear goals and will comply with tasks. Clients who see control as external to themselves may do better if they are encouraged to focus on exceptions and small steps in order to increase their sense of being in control. Clients with external locus of control may be more likely to expect that prescribed medication is going to be helpful. Internal locus of control may encourage clients to accept medication if they have initiated help-seeking themselves.

Prescribing by psychologists is being introduced by some states in North America and prescribing by nurses and pharmacists is being proposed in the UK. This has produced anxieties about poor practice, overprescribing and a reduction in medical authority. However, many countries allow over-the-counter purchase of all or most medications: Spain, Italy, Portugal, Thailand and South Africa are all examples. There is no evidence that their standard of health care has been dramatically affected by this specific freedom. Neither has respect for doctors declined in these countries. A greater risk which has been predicted is that psychologists and nurses who can prescribe drugs will no longer have the same interest in providing non-drug treatments.

Standards of health care are more affected by the general economic status of a country than by specific health care practices. Access to medication is controlled by cost as much as by prescribing. For example, the less effective drug codeine is preferred to methadone as a substitute drug in withdrawal from narcotics in Germany. This is not due to the control of prescribing by doctors but because methadone is prohibitively expensive in that country. In North America it is now common for those who are on several medications or whose resources are limited to buy drugs from other countries via the Internet because the prices are lower. This raises anxieties about the potential quality of the medication. However, many tablets issued in the UK, USA and Canada are actually made in countries on the other side of the world; pharmacists buy and supply them because the profit margins are greater on preparations manufactured abroad.

Limiting prescribing to health care professionals has not been a successful mechanism for controlling access to drugs. Illegal drugs are widely available on the street on almost every country in the world. The main product of some countries such as Afghanistan and Colombia is said to be drugs for the illegal trade. Among other risks, the supply is of poor quality and the profit margins are excessive. It has been suggested that making these drugs legal would improve quality control and defeat the illegal trade. Those countries that have legalised possession of some or all of such drugs for personal use (including 10 European countries, Chile and Argentina) have seen a decrease in crime and disease, especially HIV/AIDS. The International Harm Reduction Association put forward 'The Vienna Declaration' at their annual conference in 2010, calling upon governments to decriminalise and regulate the drugs trade (www.ihra.net).

Another category of high-risk drugs are steroids taken to enhance sporting performance. It is not difficult to obtain these drugs in the UK without a prescription. The need for constant drug-testing of sportsmen and racehorses underlines the ready availability of these substances. Making antibiotics available only via prescription is intended to limit the development of antibiotic resistance, which can have disastrous consequences for public health. Yet many animal feeds legally contain antibiotics because they encourage weight gain in livestock.

It is important not to be dazzled by claims made for medication. One frail old lady in hospital had her several drugs devotedly supervised by her doctors and nurses. Changes in her state were observed closely and linked to her treatment programme. When her bed and belongings were moved to another ward to allow the rooms to be painted, every single tablet that she had been prescribed was found in her bedside locker. It was clear that the variations in her state were not due to her medication and that her improvement owed more to nature and her own resilience than to high-quality health care.

Specific Medication Effects

It can be useful to think in terms of drugs to relieve symptoms instead of thinking in major diagnostic categories. Identified symptoms may respond to specific drugs. Antidepressants reduce the symptoms of formal depression until the episode is past. They sometimes help the mood in depressive spectrum disorders. Antipsychotics improve mental functioning and behaviour control in those with a major psychosis, thus assisting psychological and psychosocial interventions. Antipsychotics in significant doses impair mental function in those who do not have psychosis.

Many of these drugs have associated or separate actions that can be useful in symptom relief. Some can reduce anxiety (paroxetine, lofepramine, low doses of antipsychotic drugs), improve sleep (SSRIs, trazodone, tricyclics), reduce appetite (fluoxetine), reduce premenstrual tension (fluoxetine), affect sexual function (clomipramine can be used to treat premature ejaculation) or reduce self-harm (fluoxetine and the antipsychotic flupentixol).

Unwanted side-effects of medication become more significant when the person believes or is told that they will be required to take medication on a long-term basis. With antidepressants a clear treatment plan, including gradual withdrawal at a suitable time, can be reassuring. Antipsychotic medications are often prescribed for longer periods and often have significant side-effects. Common side-effects include sedation, which may be temporary or more persistent, tremor and muscular rigidity, weight gain, difficulties with sexual function and an increase in levels of the circulating hormone prolactin, which can affect the risk of other diseases. Any of these might be tolerable in the short-term but are very different issues when long-term treatment is being discussed. The issue is more acute if the patient does not regard themselves as unwell or in need of treatment at all.

The issue of diagnosis is not always of interest to clients. They may fear an illness or disability which has been reported in other members of their family. In major psychosis and affective disorder, I will tell the patient if they ask or if it is necessary to their forward planning (for example, a court order specifying 'treatment for schizophrenia' is going to make a difference to the patient). Otherwise whatever name the patient wants to call the problem is the best 'everyday' name for the illness or problem. It is rare for patients to ask what the official classifications of disease will call it, although some will find a diagnostic term useful in seeking out self-help materials and other resources. You can use this conversation to discuss prognosis and therefore likely exceptions with them. Most care providers require an official diagnostic classification, but this has little bearing on conversation with the patient.

Using Medication in Combination with Solution-Focused Thinking

Current research into combined forms of therapy concludes that for emotional disorders medication and psychological treatments have similar efficacy. Combined treatment with medication and psychological approaches are often more effective than either treatment alone but are more costly and time-consuming. The recommended strategy is to use whichever therapy is most conveniently available, proceeding to add a second treatment if progress with the first is not sufficient (Thase and Jindal, 2004).

Solution-focused brief therapy is suitable and convenient for use in combination with other treatments. It is helpful to link the proposed medication to their goals if possible: 'You hope to experience less or more of ...; this medication may help with that.'; 'I have seen others with similar stories who have benefited from ... medication. Try ... as an experiment for X days/weeks.'

Obtaining consent to drug treatment is aided by knowledge about how medication is used appropriately. The specific dose ranges required for effective treatment with individual antidepressant and antipsychotic drugs are known. Studies of drug metabolism enable prescribers to predict when doses ought to be increased and to recognise when a particular drug has clearly failed. It is then time to augment or change the treatment programme. In the same way the average time by which drug treatment can safely be reduced and stopped is known. If the plan of care can be described clearly to patients in this way, then they are much more likely to comply with the plan. Only the most determined patients can successfully follow the recommendations for more than three drugs daily.

Enquiry About Medication

During return visits it is convenient to follow the usual solution-focused sequence initially. Asking about medication prior to scaling allows the client's responses to be included in planning the next steps. Advice about changes in medication can be included in the concluding feedback.

Including Medication in Solution-Focused Reviews

Including Medication: Key Questions

What's been better for you since we last met?

If good: How did you do that?
If bad: How come that happened? How did you get through it?

What's happening with your medication now? (Allows them to say they've stopped it, changed it or hated it.)

Scaling:

How will you recognise when you are one point or half a point further up the scale?
What else will be different then?
Who will notice? And then who?
How long will it take for this?

Feedback

This sequence of 'What's better? Medication? Where are you on the scale now? What is the next step?' can be used in any medical consultation after the initial visit, even if the doctor has no other knowledge of or use for solution-focused therapy. It provides a structure and will in itself help to generate positive thinking and productive next steps for both doctor and patient.

Affective Disorders

Disorders of mood (bipolar disorder, affective disorder, manic-depressive illness) consist of episodes of elevated or depressed mood, known as 'mania' or 'depression'. Occasionally mixed states occur. The worldwide incidence is about 1 per cent of all populations studied. These disorders are marked by biological symptoms that recur in a similar pattern in each episode. A family history of the disorders is common. Antidepressant drugs can induce mania in some individuals, which confuses the diagnostic picture. A proportion of people who have had depression will later have at least one episode of mania.

Mania is characterised by elated mood, being overactive and overtalkative, and having decreased sleep and appetite. Most antidepressant treatments can induce mania and this may lead to diagnostic errors. Episodes usually last from three to six months if untreated.

Major depression is characterised by low mood; waking early in the morning and not going back to sleep; reduction in appetite, weight, concentration and interest in sexual activity; constipation; amenorrhea; and regular variation of mood over the course of the day. These bodily functions are all regulated by the hypothalamus. If at least four of these symptoms occur consistently for five days per week over several weeks, then the illness is present and physical methods of treatment such as medication may be valuable. If these features are not present, then the response to physical treatments is less predictable. An episode will last six to nine months in 85 per cent of cases. Future episodes will be recognisably similar and more common with increasing age.

In my opinion, biological symptoms of affective disorder can occur in anyone. Once a certain duration or amount of stress is exceeded, the body becomes unable to adapt and then biological symptoms appear. Shakespeare suggests the following sequence to account for Hamlet's melancholy:

Polonius: 'And he, repulsed, ...
Fell into a sadness; then into a fast;
Thence to a watch; thence into a weakness;
Thence to a lightness; and, by this declension,
Into the madness wherein now he raves,
And all we wail for.'

(Act 2, Scene 2, Line 147)

It depends on what stresses you encounter, what supports you have available and what susceptibility to mood disorder you have inherited. Depression is the more common type, but mania can also occur as a response to stress, usually in those with a strong family history of affective disorder. In either case, drug treatment can be valuable, acting to relieve distress and to enable the survival of the patient and their social and business relationships until the episode is over. Premature cessation of drug treatment often reveals continuing symptoms, suggesting that drugs help to suppress the symptoms but do not cure the disorder. There are several major classes of antidepressants but there is little difference in effect between antidepressants from the same class, so the eventual choice may be based on the client's experience of side-effects. Modern electro-convulsive therapy is safe and can be effective in both depression and mania. Its effect is often short-lived, requiring further treatments or additional forms of treatment. There has been increasing interest recently in the use of high-intensity light therapy and of sleep deprivation for depressive disorders.

In the clinic, reviewing people referred with 'depression' gives the chance to look for biological symptoms and for inadequate doses of medication. The conversation can then move easily into solution-focused work. There is no reason why medication and solution-focused brief therapy cannot be used at the same time. A knowledge of good practice with medication can be included in the consultation, encouraging compliance with suitable treatment. A 'not-knowing' perspective does not mean that you cannot propose experiments based on your own knowledge. Knowledge of standard protocols regarding antidepressant medications is useful in order to encourage clients to give the medication enough time to have an optimal effect.

Antidepressants are best given as a single dose where their properties allow this. If they are sedative, then a night time dose is best. They need to be taken in an adequate dose for four to six weeks before the dose is increased. If the maximum dose is ineffective after six weeks, then there should be a change to an antidepressant of a different class. It is not useful to persist with an ineffective drug or dose. This delays recovery and exposes the patient to the risk of drug side-effects to no purpose.

Once response has occurred, the drug should be continued in the same dose for four to six months. If cautious withdrawal allows symptoms of depression to reappear, then the dose should be returned to its previous level for another few weeks before a further cautious attempt at withdrawal. Recognising relapses and conversations about relapse prevention are useful at this stage. The dialogue about finding and maintaining exceptions lends itself to such conversations.

Case Examples

A woman asked for help with her sleep. She reported a number of formal depressive symptoms. There had been a temporary improvement with a low dose of a sedative antidepressant, after which she had stopped taking the tablets. As well as complimenting her on her existing strategies, she was advised to increase the dose of her antidepressant because this would improve her sleep and was likely to produce further improvement in her depressive symptoms.

An elderly man attended complaining of headaches and impotence. These were both common side-effects of his antidepressant tablets, which he had taken for over two years. He was not depressed at interview and mentioned no depressive symptoms when discussing pre-session changes or exceptions. In his miracle he described better enjoyment of physical activities and a better relationship with his wife. He was advised to reduce or stop his antidepressants.

Elevated Mood

In the treatment of mania the usual choices are antipsychotic drugs (major tranquillisers) and mood-stabilising drugs such as lithium, carbamazepine and sodium valproate. In most cases the antipsychotic drugs can be withdrawn once the mood has stabilised. Solution-focused conversations can include relapse prevention as well as management of the current situation. Some patients with mania require hospital admission because they are unable or unwilling to cooperate with care outside hospital. Aspects of solution-focused management of inpatients are discussed below.

Long-term medication is needed for a number of clients with major psychosis or continuing depression. Many people prefer not to see themselves as dependent on medication for health and will need time to accept the need for continuing medication.

In affective disorders relapse prevention and management often follow naturally from discussion of exceptions and of previously successful strategies. 'Recovery' can be expected in eating disorders and abuse of substances as well as in many depressive and anxiety disorders. This does not mean that clients will not sometimes have variations in their habits and symptoms, which is a part of normal life for everyone. Other problems such as chronic or relapsing illnesses may respond to treatment but can be expected to return. In that case relapse prevention and knowledge of previous successful strategies is helpful.

Psychosis

For schizophrenia there is consensus between the American (DSM-IV) (APA, 1994) and European (ICD-10) (WHO, 1994) diagnostic classifications. The illness can be diagnosed given the presence for more than one month of bizarre delusions and/or auditory hallucinations in which one voice keeps up a running commentary about the patient or two or more voices talk to each other. If these features are not definitely present, then the diagnosis may depend on the presence of other less specific symptoms such as disorganisation of speech or behaviour and negative symptoms such as flattening of emotions. Subtle neurological damage can be detected in many sufferers, and there is sometimes a relative with a similar disorder. The use of amphetamine-based drugs, alcohol or lysergic acid diethylamide can provoke similar symptoms, which may become permanent.

The incidence of schizophrenia seems to have increased early in the nineteenth century. Hypotheses to explain this include population increase or a proposed infectious or toxic agent. Examination of the careful records kept in nineteenth-century Europe shows that the prevalence of major mental disorders has not changed since then.

The diagnosis of schizophrenia is viewed by the public as catastrophic, yet 15–25 per cent of patients have only one episode in a lifetime (Gelder et al., 1996; Kumar and Clark, 2002). Many require long-term support, but follow-up studies in various countries show that over 60 per cent of those previously diagnosed with schizophrenia are stable in middle age, often without medication; many are married and/or in work (Harding et al., 1987; DeSisto et al., 1995). Their work and social function is usually below that expected for their background, but this phenomenon is not confined to those with schizophrenia. The Recovery Model in the UK is beginning to work towards these long-term goals for all sufferers. Those in whom the disorder is limited to paranoid delusions often retain all their skills and abilities (including the ability to carry out their delusional impulses).

It is now recognised that hearing voices is not uncommon in the general population. It is not directly linked with mental illness, although the UK Hearing Voices Network estimates that only 20 per cent of voices are exclusively pleasant. Help is sought mostly by those for whom the voices are unpleasant or frightening. Solution-focused approaches are helpful for those who want to modify the voices or their reaction to them. As far as mental health is concerned, it does not matter that someone hears voices provided that their external behaviour is safe for themselves and others.

When used in equivalent doses there is little proven difference in efficacy between one antipsychotic drug and another. (The exception is clozapine, which can be beneficial in schizophrenia that has been resistant to other antipsychotic drugs.) The useful differences lie in the side-effects, and this is a matter that can be negotiated in collaboration with the patient. A young man may resent erectile failure as a side-effect whereas, an elderly man may be more concerned by tremor. A patient who suspects others of threatening him is more likely to accept a drug that makes him calm and alert rather than one which has a sedative effect and thus makes him feel more vulnerable. Once again this is essentially a client choice based on their experience of side-effects.

The majority of antipsychotic drugs can be given as a single daily dose, which is convenient for most people and easier to remember. Taking the dose at night often means that the side-effects are largely gone by the morning. A period of two to six weeks at an adequate dose is needed to determine if a drug is going to be effective. When the time comes to withdraw such a drug this should be done slowly, unless an alternative antipsychotic drug is being started at the same time. It is best to stay within the recommended dose ranges. This will help to reduce side-effects, and very high doses are rarely more effective. The risk of untoward events is greater when the recommended doses are exceeded.

In the management of longstanding psychosis, clients usually have specific problems when they attend. Either they have identified the problems themselves and sought help or the problems have been noticed by someone else, such as a relative or professional. After addressing the problem using solution-focused brief therapy they are discharged or the frame is changed back to 'support' once the problem is being managed adequately. The medication should be maintained at the lowest effective dose, with increases when the situation requires it. This reduces side-effects and increases compliance.

Admission to Hospital

Inpatient admission should only be for specific indications and not as an all-purpose panacea. There are many studies showing the disadvantages of hospital care. These start with investigations into the care provided by private madhouses in the early nineteenth century. Mental health legislation was originally intended to protect the sufferer, not society. The problems of mental hospitals and other total institutions are well documented in Goffman's *Asylums* (1968) and by many inquiries in hospitals across the world since then. The film *One Flew Over the Cuckoo's Nest* (1975; Kesey, 1962) provoked many shades of response, but no-one denied that the hospital depicted might exist.

Patients with major mental illness are often acutely sensitive to changes in their social environment. They will often react to family tensions or staff changes. Because their response may be expressed in terms of symptoms or agitation, it may not be clear that there are triggers for their behaviour, and that these triggers may be open to modification. It is always useful to ask 'How come this is happening now and not some other time?' The client may not be able to answer the question, but others in the family or the social context may have suggestions.

One client with long-term mental illness moved to a new area. He refused to answer letters about his rent and became angry when confronted with this. He was on the point of being evicted and returned to hospital. We then discovered that he also had a severe reading difficulty and had never been able to deal with written communication. Once someone was able to deal with letters on his behalf, then his anger and the non-payment of rent were rapidly resolved.

Useful functions of hospital care include the assessment of complex cases and providing safe conditions for the patient and the community while assessment is done. In all cases assessment should be targeted and brief. Inpatient care may also be necessary for specialist treatments that carry risks. Our service also offered 48-hour 'non-treatment' admission on-demand for those whose lives gave rise to recurrent crises, and seven-day 'low stimulation' admissions (bed rest, no visitors, no radio or TV), for those whose goals include 'a rest'. Most of the latter soon find that simple rest is unhelpful and decide to move into more active pursuit of their goals.

Management of the Acutely Disturbed Inpatient

The incidence of violence in our secure unit was reduced once we introduced solution-focused concepts. We believe that this was due to our clients recognising our interest in their wishes as opposed to imposing external rules. Length of stay was also reduced. Whatever one's theoretical stance, many urgent admissions have been short of food, drink and sleep for some time. A day of calm and quiet with plenty of food and fluids often produces substantial improvement in understanding and collaboration. Offering medication is often acceptable at this point provided it is framed as being in part to 'help with sleep'. Several short interviews over a few days is often best, as long interviews are tiring; the individual's concentration and their recall of the agreed treatment plan may both be limited. Solution-focused methods are ideal for this style.

It is helpful to see people soon after admission. After the immediate situation has been dealt with by offering fluids, food and sleep, the next question to ask the patient is 'What do you want to get out of being here?' This begins the process of establishing a collaboration from which all parties will benefit, shifting the patient's perception from being at the mercy of the system to having some say in their own affairs. It is useful to obtain the minimum necessary information for diagnostic purposes soon after admission.

Once the 'official' diagnosis is made, the focus becomes future manage-ment. Specific symptoms will not be discussed again unless there is a good reason for doing so. Some service users have learned to use psychiatric ter-minology but others have their own names for their problem or only wish to address one specific issue. There may be target symptoms that they wish to work on or they may have goals based on their everyday life.

In acute disturbance, whether due to physical or mental disorder, simple conversations are best for understanding. The solution-focused process is ideal for this purpose. It is helpful to know if symptoms are useful in some way. Not all voices are hostile or unhelpful; nocturnal wakefulness may suit the patient or the family by reducing social stimulation to a comfortable level. One patient would only eat food which his dog had identified as safe. He could not tell us how the dog communicated this information to him. He was prepared to starve rather than risk eating food without this safety check. As a result we had to admit his dog to hospital also. (Unfortunately it brought in fleas and we had to fumigate the unit after they were discharged.)

For those who resent being in hospital or in contact with services, it is useful to talk about how they can avoid relapse or return to hospital. Over time many will come to recognise that there are actions which reduce con-frontations and hence avoid readmission. Such actions will be more likely to occur if the patient regards them as self-invented rather than forced on them by professionals or families.

Relapse: Key Questions

Have you had this problem before?
What helped you to get through it then?
Did you notice it yourself?
Did someone else notice first?
Who noticed?
What did they do that was helpful?
What things are happening now that you want to go on happening?
How confident are you on a scale of 0–10 that you can get through the day/the weekend? What would increase that by one point?

Because it is collaborative and focuses on building relationships from the start and because a detailed history is not needed, solution-focused work is particularly suitable for short-stay psychiatric units. It can be used in spite of the fast turnover of patients and the number of disturbed residents. It is difficult in such units to introduce other forms of psychological therapy and transfer out is likely to occur before any progress is made with more complex therapies, which is discouraging for staff. There is less scope for misunderstanding when solution-focused care plans are used because they are easy to summarise and to hand over to colleagues.

Steve de Shazer has suggested that therapy cannot be done unless a conversation is possible (plenary discussion, European Brief Therapy Association annual conference, Bruges, Belgium 1998). In some acutely disturbed patients, conversation is not possible initially. The dialogue may resemble a conversation but no transaction or social exchange is taking place. Whatever the interviewer may ask, the replies are couched in similar words about some preoccupation. Solution-focused therapy, like other psychotherapies, appears to be ineffective at this stage. Shakespeare observed this:

> Hamlet (to his mother): '... it is not madness
> That I have utter'd: bring me to the test,
> And I the matter will re-word; which madness
> Would gambol from.'

> (Act 3, Scene 4, Line 161)

The Uzbek author Marat Akchurin reports travelling in a truck with a man in restraints who was being transferred to a mental hospital: 'I tried to reorganise our strange exchange into a dialogue, but neither this nor any of my subsequent attempts to establish rational contact had any effect, since the old man did not listen but only spoke' (1992, p. 155). This neatly summarises one's experience of such conversations.

The use of solution-focused questioning results in quick recognition of this situation. Detailed discussion can then be delayed until the patient is ready for true conversation. Experience suggests that using their language as part of attempts at dialogue in the interim leads to rapid building of relationships later.

Case Example

An elderly man was admitted from a rented house. He was educated and financially secure but kept all his possessions in a van and moved to new accommodation every few weeks. He had called the police in the early hours because of 'intruders' outside. He had put the telephone in a box and buried it under cushions. He had glued carpet over the windows. On arrival, he said, 'They follow me everywhere. They torment me all night. I don't know how they find me again so quickly after I move.' He was politely adamant that he was not unwell and that his experiences were real. He accepted an antipsychotic drug in a single night-time dose when told that one of its effects would be to improve his sleep. Within three days he was stable and contented. His belief in the 'intruders' decreased steadily over the next four weeks. He left hospital and continued his medication as recommended.

Medication in the Inpatient Setting

We negotiate the use of medication in order to assist patients to function better. Sometimes this requires us to say: 'We respect your beliefs about medication but we believe that medication is essential at the moment. We also have goals for your stay here. We will find it hard to work with you if you do not accept medication.' Clear information about medication assists the process of negotiation. It is sometimes useful to point out that medication increases calmness and clear thought, but does not affect real knowledge. You can demonstrate this by asking 'What was your mother's name?', 'What school did you go to?' Finding that they still know the answers to these questions might show that medication reduces worrying ideas but does not alter what they know and believe. If we do not know whether medication will help or not, we present the idea in terms of an experiment with clear goals and a fixed time limit. Many patients have previous experience of medication and it is useful to ask if there were any specific medications that they found helpful or unhelpful. Patients are more likely to cooperate with prescribed medication if they feel that their views and expertise have been respected.

Many patients also know that we have the legal power to enforce medication, although this is more useful for emergencies than as a part of a regular programme. It is important that there is a clear policy for such situations because polypharmacy and excessive dosing are known to carry increased risks. The usual practice in the UK is to use oral or injected benzodiazepines, followed or accompanied by oral or injected antipsychotic drugs. There are several drugs in current use to choose from. Duration of action and the patient's previous reaction to the drug are a useful guide.

From Bulgaria, Bostandzhiev and Bozhkova report on a comparative study in a Mental Health Day Center, 2002–2005. Ninety-six subjects were included: 41 experimental and 55 controls. Group 1 (n=14; anxiety disorders, depression): solution-focused therapy without drug therapy; Group 2 (n=8): medication without psychotherapy; Group 3 (n=27): solution-focused therapy and medication; Group 4 (n=47): syncretic group therapy (recitation and discussion of problems, average 30 sessions) and medication. Groups 2, 3 and 4 included schizophrenia, bipolar disorders and anxiety disorders. Thirty-one patients (32.3 per cent) in the whole sample were diagnosed as having schizophrenia. The solution-focused input varied from one to seven sessions, with an average of 2.6.

Results are based on improvement measured by OQ45, GAF and client's scaling. Group 1: 78.5 per cent improved; Group 2: 25 per cent; Group 3: 63 per cent; Group 4: 19 per cent. From Group 4, 15 per cent showed deterioration, but none of the other groups. Thus 65.8 per cent improved when solution-focused therapy was included, as against 20 per cent without. There was rapid change in daily functioning for all diagnostic categories, ranging from coping with chores and family life to full recovery.

Continuing Inpatient Care

Psychiatric intensive care units in the UK usually offer short-term admissions of weeks rather than months. We found that solution-focused ideas were useful because relationships developed quickly. Goals and plans were easily transferred from one worker to another, making the best use of time in the unit. If the client's goal was simply to get out of the unit as soon as possible, then we described the necessary steps towards discharge. We advised them that certain behaviours were unlikely to speed their progress towards discharge. Clients appreciated the clarity of knowing which behaviours were used to judge progress. The staff used their own expertise to determine when a client could move from one level of security to the next.

Patients are often comfortable with small steps and exceptions initially. Once they become more at ease in the unit they are able to aim for larger goals and to learn what services are available that will help them to achieve them. Scaling is a valuable tool both for symptoms and for other behaviours. Although scales do not seem to work well for elated patients: 'If 10 is completely well and able to leave the hospital, what number are you at?' 'Fifteen!'; 'What number do you want to achieve eventually?' 'Twenty!' Such patients often see attempts to restrict their goals and self-confidence as being unhelpful. Sometimes they may accept that their significant others prefer them to be lower on the scale. Some elated individuals are willing to work with reversed scales in which they are at 10 now but will be accepted for discharge by others at some lower point. Others who have experienced both depression and mania can use a scale with depression as zero and mania or 'being high' as 10.

A short question set or 'microtool' for use by psychiatric inpatient staff has been developed. It is similar to question sets used for crisis intervention (Chapter 7) and for situation management as a hard-pressed manager (see Chapter 9). Little knowledge of the patient's background is needed, since the focus is on immediate problems and how to start dealing with them.

Microtool – Inpatient Conversations: Key Questions

What is the problem? (Obtain a behavioural description)

Scaling of the problem from 0–10:

What first small step will show that you are moving up the scale?
Who else will notice?
What coping skills can you use in the meantime?

This question set can be applied to problems on any scale. Its brevity allows its use in brief interactions in a ward or unit where there is little scope for detailed one-to-one conversation.

Families are often sensitive to small changes in the disturbed person because of their previous experience and their knowledge of the individual. If there are difficulties with someone's management it is often helpful to ask the family to advise on how they would address the situation. Familiar interventions may be more recognisable and therefore more acceptable to the patient. In a similar way, if a family are critical of the unit or its management it can be helpful to ask them for their advice about managing the patient. They may have knowledge of previously effective interventions, and using them as allies can be valuable in defusing situations. Equally, if the family say that they have no suggestions and that the staff should come up with something, this moves them towards collaborating with proposals made by the staff.

Not every team member wants to work in a solution-focused way. This does not give rise to conflicts as long as all points of view are respected. Research described in Chapter 6 shows that a model fitting a client's concepts and to which the therapist has allegiance will produce a better outcome. It is therefore best to have more than one approach available within the team. Many workers have their own skills and prior training. They may adopt solution-focused brief therapy as another possible option, using their own judgement as to which option to adopt with any one client. Or they may use only their preferred model, advising the rest of the team when they see a place for their specific skill.

Greenberg (1998) has pioneered solution-focused groups for clients with long-term mental health problems. He focuses on goals: 'What do you want to achieve?', scaling, the next step with the aid of advice from the group and the recurring question 'What have you achieved since the last time you attended?' He emphasises the role of the group leader in keeping up the level of activity and discussion in such groups. In his experience clients may walk in and out of the group or miss sessions without problems for the group and without detriment to the eventual achievement of goals by the client. This approach to groups is useful in supportive work and in day centres.

Vaughn et al. (1995) work in a hospital in Denver that introduced solution-focused methods throughout the hospital. As well as reducing length of stay in the hospital (see Chapter 6), they make use of various groups aimed at goal-setting and solution-building. One regular group on the inpatient unit is 'The Compliments Group'. Every week two staff members meet with all the patients. The staff identify two compliments for each patient regarding their achievements in the preceding week. They then ask the group to add any other compliments for the person. They report that this is the only group in the week that everyone attends without complaint.

Rowan and O'Hanlon (1999) co-wrote a book about solution-oriented therapy for chronic and severe mental illness. Tim Rowan is a clinical social worker and Bill O'Hanlon is a therapist and trainer in brief therapy with an international reputation. The book contains a collection of case vignettes, each showing a potential response or manoeuvre for situations that arise in work with severe mental illness. They point out that searching for 'The Cure' is not productive; they advise aiming for small changes and collaborative working. They emphasise the importance of 'both/and' conversations, to move the client from a focus on the symptom or diagnosis towards a view of themselves that allows for resources and changes.

Legal requirements may restrict options such as trial leave of absence. It can be helpful to explore issues with clients prior to legal or quasi-legal proceedings. Even if the outcome goes against their wishes, it is good for their self-esteem and confidence if they feel that they have spoken up for themselves appropriately. To the benefit of all, this also diminishes inappropriate behaviour during or after the proceedings. The question set given in Chapter 9 for use when faced with powerful vested interests can be helpful here.

Case Example

Alan X had been disturbed for several days before being detained under legal powers at his home. He resisted transfer by ambulance and was brought to the secure unit in handcuffs by the police. He was interviewed three hours after arrival.

Interviewer: [*Introduces self and nurse*] What would you like to get out of being here?

Alan: They sent me here; it's not me; they've done it before. They've got it in for me; they know what it's all about; you know too.

Interviewer: Who is this 'they'?

Alan: They know what it's all about. They sent me here; it's not me. You have it all on camera.

Interviewer: What cameras?

Alan: The cameras in my house. You know what it's all about.

Interviewer: I have not seen any cameras or tapes.

Alan: You know what it's all about. They've done it before.

Interviewer: How come it led to you coming here?

Alan: They know what it's all about. It's not me; they sent me here; they did it. You should be talking to them, not to me.

Interviewer: We will talk about it all after you have had some rest. We will give you some medication to help you sleep. Be sure to tell us if anything similar happens while you are here.

Next day

Interviewer:	[*Introduces self and nurse*] We talked briefly yesterday. We wonder what you would like to get from being here?
Alan:	They need to stop what they are doing. They want to hurt me. I can't go to the shop.
Interviewer:	What have you done about what is being done?
Alan:	I went to the town council but their man said he could not do anything unless he could hear it himself. I told him to come back at night to hear it but he would not. The police say they cannot do anything until they see something on their cameras in the street.
Interviewer:	What do you think they will see on their cameras?
Alan:	The neighbours hammer on my door and shout at night. They are clever about doing it when the police cameras are not looking.
Interviewer:	Do you think you could be mistaken about the neighbours doing this?
Alan:	No; I know it's them.
Interviewer:	Did you ever have this hammering and shouting before?
Alan:	It happened before five years ago but they stopped after I had been in hospital.
Interviewer:	Stopped … when did it start again?
Alan:	About four months ago after my medication was changed.
Interviewer:	As well as the hammering and shouting, what else has been happening in recent months that bothers you?
Alan:	I lose sleep because of the noise; I have trouble eating because I can't stay in the shops for long in case someone gets in at home. They know when I have gone out because their cameras are inside my flat.
Interviewer:	Did you manage to sleep last night in here?
Alan:	Yes; because the neighbours could not get past the night nurses. Your tablet did not do much.
Interviewer:	Did the nurses get you something to eat?
Alan:	I did not like the hot meal but the staff had some sandwiches sent over for me and they made me coffee.
Interviewer:	Are there ever specific references to you on the television or in the newspapers?
Alan:	No. There was a letter in the paper from someone called Alan but it was not me.
Interviewer:	Does all this make it difficult to keep your mind on things like reading the paper?
Alan:	No, not if I get enough sleep.
Interviewer:	[*Confirms by specific questions that John has accurate knowledge of current events, that depressive symptoms are absent and that he does not use street drugs. He has no signs of drug withdrawal. Screening of blood and urine reveals no traces of illicit drug use.*]
Interviewer:	Do you drink alcohol at all?

Alan:	If I have enough money I can buy beer at the supermarket but I don't usually go there because it is too far from my flat.

[Interviewer is now satisfied that a diagnosis of paranoid illness can be made, fixed false beliefs and auditory hallucinations being present, but with no signs of thought disorder, ideas of reference or impairment of concentration or memory. Depression and substance misuse are not present. The necessary administrative processes can now be completed, therefore the focus of conversation becomes the treatment plan.]

Interviewer:	So what helped you to deal with this when it happened before?
Alan:	I could eat and sleep in the hospital; I took the medication to keep the staff happy. Nurse Y used to come and visit; I think maybe the neighbours knew about her and so they kept away in case she saw them.
Interviewer:	How come Nurse Y stopped visiting?
Alan:	She retired and I did not want someone new.
Interviewer:	Someone took over after she retired; do you want to have them visit?
Alan:	Dunno … I would need to meet them first.
Interviewer:	We can arrange for them to come and see you here. Let us know what you think. What medication was helpful to you in the past?
Alan:	Not the blue tablets; they made my hands shake. I don't remember their name but I know what they taste like.
Interviewer:	The tablets we prefer now do not usually make the hands shake. You took one last night; are your hands shaky just now?
Alan:	No.
Interviewer:	We plan to increase the tablets tonight and again tomorrow night; after that they will stay the same until we see how it goes. Is that alright with you?
Alan:	I'd rather not take tablets; I want to get out of here.
Interviewer:	We think that taking the tablets will help you to get out of here sooner. Make sure to tell us if your hands shake or there are other problems for you. Is there anything else you want to mention today?
Alan:	They need to sort out my money; if they don't my rent will not be paid.
Interviewer:	What do they need to sort out?
Alan:	I stopped opening the envelopes so I don't know if I am due any money.
Interviewer:	How do you find out what you are due now?
Alan:	Someone could ask the Benefits Agency about welfare payments.
Interviewer:	Who could ask them?
Alan:	My sister does not speak to me now. Could I go to the phone?
Interviewer:	There is a phone in here which you can use. It is too soon for you to go out for walks with staff at present.
Alan:	I don't know if I want to use the phone in here.

Interviewer:	One of the staff has a special knowledge of the welfare system. He can talk with you about what you will say when you do use the phone to them.
Alan:	OK.
Interviewer:	So thinking about a scale of 0–10 where 10 is you out of hospital and things going well, and 0 is as bad as things were before, where are you right now on that scale?
Alan:	Nought.
Interviewer:	So how have you kept going when you are at nought?
Alan:	Getting some sleep helped.
Interviewer:	So sleep is really important for you. When you move up half a point on the scale what will be different for you?
Alan:	I won't feel like hitting people.
Interviewer:	Who did you feel like hitting?
Alan:	The neighbours and that policeman. He had no right to put hand-cuffs on me.
Interviewer:	How come the police were there?
Alan:	I told the ambulance man I would cut him if he tried to come into my flat.
Interviewer:	Have you cut anyone before? Or hit anyone?
Alan:	No; but I would have done it.
Interviewer:	How come you did not do that?
Alan:	They came in before I could get a knife from the kitchen.
Interviewer:	Do you still think about getting a knife or cutting someone?
Alan:	I sometimes think about it.
Interviewer:	How do you manage to think about it but not do it?
Alan:	I think to myself that they will put me in hospital again if I cut some-one. The neighbours might get me for it while I was sleeping.
Interviewer:	Are there specific people that you think of cutting, neighbours or anyone else?
Alan:	I felt like hitting that policeman.
Interviewer:	Have you thought about cutting or hitting anyone in this hospital?
Alan:	No.
Interviewer:	How can we tell if you are thinking about cutting someone or hit-ting someone?
Alan:	I don't know.
Interviewer:	Will you tell us if you are thinking that?
Alan:	[*No reply*]
Interviewer:	When you are thinking like that, what can we do that will help?
Alan:	Let me stay in my room; the other people here are strange.
Interviewer:	Will you tell us when you need to stay in your room?
Alan:	Yes.
Interviewer:	OK; we will ask you if we are not sure. I guess that hitting or cutting someone will not help you to get out of hospital sooner.
Alan:	[*Nods*]
Interviewer:	Anything else to mention today?
Alan:	No; I'm tired of talking just now.

Two days later

His key worker asked Alan X the miracle question during an individual interview. Alan replied that miracles did not happen. He went on to say that he did have 'a dream' sometimes about how he wanted his life to be. This dream was explored as if it was a reply to the miracle question. He described living in the same flat but with somewhere to go for social contact, 'Not pubs because the rough people come in there', and the chance to play lawn bowls. His grandfather, dead many years ago, had taken him to try lawn bowls when he was a teenager and he believed that he had a talent for this game. The dream also included having his money 'sorted out', being confident about his budgeting and being able to visit different shops for his purchases.

   Alan talked with the staff about his money and made a plan for moving towards discharge. He showed no signs of violence and did not spend much time alone in his room. Our security precautions were gradually reduced. He was able to go for walks, first with staff and then alone for increasing periods. He decided that the phone in the unit was acceptable for his calls. He took his medication, joined the unit occupational programme and wrote to the local lawn bowling club for information. His suspicions about the neighbours were rarely mentioned. After meeting the nurse from the community team he agreed to have her visit him at home. At times he would stop his key worker in the corridor and say 'I'm still work-ing on that dream!', but he rarely referred to it directly when talking with others. His eventual discharge home was successful after some five weeks in hospital. Six months later his community worker reported that he had remained on medication and was not quarrelling with his neighbours. He had been to a bowling alley once with the local day-centre members.

Solution-Focused Work Within the Mental Health Structure: Common Problems

The legal system and mental health law are both constructed around a problem focus. Formal reports for courts about offenders and in reviews of detention are required to contain problem-focused information. It can be difficult for clients to understand why the workers who talk about solutions with them all day will then offer problem-focused material to outside agencies. It is sometimes helpful in maintaining a therapeutic relation-ship with the client if compliments on their efforts to change and achieve goals are included in reports. Another option is that the senior practitioner remains problem-focused while other staff do the solution-focused work. However, this creates a split in the staff team, which may become divisive. Community support teams in the UK are often organised in the name of the senior practitioner so that collaboration may decrease if that person is not viewed as supportive by the client.

The solution-focused model addresses 'What now?'. It does not contradict client's perceptions of events, although it may offer other possible perceptions. When clients were still in contact with their families of origin, we have sometimes tried to go beyond the solution-focused approach to explore their behaviour within the family or social context (cf. Seikkula et al., 2003 and elsewhere). This has been fruitful in some cases and not in others. It appears that we have had most success with this when the whole care team has been involved in the process. When this is not the case, then traditional values and approaches have reasserted themselves and all collaborative work has become more difficult. This has not appeared to be linked to any specific features of the cases.

The Wider Hospital System

Those of our inpatient units that have favoured collaborative/brief therapy approaches have had lower bed occupancy and a rapid turnover of clients. This was not accompanied by any increase in adverse events. Similar experience with inpatient services in Colorado has been reported by Vaughn et al. (1996). Our intensive care unit was often the only such unit in the North of England that could make beds available for emergencies from other counties. Our open wards were usually able to make beds available for urgent admissions and to provide 'on-demand' crisis support, as described above. This low occupancy is uncommon in English psychiatry as bed numbers have been reduced nationally by 60 per cent since 1978. Psychiatric intensive care units in local mental health settings are the first point of contact for the most severe examples of mental illness and for mentally disordered offenders. Such patients may move on eventually to higher levels of secure care or to prison, but only after assessment and initial treatment in these local units. So if there is benefit from solution-focused thinking there, then some benefit may be hoped for in any mental illness setting.

Within the hospital, the effects of solution-focused skills were acknowledged by respect from the administration. However, the same financial and bureaucratic restraints existed for everyone. An excellent safety assessment tool was devised by a non-solution focused colleague. It took the form of three 1–10 visual scales, one each for risk of self-harm, risk of suicide and risk of violence. Each scale was marked by the client and the key worker. A new assessment could be completed in minutes whenever necessary. It was well-liked by professionals since it showed the situation clearly at a glance. The hospital management replaced it with a purchased instrument, which had no evidence base and relied on repetitive collection of factual data, while neglecting all aspects of judgement or relationship. It was therefore comprehensible to the hospital administration but did not use most of the information gathered by trained and experienced clinical staff.

Many individuals within our hospital have had training in solution-focused brief therapy. However, some units do not employ solution-focused approaches and may not continue our treatment plans or accept our formulations and safety assessments. This can delay discharge and create tensions for clients. On some occasions the hospital administration was unable to tolerate our estimates of safety and chose to place clients elsewhere instead of accepting our recommendations for discharge.

Solution-focused ideas proved valuable within the hospital management system. Their use at management level encouraged the best of existing resources, including reducing the time spent in meetings. It should be noted that for an administrator, a meeting is a social high point adding knowledge, reinforcing hierarchy and postponing less attractive activities. Whereas for clinical staff, the high point of the day is employing clinical expertise; meeting administrators who have different and sometimes conflicting interests is not valued in the same way.

Conclusion

Solution-focused therapy has advantages for use within the mental health system. The presence of major psychiatric phenomena does not prevent the use of solution-focused conversation. It can be applied without previous knowledge of the patient and is easy to share with other colleagues when a patient is transferred or discharged. Its brief and collaborative nature helps to reduce length of stay in hospital as well as diminishing conflicts with the patient.

Key Points

- Prescribing is not an exact science.
- Combining medication with solution-focused input can improve compliance with treatment.
- Coherent medication policies also improve compliance.
- Psychosis is not a unitary concept.
- Admission should serve a purpose beyond removal from the community.
- Collaborative management improves care and reduces violence.
- Brief conversations can change many things.
- Hospital systems are as resistant to change as any other institution.

Solution-Focused Approaches in
the Workplace

Contents

- Research in the workplace
- Solution-focused situation management: finding cooperation quickly
- Handling conflict in teams
- Anticipation conversations
- Solution-focused supervision
- The microtools concept
- Solution-focused coaching in education
- Solution-focused reflecting teams
- Constructive criticism
- 360° feedback
- Managing disagreement with powerful vested interests
- Bureaucracies and large organisations
- Conclusion

The world of organisation and management has become another promi-
nent area for solution-focused ideas. Coaches, consultants and change facil-
itators have become interested in these new ways of applying their skills to
interactions within companies and agencies. Each year there is an annual
conference and other events run by SOLWorld. SOLWorld is an association
of management consultants and trainers who use solution-focused methods. It was founded in Britain by Mark McKergow, Jenny Clarke and Paul Z.
Jackson. It attracts leading consultants from around the world. Many of the
consultants who attend have their own skills and are devising new ways of
applying these skills in combination with the solution-focused approach.

For those interested in learning the solution-focused model for use in the workplace, a good workbook by Jackson and Waldman is available: *Positively Speaking: The Art of Constructive Conversations with a Solutions Focus* (2010).

Research in the Workplace

Studies within business and education setting have shown significant effects from applying the solution-focused model.

Coaching

The University of Melbourne has produced a number of papers on 'solution-focused, cognitive-behavioural' approaches, some of which are discussed below. The title is used regularly by Grant and his co-workers. However, the description within the papers makes it clear that this is a solution-focused approach.

Green et al. (2007) examined a project to provide life coaching for senior high school students. There were 25 healthy student volunteers in the experimental group and 24 controls, randomised to the two groups. The experimental group received 10 individual coaching sessions over 28 weeks. Using objective tests they showed improvement on hope, hardiness and depression but not stress or anxiety.

Another study by Spence and Grant (2007) examined volunteers randomised to coaching modalities: 21 by professionals, 22 by peers, 20 controls. Peer coaches had one day of training. Measures were taken at the end of 10 weeks: there was better attendance and more progress towards goals in the professionally coached group.

Similarly, Green et al. (2006) reported a study of self-coaching in 25 self-selected students and 25 controls. Eighteen of the experimental group were followed up 30 weeks after the 16-hour training in self-coaching. There were significant improvements in goal striving, wellbeing and hope. A similar study by Short et al. (2010) found less increase in distress in 32 experimental coachees against 33 controls.

A randomised trial by Grant et al. (2009) provided a training workshop for 41 executives. Group 1 (20) received solution-focused/cognitive-behavioural therapy coaching at once; Group 2 (21) had a 10-week wait before coaching. Measures found enhanced goal attainment, resilience and workplace wellbeing, with reduced depression and stress once each group had completed the programme.

A further study (Grant et al., 2010) examined developmental coaching for high school teachers. Twenty-three are in the intervention group, with

21 controls. They found improved goal attainment, resilience and wellbeing at the end of a 10-week programme. A pilot study (Grant and O'Connor, 2010) examined the differential effects of solution-focused and problem-focused coaching questions in students. Thirty-nine had a problem-focused coaching session and then 35 of them had a solution-focused session. There was a greater increase in goal approach and positive affect in the solution-focused group.

Workplace

In one of the first studies of its kind, Hoffman et al. (2006) carried out a comparison study of solution-focused training on productivity and behaviour in the workplace. Two snack-food factories under the same company received coaching for middle managers and production staff. There were significant improvements in leadership and in productivity in the experimental factory. (The therapists were Bjorn Johansson and Eva Persson, who were also the therapists in the Thorslund study of 'return to work after sick leave' and in Klingenstierna's unpublished studies on the same topic.)

Another innovative study was carried out by Carin Mussman in 2006. She used an appreciative observation study of solution-focused leadership in organisations to examine changes in style. The published work includes feedback from employees about the changed style.

O'Callaghan and Mariappanadar (2008) have described the use of solution-focused principles in the IT industry, to deal with the unexpected failure of a computer or network hardware system or software application in a business. They aim to develop a research tool to give insight into the approaches that incident managers use to restore service.

Sparks (1989) demonstrated that solution-focused input would improve communication and task performance within existing teams.

My own special interest within this field is in managing disagreements and conflict in the workplace. As a manager I have used solution-focused methods for managing acute situations without loss of time. Work with a number of other specialists led me to effective ways to work with team conflict and change management. Peter Rohrig (2005) of Dusseldorf has devised a solution-based way to deliver constructive criticism that can be applied in a wide variety of situations when working with subordinates. There are times, for most people, when they find themselves in actual or potential conflict with others who are more powerful in appearance or in fact. It is not always possible to win such struggles, but there are ways to manage this experience which maintain self-esteem and facilitate more success next time. Each of these topics will be discussed in turn.

General points for management training include the need to begin with some brief information about the principles of solution-focused therapy and the difference between this and other approaches to people management. Often, this can best be done by an exercise or a demonstration. There are many variations that can be employed. Some begin with 'Talk with a partner about something that you did well recently at work', or 'Talk with your partner about a recent problem at work while an observer watches, then change to talking about the skills that you used in dealing with the problem.' Another option is a demonstration interview with a volunteer, which can be solution-focused only or can shift from problem focus to solution focus.

It is also helpful to share some ideas about the microskills of interviewing that are a significant part of the solution-focused toolkit. Business and management trainings traditionally focus more on what is to be done than on how to deliver the message effectively. Introducing solution-based approaches can be done as didactic teaching or by the use of exercises that highlight different conversational styles and ways of delivering messages.

Solution-Focused Situation Management: Finding Cooperation Quickly

Eighty per cent of effectiveness comes from 20 per cent of what is done, so being a perfectionist is not essential. An organisation will achieve its assigned task until it falls below 20 per cent efficiency. This is based on the performance of military units in defensive combat, quoted by Luttwak (1969). These percentages are supported by anecdotal accounts from many enquiries into failing hospitals and businesses. Thus, a team or organisation will not be recognised as ineffective until its function has deteriorated severely. By that time poor performance will be found throughout the system. This accounts for the common experience among managers that once a serious issue is investigated it is found that there are many more problems and errors in existence as well. A great deal of work will then be needed to restore effective functioning and to re-establish good practice.

Good management consists in preventing matters reaching this stage. This means dealing with a lot of small problems before they become significant. Such good management is largely invisible, because problems are averted or managed early. This point was first made by Parkinson (1965) but is commonplace in modern management texts. In advance of solution-focused theory, Parkinson also suggested that good managers do not ask 'why' questions or look at the history of the problem; they focus on what to do now.

Many managers will find that a wide variety of staff will come to their office without appointments to share various problems and anxieties. It is necessary to respond to these enquiries appropriately and respectfully, in ways that encourage self-reliance rather than dependence on management to address issues. If an immediate response is forthcoming, then the issue is much less likely to enlarge itself or to draw in other participants (Macdonald, 2006b).

When someone comes through the door, often in a state of concern or anger, immediately set aside your current task and give them your full attention. Find out who they are, if you do not already know. It is best that you do not invite them to sit down, unless they are significantly distressed. They will be more inclined to action if they are standing (see below). It is best that you remain seated, as it will raise anxiety if you rise quickly in response to their appearance. If you remain seated while they are standing it also conveys that you expect to resume your previous task soon.

Begin by asking the questions given below.

Finding Cooperation Quickly: Key Questions

What is the problem?

Ask for a behavioural description

What happens?
Who does what?
When does/did it happen?
Are we certain that this is happening?
How do we know?

Taking brief notes at this stage helps you to detect repetition and demonstrates that you are giving your full attention to the issues. It is important to discover the quality of their information about the alleged events. Usually by the time you have obtained the answers to these questions your colleague has become calm enough to think about the situation as well as reacting to it. Now you can move on to the next set of questions.

What small/first step will show us that the situation is moving in the right direction?
What can be done?
Who can do it?
What is the next step in this solution?

It is best that you only offer ideas yourself if it is essential, and only after asking for their suggestions. You want them to learn to solve problems confidently and without reliance on you. This is good for their development. It is more efficient for the business. It will also reduce calls on your time. The final questions relate to ensuring that the problem is successfully resolved.

When do we review this?
What do we do to review this?

Expect your colleague to feed back to the proper person if the situation is not resolving itself. The use of 'we' confirms that you are taking responsibility for the conversation. The proper person to feed back to may be elsewhere in the organisation but should be acceptable to both of you as a resource if needed. A brief record of the outcome of the conversation can be added to your initial notes in case you need to refer to the conversation in future. This record can be filed with matters referring to the specific department, although if a senior manager or team leader has presented the issue then I often keep the record in their personal file for reference prior to future appraisals or if such unexpected visits become frequent.

Setting a review is an important step, as you wish to be sure that the problem is truly solved following your intervention. If you have misjudged the intervention, you need to know about it soon. It is not wise to give unresolved problems time to grow and become more complex.

In general, these conversations last about five minutes. A week later you are likely to find that the problem has almost been forgotten. Of course, new problems with something else will have arisen, which is the nature of the world of management.

The best exercise to demonstrate this technique is to ask the trainees to work in pairs, or in small groups, with some acting as observers. Two play out a similar situation from their workplace, using the questions above. The observers and then the participants then comment on the difference between this and their customary approach.

Studies of human interaction have shown that many decisions are made about people within seven seconds of setting eyes on them and most major conclusions about them are made within 90 seconds. In the street, as someone approaches, a number of clues such as dress, age and familiarity will determine how you greet or do not greet them as they get closer. The importance of this for managers is that such instinctive responses may lead to poor relationships with, or lack of information about, key colleagues. So if there is a time in the day with no specific task, managers are well-advised to go and talk to the person they would least like to spend time with. Surprisingly often instinctive personal responses will turn out to have been inaccurate. This may not matter in social situations but it can be crucial in business and personnel matters.

Action-oriented transactions often take less than 90 seconds, so that conversations about specific decisions can be brief. 'Shall I put these on this shelf or that?' If the question has a known answer in the context of the participants, then no more information is required. Such action-oriented planning is facilitated if participants are standing or walking. Some expert managers conduct their Monday morning reviews with all present standing-up to take advantage of this. Very few military conversations take place in a seated position. Even military gaming is usually carried out from a standing position. Cocktail parties are largely standing affairs because their function is to maximise social contact. They are designed to encourage movement and mixing among the guests and to reduce lengthy and intellectual activities. The sitting position is more reflective, therefore committee meetings and therapy sessions are mainly seated activities. The lying position is the most contemplative, thus it is used in hypnosis, in relaxation training and in the traditional free association of Freudian psychoanalysis 'on the couch' (Wainwright, 1985).

A social contact sequence lasts four to five minutes, after which we know if we want further contact (Zunin, 1972). If a conversation lasts less than this time, comments are made such as 'We did not have time to get to know one another properly', or 'We did not have time to discuss it adequately'. Conversations and relationships are made up of successive sequences of a few minutes each. This means that in a business setting most useful transactions need occupy only a few minutes. For example, learning about a proposed purchase can take much time, but formal price negotiation usually only takes four or five conversational exchanges.

The sequence described above for analysing and resolving problems takes long enough for your colleague to become calm and to feel that a conversation of sufficient length has taken place. They should leave believing that they and the situation have been taken seriously and dealt with appropriately. At the same time they will recognise that they themselves provided the means by which the problem was addressed. This is good for their self-confidence. They will have more confidence in a manager who accepts their unexpected arrival calmly and who requires concrete information at once.

As the manager, you have quickly gained enough information to move things forward, hopefully without leaving your chair. At the same time, you have clarified your understanding of interactions within your organisation. This information may be useful in the future. There is a minimum of unfinished business which you have to keep in mind and so it is easier to return to your previous task.

Handling Conflict in Teams

There are many times in any organisation when changes are supported by some and opposed by others. There are times when there is a dispute about what sort of organisation should exist. Sometimes these can be addressed by straightforward negotiation techniques, but this is not always effective and it may be necessary to use other techniques.

Miles Shepheard of New Zealand acts as a consultant to governments and political organisations. He has described techniques for working at this level of organisation. For major disputes on political or other issues, he suggests that all who are interested in the disputed topic are brought to meet together. The rules for the meeting are that each person may speak once: they may say anything about any topic for as long as they like, but then they have made their contribution and cannot speak again. They are reminded at the start that criticism of others is likely to draw criticism in return.

Another facilitator who works at a similar level is Loraine Kennedy (www.lkdevelopingpeople.co.uk). During all such meetings she has a large notice on the wall bearing the word 'RESPECT' in the appropriate language. She will point to it when necessary; the non-verbal impact is greater than direct criticism of the speaker. Others in the meeting will also point to it rather than responding verbally, which maintains a more amiable level of discourse in the room.

Where there is a clear conflict between two groups about the way forward, one option is to ask all the parties to meet together to discuss the matter. Two independent sets of minutes are taken, each by someone committed to one or the other side of the conflict. After the meeting, both sets of minutes are circulated to all participants. It is usual to find that there is a great deal of common ground between the two sets of minutes. Once these agreed areas have been identified, then more work can be done on the unresolved issues if necessary. This may require another meeting, but often the points of disagreement have become less contentious and the matter can be settled without a further meeting. This technique has some aspects in common with 'principled negotiation', where each party withdraws to prepare a list of their specifications and then the two sets of specifications are compared.

On some occasions the solution-focused worker is a lone voice in a problem-focused organisation. For this situation the work of Herman de Hoogh (2000) is of value. He has constructed a list of identifiable problem-focused behaviours with their solution-focused counterparts (see Table 9.1). The list was designed originally for medically-dominated case conferences and ward rounds. It has been modified slightly to be suitable for business meetings. The list can be used to monitor events in meetings by scoring the presence or absence of each element. It can also be used as a cue sheet for the solution-focused worker who can say something solution-focused in the hope of gradually interrupting the problem sequences to which others present are accustomed. This does not depend on the hierarchy within the meeting; even if the senior person present adopts a solution-focused stance,

TABLE 9.1 *Meeting: problem or solution?*

Problem focused	Solution focused
1 Complaints	1 Individual/team/client goals
2 Hypotheses about problem	2 Positive characteristics plus resources of individual/team/client
3 History of problem or blame	3 Earlier achievements or successes of individual/team/client
4 Questions about the past	4 Suggestions given by individual/team/client and used
5 Prediction, not action	5 First step planned by individual/team/client
6 Advice based on problem focus	6 Advice based on solution focus

Optional actions by observer/participant:
Assess on which side the communication is happening.
If problem focused, give comments/questions based on right-hand column.

Source: Adapted from de Hoogh (2000)

the system and the accustomed pattern of the meeting will change only slowly. A less senior person has an equal chance of changing the pattern.

When this technique is being shown to teams, it is useful to ask them to demonstrate a typical meeting, with some acting as observers who count the problem-focused comments. After a few minutes they are asked to change to a solution-focused conversation, with comments being counted in the same way. The count will demonstrate to them how easy it is to slip back into problem-focused talk, while the participants will usually report a preference for the solution-focused conversation.

Another possible exercise is to discuss some topic in the group as they normally would. Then the rule is given that they can use the word 'and' but never the word 'but'. They will notice a change in the conversation and in how many ideas they can generate in the conversation.

Anticipation Conversations

A good community team will try to limit the number of people working with one client or family. This is less confusing for clients and is more efficient in managerial terms. In some countries the extensive welfare system makes this difficult. If someone is referred who already has workers or therapists in place, it can be assumed that the existing therapy plan is not successful – otherwise referral to you would not have occurred. Then the care plan can be renegotiated with the other therapist(s) and the client. It can be suggested that if current inputs have not been sufficient, they should be stopped until a case review, following a trial of solution-focused brief therapy. Most colleagues will accept such plans provided they are phrased as alternatives and not as criticism. Sometimes a break from therapy with the other therapist is acceptable; sometimes legal issues require the other worker to remain in contact, but perhaps less frequently.

Jaako Seikkula et al. (2003) from Finland wanted to reduce excessive use of traditional mental health services in their rural area. The resources of the mental health service were not sufficient to meet local needs. In Scandinavian practice there are usually numerous workers from various social agencies involved in each case, but this can lead to inefficient use of time and skills. They devised a system whereby a crisis meeting was held involving all parties prior to any hospital admission or as soon as possible thereafter. Their technique has much in common with the solution-focused approach. It has been adapted here to fit business situations in which team conflict or change management are the central issues. (Andersen (1995) has described reflecting team approaches to this issue.)

The family and the workers or the two groups within the business sit at two tables in the same room. Each person in turn is asked the following questions by one facilitator, to be answered in as much detail as time permits while the others listen. In family and health care issues it is best to begin with the workers' group and then move on to the family. In business settings it is best to begin with the group that perceives themselves as less favoured or the subject of discrimination.

Anticipation Conversations: Key Questions

Describe what it will be like in one year when all is going well/better:
What was done to achieve this?
Who helped to reach this point?
What did they do?
What were you worried about a year ago?
What lessened your worries?

After these questions the facilitator recapitulates the responses. Notes are made of this good future and the suggestions offered to achieve it.

The same questioning process is repeated with the other team. This process is assisted if a second facilitator is available.

Describe what it will be like in one year when all is going well/better.
What was done to achieve this?
Who helped to reach this point?
What did they do?
What were you worried about a year ago?
What lessened your worries?

After these questions the facilitator recapitulates the responses. Notes are made of this good future and the suggestions offered to achieve it.

This is followed by general discussion of the proposed plan between all present. This helps to restore overall shared interest between the groups. By this time both sides will be aware of the arguments of the other side and of the commitment of all parties to finding solutions. Two sets of minutes, as described above, can be used as a tool if it has not been possible to air all the issues in the one meeting. The length of the process varies depending on the issues involved, but mental health and family issues often require one to two hours, whereas well-established conflicts in business and industry may require a full day or more.

If too many workers are involved in a scheme or problem to follow the above process within the available time, then this shorter version can be used. It is good for change management but less effective where there is open disagreement.

Sit everyone in the affected group around a table. Each person in turn is asked the following questions by the facilitator.

- What if you do nothing?
- What could you do to help?
- What would happen if you did that?

Then decide on a minimum plan as to who will do what with whom next.

When teaching this technique, ask the trainees to practice it with a real or imaginary situation. After the exercise is completed, ask all present to identify two differences between the approach demonstrated and the methods that they would normally use.

Solution-Focused Supervision

Supervision forms one tool for introducing and implementing solution-focused approaches within institutions and corporate systems. Supervision in solution-focused work has been described in O'Connell (2005). He recommends the same process as is followed in therapy, with the supervisor being respectfully curious about the trainee and the progress of therapy. Thomas (1996) has enlarged on these aspects of supervision. Each session begins with negotiating goals, followed by looking at the trainee's strengths and solutions, thinking about future management of the case, scaling progress and ending the session by asking the trainee to sum up the session and to state what they will be taking away with them. Hogg and Wheeler (2004) give a good account of the effects of introducing solution-focused training and supervision into child protection teams within social work.

Resources and time for supervision are often limited. Supervision in groups is one common solution. The Solution-focused Reflecting Team (see below) is a good way of addressing this in an equitable and creative fashion. There are strengths in group supervision that often make it more effective than one-to-one meetings. A group can support each other and can propose additional ideas. Case knowledge is widened as the group hear each other's problems and successes. In this way the benefits of supervision are increased within a reduced number of supervision hours.

Solution-focused thinking can also be used to review a large number of cases rapidly if this is all that time allows. In a group of trainees, ask each one to think about their most difficult current case. Each one is asked to state aloud where on a scale of 0–10 they would place their last session, if 10 is that everything in the therapy is going well and the client is making progress rapidly. Each then reports to the group what will be different if the next session has moved one point up on the scale and how they will recognise this. The conversation will reveal enough about each case to allow group members to offer additional ideas. If time permits, the process can be repeated for their 'second most difficult' case. This structure has proved useful when real-life obstacles have meant that the group's time for supervision has been unexpectedly curtailed.

The Microtools Concept

Microtools were conceptualised by the Swedish therapist and consultant Michael Hjerth (2008). He suggests that for any given application, a very small question set will be sufficient when combined with a solution-focused approach to language and solution-finding.

Michael Hjerth's first example is a microtool for coaching.

Two Minute Coaching: Key Questions

How will you know that this coaching session has been helpful?
Which of your qualities will you use more after this session?

Repeating these questions in combination with language matching and the use of 'What else?' questions will often be remarkably effective.

Similar microtools exist for numerous topics. The situation management tool described earlier in this chapter is one example of such a device. Another one, this time for mediation, is the work of Fredrike Bannink (2008) from the Netherlands. More detail about this tool and other aspects of conflict management can be found in Bannink (2010).

Solution-Focused Mediation: Key Questions

P: Platform

What are you hoping to get from mediation?

L: Look at the possible future

What difference would that make?
What is already working in the right direction?

S: Stepping the scale

What would be the next step/next sign of progress?
What can you do yourself?
What do you want from the other(s)?
Collect three things that work best and write them on sticky notes.

Solution-Focused Coaching in Education

For education settings, Lee Shilts and Insoo Kim Berg (Shilts, 2008) devised the WOWW classroom coaching method, which can be summarised in a microtool form. This intervention can be initiated in the interests of specific children or for a whole class or group of classes. The coach may spend one or two periods weekly in observing the class, so the method is cost-effective. It has been reported to have excellent results.

WOWW Classroom Coaching

Coach observes class; records positive events and interactions.
Coach feeds back to class and teacher about what was done well, mentioning some by name.
Week 3 or after: Coach helps children set goals for 'good classroom', using scaling.
Teacher and class predict scaling results.
Progress reviewed at end of each week by teacher and class.

Solution-Focused Reflecting Teams

The Solution-focused Reflecting Team concept was developed by Harry Norman et al. (2005) from the Bristol Solutions Group. It is a valuable tool for widening the use of solution-focused thinking beyond the immediate context of therapy and coaching. It arose out of experiments with different methods of providing supervision including the Reflecting Team format (Andersen, 1991). The model opens with a brief PRESENTATION by the therapist/customer during which no-one else speaks. Then questions are asked by others, one at a time and in turn, to CLARIFY the situation. Each member then AFFIRMS the therapist/customer by describing what they have found impressive about him/her in the situation; the therapist remains silent. In the REFLECTING stage, each team member in turn offers a reflection or idea about the situation or what to do next. The therapist/customer remains silent unless there is a clear misunderstanding in the reflection, in which case a brief comment is made. In CLOSING the therapist/customer comments briefly on what seems applicable or what the plan of action will be.

This model maximises the use of time and inhibits domination by one person. The model has been used for coaching, establishing learning sets and as a tool for business management. Some who have encountered it first as a method of supervision go on to use it in other areas of their practice, such as team meetings.

Constructive Criticism

Constructive criticism is not usually seen as a solution-focused technique. However, there are many situations in business and education in which feedback is needed. Sometimes the feedback will have to include requests for changes in behaviour in order to improve personal or business performance. It is valuable to have methods of addressing these situations effectively. The approach described below draws on work published by Peter Rohrig (2005), a management consultant from Dusseldorf.

The first step is to think about what is already done well. Many people have anxieties about confrontations and the process of criticising others even if it is a required part of their duties within their contract of employment. Nonetheless, most people have developed some skills which can be applied in this situation. A good beginning is to think about where you would place yourself on a scale of 0–10 in terms of 'How good are you at criticising someone in such a way that he or she has accepted this criticism without being hurt or insulted? In other words, where the criticism has had the consequences that you hoped for' This can be put to people working in pairs or as a large group. A brief conversation will often reveal a substantial variety of skills in the individuals. Most people enjoy the chance to discuss this topic in a relaxed setting and to consider how to develop their skills.

An important learning point is that if colleagues are praised appropriately, it is easier to criticise when criticism becomes necessary. Five compliments are needed for every one criticism. These skills can be learned and improved by practice in order to be more effective for guiding colleagues. In the training of more senior managers, feedback can be used as a form of dialogue. It tells others how you see them and helps you to learn how others see you. Similarly, feedback can be a very effective instrument in order to learn from concrete experience in a training group.

A solution-focused view relieves you, as a supervisor, of too much responsibility. It is not you who has to offer a solution about how your colleague will achieve more in the future. Instead, your colleague has to take the responsibility of finding a solution with which both of you can be satisfied.

The following exercise is useful in order to practice these techniques in training groups. Identify a participant in the training group who wants to practice a difficult conversation that involved criticising a colleague. As an example he can take a conversation in the past that did not end satisfactorily for him. He could also choose an imminent conversation for which he would like to be better prepared.

The trainer selects someone from the training group who will act as the colleague in practicing the conversation. For senior managers this role offers the chance to experience the criticising conversation from a neutral perspective. By listening to the trainee working on his goals the colleague learns about the situation and his role. Through further questions he will receive the information he needs in order to play the part of the criticised person.

The trainee has to develop individual goals for the conversation. It is necessary to find sentences suitable for both the exercise and the real situation. The formulations are polished until they really fit the situation and the style. You are not content with specified current behaviours; you want concrete change; you are confident that they can do it.

Of particular importance is the formulation of the statement in which the trainee says clearly what he wishes the colleague to do or to change in the future. This sentence will begin with 'I want you to ...' or 'I expect you to ...'. It must correspond with the conversational style of the trainee. The sentence with which the trainee expresses his confidence that the colleague will find a solution also has to be authentic. Experience shows that sentences which suggest competence to the colleague are suitable: 'You have probably already considered how you could change that. What do you suggest?'

After this sentence you must have patience and bear a moment of 'solutionlessness', even if this is not part of your usual style. It is useful here to sit as still as possible and to make no sound for five to ten seconds (see Chapter 1 in relation to the duration of silences). Even if the colleague does not offer suggestions that satisfy you, remain friendly, steadfast and interested in those solutions he offers. If nothing satisfying comes, arrange a new conversation with the colleague in two or three days and give him the opportunity to develop an excellent solution.

Constructive Criticism: Key Questions

Beforehand

What do you [as manager] want from the process?
When you leave the room, what do you want to look back on as successful about the interview?

At interview

I am not content with [specified current behaviours].
I want you to …/I expect you to … [concrete changes].
I am confident that you can find a way to do this.
You have probably already considered how you could change that. What do you suggest?
Explain to me how that will work/help.

Next step

If nothing satisfying comes from the colleague, arrange a further interview in two or three days to give time for solutions to be developed.

When goals based on the above concepts are clearly formulated, the main sentences can be written on a flipchart and placed where the trainee can see them while they are trying out the conversation with their colleague.

With simple props (table, seats) the trainee sets the stage for the demonstration. While doing that, it is useful to clarify the following questions, which are of importance in preparing for the conversation: 'In which room will the conversation take place?', 'How can it be held without disturbance from outside?', 'How is it introduced?', 'Where will the conversation partners be seated?' The trainee as manager can control many of these factors, which is helpful in giving them confidence in the real situation as well as in the demonstration.

Once this is done, the trainee and his 'colleague' carry out the demonstration. It may be necessary to remind the trainee to use the questions from the flipchart. This will encourage them to use the new sentences instead of their usual techniques. This exercise is also helpful because the colleague's responses may predict some of the things that will be said in the real conversation.

Any responses from the colleague in the form 'Yes, but ...' can be understood as 'No'. This interaction is discussed in more detail in Chapter 1.

Eye contact is important in these conversations. Studies of non-verbal behaviour have shown that 'business' gaze means looking at a person's eyes and forehead. 'Friendly' gaze looks at the eyes and lower face, because more emotional expression is registered in the lower part of the face. As conversation becomes more intimate, the gaze falls to neck and chest, then lower down the body. If we think a person may be attractive we often look them up and down as they approach us. Such signals are usually processed without our awareness. A commonplace example is in movies in which someone is shot in the forehead. For ballistic and anatomical reasons this is rare and inefficient in real life. However, the emotional significance of this enhanced 'business gaze' is unmistakable.

Using a 'friendly' gaze when delivering a business message can weaken the effect of our message, thus it is important to make eye contact or look at the colleague's forehead when delivering instructions or requests. If eye contact is difficult for the trainee they can look at the nose or ear because most people cannot distinguish this from eye contact (Smith, 1981).

The formula for solution-focused feedback, devised by Peter Rohrig (2005), is given below. It is useful as a conclusion to many demonstrations and exercises. It is especially useful for situations such as constructive criticism, because the protagonist is not asked to say much about their own reactions. It is important to protect the self-esteem of those who have volunteered to take part in demonstrating challenging situations.

Solution-Focused Feedback: Order of Questions

1 Observers liked what?
2 Criticised person liked what?
3 Protagonist liked what? What will they do in the real situation next time?
4 Advice now from observers but protagonist only listens; may say 'thank you' but will not comment otherwise.
5 General discussion: What was helpful? What will I try out myself?

360° Feedback

Many organisations now seek 360° feedback, by which they mean that opinions are sought from a wide variety of stakeholders about performance, not only from a manager or from the company. In terms of 360° feedback for customer service and health care organisations, a simple tool for written responses has been found useful.

360° Feedback Tool

1   Please record your score for your contact with Mr/Ms X over the last year by making a single mark on the line below.

0 --- 10

(very poor)   (could not be better)

2   What single change over the next year will increase your score by one point?

Please give your name or job title if you wish.
Thank you for your help.
Please return the form in the envelope provided.

This instrument can be completed quickly. Longer question sets tend to generate responses which do not lend themselves to easy analysis, whereas this tool generates practical replies that can easily be collated and grouped if necessary. Sending it to all concerned produces detailed results, whereas sending it to a selected sample allows repeated sampling from the same workforce or client group. It can be modified to focus on a specific skill or element of a task if necessary. Most people are willing to give their names or job titles, allowing the replies to be linked to specific groups or departments. For clients, a useful randomising procedure is to send it to the first in the database from each letter of the alphabet. Then the next time the exercise is done it can be sent either to the same sample to obtain feedback on the actions taken, or to the next ones in each alphabet group to obtain results from a similar but new group.

Managing Disagreement with Powerful Vested Interests

It is detrimental to our self-esteem and efficiency to believe that we can say or do nothing to express our opinions when we believe that mistakes are being made. The techniques so far described are useful in situations in which you have some degree of influence or responsibility. However, situations can arise in the workplace where change is being imposed by those who have the power to compel compliance. On occasion, leaders are constrained by budgetary or political considerations which restrict the use of ideal solutions. It is important for self-esteem and organisational efficiency to share your opinions if it is possible that new policies or proposals may create difficulties. At the same time you are aware that your power is limited and that there are risks in being too assertive. Clients in legal or child protection proceedings and patients being managed under legal powers are in a similar situation. Some episodes of bullying or harassment also follow such a pattern. When faced with these situations, it can be helpful to prepare yourself beforehand by considering some of the following questions.

The first section looks at planning for the conversation beforehand.

Managing Disagreement: Key Questions

What do you want from the process?
What do you want to ask the manager about their proposals?
What do you want to ask the manager about your choices?
What alternative proposals or ideas do you want to put forward?
When you leave the room what do you want to look back on as successful about the discussion?

The next questions are useful if you hope to use the information you have gained to modify or change the decisions or plans being made (Crosby, 1981).

Changing Minds: Key Questions

If the manager's ideas remain unchanged, what comes next for you?
Whose mind do you need to change to alter the plans?
What does that mind think now?
What is the best method to follow to change that person's thinking?
How can you prevent this from happening again?

The 'salami' metaphor for managing situations identifies a method for approaching a major task in small 'slices', which can be dealt with one after the other. In dealing with organisations a useful metaphor for the internal hierarchy is the 'lasagna' structure. Lasagna is formed of ingredients arranged in a number of different layers. In organisations there are people who like to say 'Yes' to things and there are people who like to say 'No'. They are distributed through the structure in more or less equal numbers as otherwise the organisation could not function. The usual style of each manager will be known by reputation within the organisation. If you wish to achieve something and the person you approach is a 'No' sayer, then it is likely that their superior or their deputy will be a 'Yes' sayer. So you need to advance your proposal or request when that person is in charge. A period of holiday absence is often useful in this regard. This will allow your proposal to go forward or at the least to move up to the next level of consideration. Equally, if you are asked to put forward a proposal or idea about which you have reservations, knowing who in the hierarchy is likely to say 'No' can be helpful in delaying things until more consideration has been given to the matter. It is helpful during negotiation to remind yourself that someone who rejects your proposal may be doing so because they prefer to say 'No' rather than from any specific hostility to you or to your proposal.

If you have explored the situation and determined that nothing more can be done, there are other questions to ask yourself. It is useful to have thought about these choices before going into disputed situations.

- What can you live with?
- What do you do next?
- How do you know that you will be OK in the long term?

In some legal processes clients may be overawed or not allowed time to say all that they want to say. The questions below incorporate the key points from the lists above for use in these circumstances.

Questions Prior to Legal Process

When you leave the room what do you want to look back on as successful about the interview?
What is the minimum you can accept?
If it goes against you this time, what can you do to improve the outcome next time?

There are a variety of exercises that are useful in practising these questions. Trainees can work in pairs on a past or present situation, using the questions suggested above after a brief description of the issue. Or, one protagonist can describe a situation, after which the group in turn each offer one idea useful to the protagonist until no more ideas are forthcoming. Many people have experience of such situations and can contribute ideas. The more ideas you have, the more flexible your response can be when exposed to similar difficulties in the future. The protagonist can comment on the ideas or simply make note of them for later consideration.

Bureaucracies and Large Organisations

Another set of behaviours can be used in dealing with bureaucracies and organisations. If the situation is face-to-face, such as finding workmen digging up the pavement right by your property, then approach politely with paper and pen. Ask who they are, including asking specifically for the name of the person you are talking to. Write the name down along with any information written on their uniforms or vehicles. Say that you are worried that your property will be affected and ask what is going on. If they say they do not know the plan, ask 'Who does know?', 'Who gave them their instructions?', 'What is the phone number of that person?' Note it all down and ask them not to do any more work until you have telephoned this person. Remain polite and helpful throughout. Most people prefer to pass on responsibility if there are problems, so they will be happy to direct you to their superiors.

With telephone calls to large organisations, start by setting aside time and limiting interruptions. Settle yourself comfortably with your cup of coffee, paper and pen and any information that you have already, such as reference numbers or the sometimes unlikely names of departments. You may wish to write your questions down beforehand. If you do so, leave space on the paper so that you have room to write the answers beside the questions, otherwise you run the risk of missing some information or forgetting one of your questions. Remain calm and patient throughout. As you speak to each person ask for their name and their telephone extension number. Write this information down. Those who work within bureaucracies dislike being identified personally, so this encourages them to deal with your enquiry or to pass your call on to someone else. It is not uncommon to find yourself after about five changes to be sent back to someone to whom you have already spoken. Your list of names and numbers will alert you to this. If they say they cannot answer a question, ask them who can answer it (name, post held, telephone number or preferably all three). Then ask to be connected to that person. Never end the call until you have a specific appointment to call them back or an arrangement to contact the next person higher up the chain. It is best if you call them rather than wait for them to call you, even if it is more expensive, otherwise you may wait a long time for your call to be returned.

At the end of this process you will have a list of names and numbers representing part of the 'table of organisation' for their office. This will make it much easier to pursue your enquiries further if that is necessary.

Conclusion

This chapter has addressed how to find cooperation quickly in the workplace and how this can be done by the busy manager. Methods to deal with change management and conflict within teams have been presented. The use of supervision and constructive criticism in appraisal and elsewhere has been considered, as has 360° appraisal. A number of microtools for specific situations have been described. Finally, surviving situations in which others have more power has been examined. General points about interaction are discussed throughout.

Key Points

- Studies have found solution-focused approaches to be effective in coaching, workplace and employment issues.
- Short dialogues for urgent situation management are effective and productive for the manager.
- Other microtools for specific situations have also been devised.
- The lone solution-focused practitioner can influence meetings towards useful change.
- Anticipation conversations facilitate good practice within health care and reduce conflict in other organisations.
- Solution-focused 360° appraisal produces effective information.
- Constructive criticism is a necessity of management and can be facilitated by solution-based techniques.
- Disagreement with powerful vested interests includes legal issues as well as defence against bullying and harassment.
- Dealings with bureaucracies and large organisations can be done in a structured and effective way.

Common Questions about Solution-Focused Approaches

Contents

- Objections to solution-focused therapy
- Solution-focused therapy and emotions
- Cultural issues
- When not to use solution-focused approaches
- Theory and the solution-focused approach
- Conclusion

This chapter seeks to address some common questions and issues about solution-focused therapy. These questions are often asked by those in training, especially those from other major schools of therapy. They are also raised by families, often those who have experience of other counselling models. They are rarely raised by those whose experience of counselling is limited to television dramas, in which rapid recovery is commonplace. Solution-focused therapy fits the preconceptions of the public, who have been reported to expect therapy to last for five to six sessions of about half an hour each (Garfield, 1986). This may help its acceptability to clients, which we have seen in Chapter 6 to be a strong predictor of good outcome.

Objections to Solution-Focused Therapy

Some reviewers have suggested that solution-focused therapy is regarded by many as too short, emotionally shallow and gimmicky. However, much of this criticism comes from workers with allegiance to other trainings. Like most of us, they keep up with their own subject but do not read the evidence for other approaches to therapy. Those workers from any discipline who have had some training in solution-focused work recognise that it is respectful of the client's autonomy and that it is not 'a quick fix' for every case.

A common question in workshops is 'Will it work with X diagnosis?'. In fact, a very large range of diagnoses have been the subject of research. All we can say is that no-one has yet found clear links between diagnostic categories and the response to talking treatments of any kind. There are some guidelines, but these appear to be about general and client-specific factors, not about diagnosis as an entity. In a training workshop, further enquiry usually reveals that the questioner is thinking not of a specific diagnosis but of a specific 'stuck' situation with which they are working. A clinical discussion about how to apply solution-focused methods to the situation may provide some new ways of moving forward, or reveal that no-one could do any more at the present time, whatever their model of care.

Another finding from this wide variety of research is that it appears to be feasible to combine solution-focused thinking and talking with other approaches to managing situations (McKergow and Clarke, 2007). Business consultants use their own interpersonal skills, sometimes combined with existing analysis tools. These may include Appreciative Inquiry or existing management systems as well as solution-focused practices. Therapists display the Rogerian common factors of warmth, empathy and genuineness, as well as skills derived from other trainings or through advice from colleagues. Combined treatments are common in mental health care, especially at the severe end of the spectrum. Someone in a secure unit may be subject to legal detention and also receiving rehabilitation, occupational therapy, medication and treatment for physical illness all at the same time.

Solution-Focused Therapy and Emotions

Experiencing emotion is thought to be the key to change in some schools of therapy. There is no doubt that emotion, positive or negative, often occurs at times of change, but which element is causative? Those with post-traumatic stress disorder constantly re-experience the emotions associated with the initial trauma, which they find distressing, not helpful. The events recalled have failed to become detached from the emotion of the moment and remain painful and frightening. The dearest wish of the sufferer is to reduce or stop such emotional experiences. Similarly, persons with bipolar affective disorder may have prolonged elevation or depression of mood. This does not appear to be a maturational process or a helpful one. Brain injury and Alzheimer's disease are often accompanied by labile and short-lived emotions with no visible benefit to the sufferer.

As discussed in Chapters 1 and 2, questions about emotions are not asked in solution-focused therapy unless the client brings them up, in words or in behaviour. This is not the same as denying the expression of emotions by the client, which would be disrespectful. Everyone has emotions: we all experience every one of the major emotions at least fleetingly every day. However, there is no good evidence that enlarging on these experiences is helpful in bringing about change. What can be helpful within the solution-focused model is to ask about what feelings might be experienced instead and how that will show itself to others in the person's life. The process is the same as addressing the person's goals for recovery instead of reiterating the details of the problem. This aspect of solution-focused work is well discussed in de Shazer et al. (2007). Sometimes it is useful to reframe emotions, for example describing generic signs of emotional arousal as 'anticipation' instead of 'fear' or 'anger'. It can also be useful to use conversation to change the context of emotions, for example asking 'how do you do sadness?'; 'how will your colleagues know when you are confident?'

Cultural Issues

Another comment sometimes made about solution-focused models is that they are 'too American' and not suited to British clients. This may be compared with the comments about Positive Psychology (see below). Naturally, the sensitivities and attitudes of clients have to be taken into account in all therapies. Some practical aspects of this have been addressed in earlier chapters, since a major part of solution-focused therapy is its emphasis on the client's perspective and language.

So far, solution-focused work appears to be appropriate for many countries and cultures. We have seen comparison studies from China, Korea, Iran and Mexico. The Health Promotion system in Hangzhou, China, is adopting solution-focused models; textbooks are being translated into Mandarin and Cantonese. Fujioka (2010) has published a Japanese textbook of solution-focused psychiatry. Insoo Kim Berg (1991) was herself a Korean native and taught widely in the Far East. India, Hong Kong and Singapore have had training workshops. Solution-focused management conferences have been held in Japan and South Africa as well as Europe. Doctors Without Borders, the American Red Cross and other aid agencies employ solution-focused trainers to assist their work in African and other impoverished countries.

When not to Use Solution-Focused Approaches

This aspect was addressed by the Dutch management consultant Coert Visser (http://solutionfocusedchange.blogspot.com). In 2009 he identified three settings in which solution-focused approaches might be less relevant.

- **If you have reason to think that the complaint primarily has to do with physical causes.** For example, if the client complains about chest pain radiating to their left arm, suggest that he sees a doctor fast instead of asking the miracle question. Similarly, if the problem of the client has to do with some kind of technical defect, such as a computer not working, it may be wiser to check the cables than to ask for exceptions to the problem.
- **If there is a proven standard approach for the type of problem.** If your client asks you how to compose a job application résumé, you might just hand him some examples instead of asking him scaling questions.
- **If there is an urgent situation or danger.** In those cases you may not have enough time to lead from behind. Instead, you may first need to take some direct action. Perhaps after that you may continue the solution-focused conversation. For example, if a client discloses information about current sexual abuse, the rules of evidence and the possible summoning of other agencies may be relevant before you can proceed with any therapeutic activity.

In child protection and other situations of danger, there are differences from the therapy situation. In therapy the client is the person sitting opposite the therapist and the therapist's job is to help them to make their desired changes. In safeguarding children and vulnerable adults, these people are the client, present or not, and their needs are the primary focus. The protocol for safeguarding is different from any therapy protocol and is derived from legal statute. A worker may seek to balance both roles, but safety must always come before therapy. If during therapy it becomes clear that another is at risk, then safety comes first, even if this requires the breaking of confidentiality or action by the police.

The application of solution-focused ideas in cases of long-term disability or illness has been discussed in Chapter 2.

Sometimes clients do not respond to solution-focused therapy. In 2007, Margarita Herrero de Vega and Mark Beyebach presented a study of 'Solutions for "stuck cases" in solution-focused therapy' at the EBTA annual conference in Bruges, Belgium. They had identified 80 'stuck' cases in their practice, 'stuck' being defined as a failure to increase on the client's scale (0–10) by session three. Their analysis of the cases suggested that those stuck at 5 or higher will respond to a change of therapist or to a different style of therapy. Those stuck at 3 or lower showed more response to a change to another style of therapy than to a change of therapist (see also Lambert et al., 2001). The use of feedback to therapists as a way of reducing 'stuck' cases from any model of therapy has been discussed in Chapter 6.

Sometimes a client will themselves identify that another treatment model or a medication has been more helpful to them in the past than their current model of therapy. In that case it is often wise to follow the client's plan, at least on a trial basis. Yvonne Dolan (2000) has described a case in which a woman had been in psychodynamic therapy until her therapist had moved to another city. The woman insisted that Yvonne provide the same type of therapy. Therefore as each issue was raised, Yvonne asked her what advice her previous therapist would have given and then repeated that advice back to her. The woman reported that this approach was successful.

The author's children used to say 'Don't use that brief therapy stuff with Me!' They wanted a parent's response, not that of a professional.

Theory and the Solution-Focused Approach

There has been criticism of the solution-focused approach because it is said to lack 'a theory of change'. Such criticism comes mostly from the psychodynamic and humanistic practitioners, whose work is based on complex theories about human cognition and behaviour. They do not accept models of therapy which do not produce a detailed and often painful narrative of human life. This might be thought of as the Romantic movement within psychotherapy. These views are held even though it has been clearly shown that all models of therapy are equally effective. The mental mechanisms identified by Freud and others do appear to be real events which occur within all of us. However, change occurs without our requiring any knowledge of these mechanisms, and knowing about them does not resolve all the problems of daily life.

The opposite of the Romantic movement in literature is the Classical. For behavioural and cognitive-behavioural theorists, the theory of change is that inappropriate behaviour can and should be changed. As we have seen in Chapter 5, the basis of stimulus–response Pavlovian conditioning is not a complete support for this. Also, human beings prove remarkably resistant to changing behaviour in spite of recognisable damaging consequences. This applies in such examples as returning to violent partners, relapse of substance misuse, changing eating habits or choosing not to support a dictator. There are many studies of cognitive-behavioural therapy, mostly in depression and anxiety but in many other disorders also. By no means all of these studies show positive results, in spite of frequent assertions about the evidence base for this therapy. Solution-focused therapists believe that their work is unlike cognitive-behavioural therapy. They do not adopt an expert stance in relation to the client. They are aware of the relative inefficiency of solutions generated by the therapist compared with those generated by the client. As solution-focused brief therapy became better known in the UK, the textbooks and literature of cognitive-behavioural therapy have gradually become more collaborative and client-centred. My colleague Kate Hart is a CBT trainer and describes her solution-focused therapy as 'CBT by stealth'.

Steve de Shazer was a respected proponent of the work of Wittgenstein. Some of his books (1994; de Shazer et al., 2007) present what amounts to a theory of the solution-focused approach in Wittgenstein's terms.

A new concept within cognitive-behavioural therapy is mindfulness (Hayes et al., 2004). Mindfulness is drawn from the Zen Buddhist tradition of the 'here and now', which in turn developed from 'Right Mindfulness', one of the elements of the Noble Eightfold Path taught by the Buddha. It was integrated as therapy in the Western tradition by Linehan as a part of the Dialectical Behaviour Therapy form of cognitive-behavioural therapy (Linehan, 1993). However, we do not yet know if mindfulness-based approaches have anything to offer Eastern cultures, since such approaches have been used there for many years. Clients in the East are likely to have considered these before they think of addressing any Western ideas of treatment.

Mindfulness, solution-focused therapy and cognitive-behavioural therapy all change feelings through cognitive and behavioural routes. Methods for changing feelings directly are less common. Eye movement desensitisation and reprocessing (Shapiro, 2001) and hypnotherapy are sometimes effective in changing feelings directly without the involvement of cognitive processes and in advance of behaviour change. Although talk between client and therapist is used in these approaches, the talk need not focus on behaviour change or mood change (Peacock, 2001; Måhlberg and Sjöblom, 2004). Cognition follows afterwards or not at all (Isebaert, 2005). The use of Ericksonian hypnotherapy techniques in combination with solution-focused therapy is described by Dolan and others (see Chapter 9). Similarly, many therapists combine narrative and solution-focused approaches.

Narrative therapists believe that change will come about through certain sorts of conversations. However, they do not prescribe change and have no specific theory about how change will be achieved. They look to the client, the family and the community for resources and ideas. Their methods are well liked and respected by clients and communities.

In both therapy and business, motivational interviewing, Appreciative Inquiry and Positive Psychology all have features in common with solution-focused therapy and are combined by some workers (see McKergow and Clarke, 2005, 2007; Mintoft et al., 2005). Motivational interviewing is used in the first stages of change; for action and maintenance one moves to other models. Appreciative Enquiry as a method can be enhanced through the use of the specific language skills and techniques found in solution-focused teaching.

Positive Psychology (Seligman, 2002) highlights exceptions in the form of happiness and good moments in everyday life. It looks for the development of strengths and socially constructive actions as a form of therapy against depression, isolation and anxiety.

Positive Psychology emphasises self-esteem and confidence based on one's existing skills and resources. The assumption is that clients will be reassured by this and will move to resolve their difficulties. Again, the theory of change is limited and the emphasis is on helpful, goal-directed conversations. It has been described as a rather grand way of saying 'Pull yourself together'. Extensive research projects, books and articles have been published. However, in daily life we see that most people are over-optimistic already. This appears in estimates of journey time and hopes for the sale price of our house. A quote from a Romanian audience: 'Hope is the biggest slut in the world: everybody lives with her.' (SOL 7/5/10, Bucharest). Positive Psychology has had considerable success in the USA and in the business community. Those from more reserved cultures, such as the British and North European countries, may find the style uncongenial.

Hubble et al. (1999) and Duncan and Miller (1999) are well-known for championing the importance of common factors in all therapies, against the concept that any specific therapy has 'the answer'. However, this does not invalidate the finding that therapists like one approach better than another, as do clients. If a therapist favours a particular model, then his or her success rate with that model is higher (Wampold, 2001). Seligman (1995, 2002) finds that the client's choice of a model is also linked to outcome. Any one approach has a success rate of 60–70 per cent, thus at least two approaches need to exist in order to help the majority of clients. Therefore, the need for different models and techniques is likely to remain.

An example of a project which examined different therapy models is given by Rhee et al. (2005). Fifty-five callers to a suicide hotline were allocated to solution-focused therapy (16), common factors therapy (17), or a waiting list (24). The authors found significant improvement on 10 of 14 measures for the treated groups, with no between-group differences.

Solution-focused therapists have become more willing to combine their work with other approaches if the situation requires it (Milner, 2001). Both sides still regard themselves as separate and different, but the techniques practised appear to be moving closer to each other.

In fact, some other widely accepted models of psychotherapy have no theory of change, nor any theory at all. Interpersonal Psychotherapy (IPT) (Klerman et al., 1974) was invented using psychodynamic language. It was intended as a sham treatment for comparison with cognitive-behavioural therapy (CBT) in a joint trial of amitriptyline combined with talking therapy. In the trial IPT was found to be more effective than CBT. This may have been due to an allegiance effect in that generation of practitioners, who were mostly trained in psychodynamic styles. The trial outcomes led to further studies of the effectiveness of IPT and it is reified now as a treatment in its own right, solely on the basis of effectiveness in practice. IPT was not based on any theory of change, and no personal therapy is expected of trainees. It is quick to learn and it is easy to obtain accreditation. IPT is one of two therapies approved by the NICE guidelines of the Department of Health in the UK for the treatment of depression (the other is CBT).

Conclusion

It seems that lack of theory is not a bar to respectability, and that extensive theory does not guarantee success for our clients. However, we may be entering a period in which any specific therapy model is not clearly separated from other models. The responses of the client may become the driver for the use of any particular technique or approach.

Interestingly, this will bring psychotherapy back towards the traditions of the medical model, in which improvement in the patient was the key variable because little was known about physiology or the means by which treatments produced benefits.

Key Points

- Allegations of being 'shallow' or 'gimmicky' do not seem to affect client's reactions to solution-focused therapy or the overall outcome of therapy.
- Emotions are present in solution-focused therapy as they are in all human affairs, but the response by the therapist is somewhat different.
- Issues concerning diversity and equal opportunities appear to be less significant in solution-focused work.
- There are situations in which solution-focused therapy is not the first step to take and there are situations in which another therapy may be a more effective next step.
- In safeguarding work, the rights of others may take priority over the therapeutic work.
- Schools of therapy may emphasise internal mental processes or solely external behaviour. The success of intervention is not clearly linked to these factors.
- Narrative therapy, Positive Psychology and mindfulness all share some aspects with solution-focused therapy.
- A theory of change does not appear to be an essential part of therapy, nor to be an essential requirement for credibility in the market-place.

11

Future Directions in Solution-Focused Therapy

Contents

- The future for therapy
- Training and accreditation of therapists
- 'Official recognition' of solution-focused therapy
- Research and evidence base
- Future developments
- Conclusion

Solution-focused approaches have revolutionised therapy in many countries and are now being integrated into the mainstream of care provision for mental and physical health. The training required is less onerous than for most other effective therapies. Accredited and proven training courses are available in many parts of the UK. Governments and agencies are beginning to recognise the significance and effectiveness of solution-focused approaches in addressing many issues that concern the public and the professionals who care for them. Research into psychotherapy is now an accepted necessity, whereas 60 years ago it was considered irrelevant or unachievable. Solution-focused workers are playing their part in the drive towards an evidence base for psychotherapy and towards a better understanding of its use for the maximum benefit to our varied client groups.

The Future for Therapy

Solution-focused therapy is now well-established in the UK with many thousands of workers trained in its use. It is used in the mental health field by community teams and inpatient units. Forensic and probation services make use of it and it is proving useful for those struggling with the issue of substance misuse. In education there are specific initiatives to incorporate solution-focused approaches into policy. Educational psychologists and guidance teachers are finding it helpful as they face increasing demands from schools and parents for effective results with difficult children. The work of Andrew Turnell (Turnell and Edwards, 1999) and other colleagues such as John Wheeler (Hogg and Wheeler, 2004) has been adopted by numerous child protection teams around the UK.

All care agencies in Britain are struggling with increasing demands from rising caseloads, restricted funding and the ever-changing requirements of new legislation. More than ever before the public are aware of the possibility of effective help, while the available funds for such help are decreasing, due to rising populations and other social and demographic changes. Solution-focused approaches offer the hope of more effective interventions for some of the most demanding areas of social distress: substance misuse, domestic violence towards partners and children, self-harm and personality disorder.

Two recent studies of alternative care services for mental illness in England (Howard et al., 2010; Osborn et al., 2010) showed that there are better results when service users have a choice about the model of care that they receive, and that they prefer to have autonomy and a voice in what they are offered. This suggests that the findings of Wampold (2001) and Seligman (1995) may be generalised to the experience of care overall, not only to psychotherapy.

Training and Accreditation of Therapists

Within the UK there are now many established trainings in solution-focused brief therapy. BRIEF in London estimate that they have trained at least 60,000 professionals since they came into existence. They offer a one-year Diploma in Solution-focused Practice as well as shorter courses and projects focused on organisational consultancy. St Martin's College in Carlisle has offered an accredited module in solution-focused therapy since 1997, training about 20 workers in each course. There are shorter accredited courses in Reading, Canterbury and Preston. Many experienced trainers offer local courses, for example those based in Cardiff and Dorset.

The meta-analysis by Kim (2006; see Chapter 6) showed that an average of 6.5 sessions was required across the included studies to produce beneficial effects equivalent to those of other therapies. On the basis of the effectiveness demonstrated by different studies, Kim in his dissertation suggests that competence in solution-focused therapy requires in excess of 20 hours of training. This is still much less than that required by other models of therapy but the finding is important for future planning and accreditation.

Many other European countries have solution-focused training courses for professionals from many disciplines. Some university departments of psychology provide degrees based on solution-focused training. A specific issue for solution-focused brief therapy is that most practitioners and trainers believe that adequate skill in solution-focused practice can be achieved with far less training time and experience than is the case for other psychological therapies. This means that many practitioners use the approach daily in their work but cannot qualify under any current schemes that recognise and regulate psychotherapists.

In the USA, registration within each state is governed by the original discipline of the practitioner. So nurses, psychologists and social workers are governed by their parent bodies. There are many established courses and trainers in solution-oriented methods.

In Canada, solution-focused brief therapy is recognised by some counselling organisations, which will accept some 100 hours of training and supervised practice as adequate for registration. Finland has a nationally recognised training scheme for solution-focused practice, established by Ben Furman and his colleagues, which requires some three years of study. In Germany, official recognition is only granted to psychodynamic, systemic and cognitive-behavioural approaches. France has no national recognition of psychotherapies, but many private training organisations offer extensive training programmes.

The European Brief Therapy Association has considered an international standard for solution-focused accreditation on several occasions. However, there are major difficulties internationally in achieving recognised and respectable standards valid for every country. Medicine proper has not yet achieved this, so there may be a long road ahead for therapists of any persuasion. Having said that, the international Association for Quality Development of Solution Focused Coaching and Training (SFCT) has a process by which pieces of work are reviewed and validated by two assessors to determine if they fit the agreed criteria for solution-focused practice. Once approved, the reviewed worker can record this on their résumé and elsewhere. The criteria for approving work can be found on the SFCT website (www.asfct.org). This process appears to be efficient and to add value to the work of members of the organisation. However, the ethical standards required of therapists may make a similar process unsuitable for international therapy accreditation.

Within the UK there is currently no universal registration scheme for psychotherapists. There are a number of groups that provide registration which is accepted by national bodies. Some solution-focused workers are registered with the UK Council for Psychotherapy (UKCP) through registration with the Association for Family Therapy and Systemic Practice. The British Association for Counselling and Psychotherapy (BACP) has national criteria that allow practitioners with adequate training in solution-focused therapy (about the equivalent of a four-year Master's course) to register with them.

Thirteen health care groups are currently regulated by the government's Health Professions Council (HPC), and both counsellors and psychotherapists are likely to come under their regulation shortly. However, the current standards of the HPC are equivalent to full UKCP or BACP registration, which leaves the question of lesser training levels unresolved. The UK Association for Solution-Focused Practice is looking at the possibility of a one-year qualification as a Solution-focused Practitioner, which could then be followed by further training to reach the BACP level of registration.

So the future of solution-focused therapy as a registerable qualification remains unclear. However, it seems unlikely that an approach that has attracted so many competent practitioners will simply be sidelined. There may be prolonged negotiations within psychotherapy and health care before a structure is devised that respects the ways in which solution-focused brief therapy differs from the more traditional therapies.

'Official Recognition' of Solution-Focused Therapy

Within the USA, solution-focused therapy is identified as a recognised treatment by the Federal Government (www.samhsa.gov; www.ncbi.nlm.nih.gov/books). It is an approved treatment in the State of Washington and approval is being sought in the State of Oregon (www.oregon.gov/DHS) and the State of Texas. Solution-focused therapy is included in evaluations by the Rand Study Group, an influential 'think-tank' (Morral et al., 2006).

Despite the lack of a formal registration structure in the UK, solution-focused brief therapy is clearly influencing planning and policy within health and education.

Solution-focused brief therapy is included in Professor Glenys Parry's review of psychological therapies' for the Department of Health (Parry and Richardson, 1996). The Department of Health is accepting advice about solution-focused approaches to self-harm and substance misuse. The *Improving Supportive and Palliative Care for Adults with Cancer* guidelines (NICE, 2004) explicitly recommends solution-focused approaches. The Scottish guidelines for cardiac rehabilitation (SIGN, 2007) recommend solution-focused brief therapy for depression following cardiac events. Several mental health and care NHS Trusts are employing the approach throughout their whole organisation. The use of solution-focused therapy in learning disability is included in a Council Report of the Royal College of Psychiatrists (2004). Sladden (2005) advises junior doctors in the National Health Service to seek training in solution-focused work, cognitive-behavioural therapy or psychodynamic psychotherapy. In the UK, the National Institute for Clinical Excellence (NICE) sets guidelines for the treatment of disorders within the National Health Service. It rarely refers to solution-focused therapy because the NICE evaluation system relies on searches based on diagnostic categories, and few solution-focused studies are conducted in this way. Studies may address social categories such as children who drop out of school or domestic violence offenders, but these categories do not overlap with medical diagnostic classifications.

In 2007 a new initiative was launched in England to make psychological therapies accessible to more people with depression and anxiety: Improving Access to Psychological Therapies (www.iapt.nhs.uk) privileged unvalidated brief training in cognitive-behavioural therapy (CBT) over all other forms of psychological therapy. The programme called for 'existing psychological workers' to be among those trained in CBT. In practice many have simply lost their jobs, apparently because they are not CBT trained already. Membership of the British Association for Behavioural and Cognitive Psychotherapies (BABCP) has become a recommended qualification, and the equally rigorous BACP membership has become largely disqualified. There has been heavy expenditure on teaching this untried brief model of CBT, which has become the only treatment available in certain localities, even if there is no evidence for its effectiveness in some disorders. This flies in the face of what we know about outcome variables in psychotherapy since neither client nor worker have a choice about which therapy is offered. It also means less choice for the 30 per cent or more of clients who do not respond to one particular model.

At the request of the Department for Education and Skills, BRIEF has written policy documents for primary and secondary school staff. These include advice about bullying and about staff development (2003). Within children's services, the Common Assessment Framework for Children and Young People highlights the need for a collaborative approach identifying strengths as well as problems; it looks for behavioural evidence of strengths and signs of safety (Department of Health, 2006). These values have much in common with the solution-focused approach and it is straightforward to apply the solution-focused dialogue to exploring these issues.

We saw in Chapter 5 that much of the reputation of psychodynamic psychotherapy arose from client word-of-mouth. This is a powerful mechanism in countries with a well-developed free market system for health care. It is less relevant in the UK where choice and knowledge are restricted. Experience suggests that where there are private therapists available from any discipline, then they seem to be effective, because it is uncommon for their clients to present themselves thereafter to public health services. Studies have shown that clients are unlikely to recommend a specific method of therapy. They are more likely to recall the therapist as a person and to recommend them by name. Most of the current support for any talking therapy in the National Health Service comes from client pressure groups demanding something other than medication. The voices of individual staff members have been less effective in attracting the support of management, however much the evidence base for solution-focused therapy is publicised.

There is no doubt that the recognition of solution-focused brief therapy by the commissioners and purchasers of care will be important for the future of the model. It appears that the model is easier to teach than some other models and requires less therapist time to deliver effective care. In that case it is important to a world with scarce resources that it is recognised and used appropriately. Because solution-focused therapy is more effective for lower socio-economic groups than are other therapies, active promotion of the model is essential to enhance services for this segment of the community. The improvement in morale among therapists who become solution-focused is important because it helps to conserve a useful resource for the community at large.

Research and Evidence Base

In the last three years the published evaluation studies of solution-focused approaches have risen from 50 to 97, and this increase seems to be continuing. The model is as effective as other therapies. It requires less therapy time than most other models. The basic skills can be learned in a short time. A major research handbook is in preparation, which will bring together material from around the world (Franklin et al., in press). Microtools represent an interesting way of mobilising the model for specific tasks, once the basic skills are available. Many countries around the world have reported success within their cultures and with a wide variety of problems and situations. Management and coaching have found the model to be helpful.

However, many therapies have an evidence base and many therapies have none, so this is not the whole story. If the scientific community is to accept the potential of solution-focused approaches, then further research is needed.

The European Brief Therapy Association seeks to encourage research into solution-focused therapy by offering an annual grant to small projects. Projects supported so far include: part of a larger study of rehabilitation of patients with long-term mental illness in Bulgaria (Bostandzhiev and Bozhkova, 2004–2006); a follow-up study of outpatients attending a psychology department in Germany by Frederic Linssen; and a Norwegian study seeking to increase self-efficacy in schoolchildren who are being bullied (Kvarme et al., 2010). The important study of medication compliance in schizophrenia by Panayotov, Anichkina and Strahilov (in press) was funded by the European Brief Therapy Association. Also supported was the Swedish study into unemployment (Thorslund, 2007), which has led to a wide use of solution-focused approaches within the relevant local authority.

Projects now in progress include investigating the effects of solution-focused therapy in cardiovascular disease patients, microanalysis of the miracle question by Janet Bavelas and her colleagues, a study of treatment for post-traumatic stress disorder and an evaluation of a group programme for men convicted of domestic violence.

The Norddeutsches Institut für Kurzzeittherapie (NIK) team in Bremen, Germany, offer a wide range of therapy, teaching and consultancy services. They are conducting outcome research on problem drinking. They are also carrying out a study to examine the consequences of events that occur within therapy sessions.

Dr Luc Isebaert of the Korzybski Institute in Bruges, Belgium, is undertaking a four-year follow-up study of alcohol misusers. The study will include measures of personality, formal DSM-IV diagnosis, their current relationship state and the level of alcohol use. Dr Isebaert and his team are preparing the protocol for a randomised controlled trial comparing solution-focused therapy with mindfulness therapy for depression and chronic anxiety. This includes devising solution-focused and Ericksonian techniques for the benefit of those who experience frequent relapses.

It is of concern that there are few studies of solution-focused work with the elderly in any country. Around the world the elderly form an increasing part of the population, and an increasing part of the population in need of health care. The elderly have been shown to value psychotherapy and to make good use of it, yet studies are few.

Future Developments

In parallel with these developments, more and more voices are raised to point out that a therapy with a good evidence base may not help any specific client and that variables such as therapist skill and client motivation are being neglected. Some of the following research ideas may continue the process of enquiry into these issues.

Future studies might use deconstructing methods such as the formula first-session task, or might compare solution-focused therapy with solution-focused therapy plus one new question, in a similar process to that undertaken by Steve de Shazer and Insoo Kim Berg and their original team. Or a study might look for differences according to whether pre-session change is present or absent (cf. Beyebach et al., 1996). Do clients see a connection between pre-session changes and success in treatment?

What about presuppositional questions such as 'What's been better?' in second and later sessions? Do they increase the effectiveness of therapy overall? It has been suggested that the miracle question is more effective if exception questions are asked first; is this true? (See McKeel, 1999). Many skilled practitioners do not follow this sequence.

No-treatment groups may not be ethical now that solution-focused brief therapy is a recognised treatment. However, some studies have used waiting list controls, who are then offered therapy later. Or clients can be used as their own controls by applying objective measures for a period before therapy starts. Multiple outcome measures will improve credibility and reliability. For example, combinations of: ratings and replies by clients and therapists; objective questionnaire measures; hard measures of outcome such as reoffending, relapse or increase in use of health care services. Relapse and therapy cost are of interest to managers and commissioners of services because they are seen as measures of outcome and cost-efficiency.

The research on psychotherapy generally shows that the therapeutic alliance is central to good outcome. Clients agree with this (Seligman, 1995; Wampold, 2001). What identifies a good alliance in the client's mind? In the therapist's mind? If the attenders are a couple or a family or friends, do all the clients present need to believe that there is an alliance? Beyebach and Carranza (1997) have identified specific interactions between therapist and client that predicted drop-out from therapy by clients.

Wettersten et al. (2005) examined associations between the working alliance and therapy outcome. With 26 solution-focused clients and 38 receiving brief interpersonal therapy, they found no differences in outcome. The working alliance predicted outcome in brief interpersonal therapy only. So the alliance between therapist and client may be good in solution-focused work, but perhaps this is a general property and there are other variables which will predict outcome.

Sometimes clients are clearly proud of a single skill or recent event which can then be highlighted or emphasised in the feedback. At other times we group a number of positives to form a compliment about an aspect of character or a talent. It may be that compliments which identify enduring characteristics rather than single events are more likely to produce change. This could form a simple research project within day-to-day practice. Also, children in treatment appear to prefer specific behaviours to be highlighted rather than general characteristics, so a comparison study might be of interest.

A concept, which has yet to be pursued in detail, is raised by Steve de Shazer in *Words Were Originally Magic* (1994). He says that interviews of half an hour are enough to produce a relevant closing statement and to facilitate useful change, even if the content of the session is not enough for the therapist to know all the details of the problem and the goals. He further suggests that goals are related to the problem, while the miracle and scaling are related to the solution. These propositions could be tested within a clinic's usual practice.

As an aspect of applying solution-focused therapy beyond individual therapy in mental health Duncan et al. (2007) have developed a solution-focused measure of occupational function. Their book describes this tool and its application within occupational therapy, as well as providing useful worksheets.

Wells et al. (2010) have carried out a study to examine the effect of solution-focused techniques in regard to mental health and employment outcomes. In an experimental group of 82, of whom 64 completed the programme, they found improved mental health scores, self-esteem, expectation of ability to work on objective measures and scaling; 41 (64 per cent) of the experimental group moved into work or work preparation. This was not different from the control group at four months, suggesting that a variety of approaches can be used in employment practice.

The testing of some of these propositions may improve the effectiveness of solution-focused brief therapy still further, while also improving our skill in teaching and delivering the model. Its benefits for those groups unsuited to other psychological treatments gives it a greater importance than other therapies as a field for development.

Conclusion

There is now a substantial and increasing literature on solution-focused approaches. If you search on the term 'solution-focused', as well as finding many interesting papers on the topic, your search will bring up papers from therapists who espouse other models of therapy. These will include quotes such as 'Cognitive-behavioural therapy has always been a solution-focused therapy', 'positive psychology includes narrative therapy, solution-focused therapy, mindfulness', 'psychoanalysis has always had a solution-focused view'. 'Solution-focused' is not a perfect title for our model, as in practice we rarely use the word 'solution' in conversation with clients. Nonetheless, there is a clear shift in direction revealed by these quotes. Evidently, every therapist is now either a solution-focused therapist or would like to be a solution-focused therapist.

Appendix I

Useful Links and Addresses

The author's website includes information about the author, the European Brief Therapy Association therapy research manual and an annotated bibliography of published outcome and evaluation studies. Some otherwise unobtainable papers are provided there in full.
www.solutionsdoc.co.uk

The Solution-Focused Brief Therapy Association (SFBTA) of America was founded in 2002. They have acquired copyright to the teaching materials developed by Steve de Shazer and Insoo Kim Berg Family Therapy Center in Milwaukee. The website provides extensive information about solution-focused therapy in the North American continent, including details of the annual conference. Programmes and training events are also listed. The site provides mail order facilities to obtain teaching tapes and literature.
www.sfbta.org

The European Brief Therapy Association (EBTA) is a worldwide group that has provided an annual world conference since 1993. It sponsors research and publicises matters of interest to solution-focused therapists in all countries.
www.ebta.nu

The Swedish SIKT website provides teaching information and access to the STF-L discussion list as well as to the list archives. The STF-L list members provide a wide range of knowledge and advice. Harry Korman of Sweden is the STF-L listmaster.
www.sikt.nu

The Dutch speaking network of solution-focused workers, Netwerk Oplossingsgericht Werkenden, is open to interested parties.
www.solution-focused.nl

Fredrike Bannink is a widely experienced negotiator and international trainer. She has published several books and articles in English and Dutch.
www.fredrikebannink.com

Coert Visser at the Solutions Centre in Amsterdam works mainly in management consultancy; however, he provides many resources through his website.
www.solutions-centre.org

The SOLWorld organisation for solution-focused approaches to organisations began in the UK. There is a discussion list for members. Their website provides details of their annual world conference and their Summer University.
www.solworld.org

The Association for the Quality Development of Solution Focused Consulting and Training has close links with SOLWorld. Their German-based group review solution-focused work and approve it when the criteria are met.
www.asfct.org

Mark McKergow and Jenny Clarke use a solution-focused approach with organisations. The Centre for Solutions Focus at Work website provides information on the foundations of their work and training events along with an interesting collection of articles, tips and examples.
www.sfwork.com

Paul Jackson and Janine Waldman at The Solutions Focus provide workplace training in solution-focused approaches.
www.thesolutionsfocus.co.uk

The United Kingdom Association for Solution Focused Practice (UKASFP) was founded in 2003. There is an annual UK conference and the Association maintains a directory of members. There is a discussion list on the Internet for members and a website. The UKASFP publishes an online newsletter *Solution News*, which attracts a substantial readership from outside the UK.
www.ukasfp.co.uk
www.solution-news.co.uk

Bill O'Connell established the former four-year MA course in solution-focused therapy at the University of Birmingham. He has also written a number of influential textbooks. His training and supervision agency Focus on Solutions' website provides details of available courses.
www.focusonsolutions.co.uk

BRIEF is the largest solution-focused training agency in the UK. It provides a full range of trainings in solution-focused brief therapy ranging from one-day introductory courses to a one-year Diploma course.
www.brieftherapy.org.uk

Brief Therapy North East (BTNE) is an influential group of practitioners and learners within the North-east of England. They arrange study days and international presenters every year. They have close links with Andrew Turnell and the 'Signs of Safety' approach.
www.btne.org

The website of John Wheeler, one of the founding members of BTNE. John's site includes a list of his publications, some of which will be download-able in the near future, along with details of the solution-focused training, supervision and consultation he offers.
www.johnwheeler.co.uk

The website for Ioan Rees et al. provides information on training events and workshops, mostly in Wales, conducted by their company Sycol Ltd.
www.sycol.org

Yorkshire Solution Focused Brief Therapy Group is a professional interest group whose aim is to assist in the spreading of SFT skills as widely as possible around the Yorkshire region.
www.yorkshiresolutions.org.uk

Professor Wally Gingerich was an early member of the Brief Family Therapy Center in Milwaukee. His homepage offers useful links and research reviews.
www.gingerich.net

Michael Durrant was one of the original exponents of solution-focused brief therapy within education in Australia. The website of the Brief Therapy Institute of Sydney is an outstanding source of useful links.
www.briefsolutions.com.au

Professor Ron Warner was instrumental in the development of solution-focused practice in Canada. The Canadian Council of Professional Certification offers recognition to courses and therapists from Canada and other countries.
http://home.oise.utoronto.ca/~rewarner/
www.ccpcprofessionals.com

The Brief & Narrative Therapy Network (BNTN) is a Canadian network for solution-focused practitioners. This ever-growing website includes a useful collection of articles and interviews.
www.brieftherapynetwork.com

The Institute for Therapeutic Change in Chicago is one of the leaders in the 'Common Factors' movement in psychotherapy. Solution-focused practice is one of the key elements in their development and the Heart & Soul of Change Project website offers useful information to the interested practitioner. Research tools, an American-based discussion list and book sales are accessible through the site.
http://heartandsoulofchange.com/

Ben Furman and Tapani Ahola's Helsinki Brief Therapy Institute website illustrates the various adaptations of 'solution talk' and 'reteaming'. Child workers will find Ben's 'Kids' Skills' to be of particular relevance, along with 'THE STEPS OF RESPONSIBILITY: How to Deal with the Wrongdoings of Children and Adolescents in a Way That Builds Their Sense of Responsibility'.
www.benfurman.com
www.kidsskills.org

Bill O'Hanlon's website explains his particular slant on solution-focused work and includes a section with various handouts and lists.
www.billohanlon.com

In Poland, Tomasz Switek has contributed to the solution-focused world by producing his Deck of Trumps, which can be found on this website. The site also includes research into the personal impact of becoming a solution-focused practitioner.
www.centrumpsr.eu

Appendix II

Hyperventilation: a Curable Cause for 'Anxiety' Symptoms

(Macdonald, A.J., *Journal of Primary Care Mental Health and Education*, 2004, 7: 105–8. Reproduced with permission)

Abstract

Hyperventilation has been recognised as a cause of anxiety-like symptoms for many years. The diagnosis can easily be made in the consulting room but is often missed. Such patients benefit from breathing exercises but not from psychological or pharmacological treatments. If untreated these symptoms are a cause of much distress and lead to increased demands on the general practitioner. Hyperventilation can be a factor in the onset of many common physical disorders. Advice on diagnosis and treatment is included, with a handout of breathing techniques for patient use.

Introduction

Walton[1] asks if anxiety symptoms will overwhelm the NHS. In 1979 a senior colleague introduced us to the idea of hyperventilation as a cause of unexplained 'anxiety' symptoms. This placed my medical training in competition with the teaching which I received as a psychotherapist, in which all 'neurotic' phenomena were ascribed to hidden unconscious motives.

Medical textbooks[2] and psychiatric textbooks[3] describe hyperventilation as a feature of 'panic disorder'. However, in some patients hyperventilation may itself be the cause of the panic and may respond to direct management. Lum[4] gives an account of the physiology of hyperventilation and of the historical background to its association with anxiety.

Physiology

Hyperventilation lowers pCO_2 thus producing a variety of physical changes. These can include dizziness, being lightheaded, feeling faint; headaches;

tension in the head; trouble thinking clearly; being easily tired; ringing in the ears; blurred vision; dry mouth; 'a lump in the throat'; sweating; shortness of breath; tachycardia; palpitations; vague chest pain; shaking hands; numbness or tingling of the hands, feet or face; aches and pains in the limbs; apprehension, tension, agitation. Rarely carpo-pedal spasm will occur. Many of these frightening physical changes mimic those produced by epinephrine release and by other states of heightened emotional arousal.

The condition is easily diagnosed in the acute episode and a history of overbreathing is often available from the patient or onlookers. However, it is less recognised that chronic hyperventilation can also occur, producing similar symptoms in a more insidious way.

Respiratory rate is controlled mainly by pCO_2 with pO_2 as a secondary driver. Those who habitually overbreathe maintain their pCO_2 at a lower level than is usual. A small increase in respiration lowers pCO_2 rapidly, and recovery to a stable level is delayed. Infusions of sodium lactate or inhalation of carbon dioxide produce panic symptoms, which has been taken as evidence of a biological sensitivity in those with panic disorder. However, these interventions also increase respiratory rate in those with low pCO_2 so that their sensitivity may have been acquired through habitual overbreathing rather than being an inherited characteristic. A low venous phosphate level is identified by Klein[5] as being both a sign of chronic hyperventilation and a powerful predictor of panic attacks.

Frequent sighing or yawning can add to the problem. If aerophagy is present then bloated stomachs, vomiting, pains in the stomach, diarrhoea, and chronic flatulence can be present.

Clinical Features

I expect to see at least 8–10 such patients every year. I have found the same proportion while working in several different parts of the UK. The rate does not seem to be affected by the availability or otherwise of psychological treatment services.

Referrals are made when a clinician is puzzled by a patient who describes 'panic attacks' with no evident precipitant, or recurrent physical symptoms for which no physical cause can be found. The patient does not show signs of anxiety at other times. They have often been stable and competent previously. They feel out of control and ask 'Am I going mad?'

The disorder sometimes follows a bereavement or a major social stress. It is more common in women. One hypothesis is that pregnancy encourages thoracic breathing, which is more likely to induce excessive ventilation. Those accustomed to abdominal breathing through training in music or meditation are less likely to present with symptoms.

The patient is often pale, with frequent sighing respirations or yawns. Speech is fast and accessory muscles of respiration may be visibly in use. Specific enquiry will reveal some of the symptoms listed above. Aerophagy may have led to bowel symptoms and sometimes a diagnosis of irritable bowel syndrome. Disturbed childhoods and features of emotional disorder are usually absent. However, you may be told that 'my mother (or father) was just the same'.

Diagnosis

Measurement of arterial or capillary pCO_2 is not convenient in general practice or in the psychiatric clinic. However, a voluntary provocation test is almost invariably diagnostic.

The patient is asked to sit comfortably and to breathe deeply through the mouth for 20 breaths. They are overbreathing successfully if their pulse rises, they become pale and sweaty and their pupils dilate. Severe cases will destabilise within a few breaths and persisting to 20 breaths is unnecessary (and unpopular with the patient!). The patient is then asked to breathe slowly through the mouth until their pulse settles and their colour improves. Because reducing pCO_2 produces cerebral vasoconstriction and therefore impairs cognition, you must wait until their pulse settles before asking for or giving information. They should not speak until their pulse has settled to a near-normal level.

The test is positive if the patient recognises that the symptoms induced by the experience are similar to the early stages of their attacks. The test is both diagnosis and treatment since it demonstrates that the symptoms can be summoned and removed by voluntary actions. I tell them briefly about the effects of overbreathing, reassure them that they can learn to deal with their symptoms and give them the handout reproduced at the end of this article. (See also Clark, Salkovskis and Chalkley[6].)

A second consultation is rarely necessary. A few fail to carry out the recommended slow breathing exercises properly; asking them for a brief demonstration will clarify this. A common error is to take a long slow breath and then hold it in inspiration. If patients wish to pause in their breathing they should do so at the end of expiration, not inspiration. If there is a long history then the patient may achieve improvement but not recovery. Even if the patient also has genuine anxiety disorder, the ability to control some aspects of their symptoms is a comfort to them. Paper bag rebreathing may help with the exercises initially or can be used in acute attacks. (The NHS Medium Dressing Bag is an ideal size.) One of my patients complained that the bag was unhelpful. Asking him for a demonstration revealed that his fear of asphyxia had led him to make a large hole in the bag as a precaution, thus reducing its effectiveness.

Physiotherapists have skills in the treatment of hyperventilation but not all departments of physiotherapy have the capacity to undertake this task.

Psychological services provided by non-medical staff often fail to recognise the role of hyperventilation. As a consequence, ineffective treatments are offered, which leads to a waste of valuable resources.

Comments

Some patients become briefly tearful when the diagnosis is made. This may be relief at having a clear diagnosis. However, it has been proposed that overbreathing is learned in childhood as a means of suppressing negative emotions of which the child's carers disapprove. It is a common observation that a child who is rebuked briskly for crying will inhale deeply or hold their breath briefly. Bioenergetic psychoanalysis encourages healthy breathing patterns; emotional release through tears is a common part of this process.

It has been suggested (Klein[5]) that hyperventilation is an oversensitive response by a biological system which exists to protect against the threat of suffocation. However, suffocation as a form of child abuse was described by Oliver[7] in 1988. It has been confirmed by many other workers since. So a fear of suffocation may be acquired rather than inherited.

Hyperventilation leading to vasoconstriction may be the final common pathway in migraine attacks, transient ischaemic episodes, epileptic fits and cardiac ischaemia. Asthmatic episodes may also be triggered by hyperventilation. Perhaps the characters in nineteenth century novels who have an apoplexy on receiving bad news are experiencing the effects of hyperventilation induced by emotion?

In sports medicine some fit and highly motivated individuals overbreathe before competitive events. This can lead to cognitive impairment and physical symptoms. Training Red Cross workers at public events to say 'Breathe slowly' instead of 'Breathe deeply' would make a useful difference. Many of the benefits of relaxation training and meditation may be due to the slow breathing component rather than the other aspects.

Smokers who overbreathe often report transient improvement on lighting a cigarette, possibly because of the high carbon dioxide level in the inhaled smoke. Chronic hyperventilators who smoke can be recognised in public areas because they inhale the first puff very deeply. Their metabolism readjusts after a few minutes of smoke-laden air and symptoms may reappear.

Diazepam reduces respiratory rate and initially may relieve symptoms due to hyperventilation. However, tolerance to the effect soon develops, followed by requests for dose increases. Beta-blockers relieve some of the symptoms but most patients do not find this enough. Fatigue induced by beta-blockers is common and can make matters worse. Certain antidepressants have been recommended for panic disorder. Naturally, research by pharmaceutical companies has focused on presumed biological mechanisms rather than on psychological features.

Conclusion

Symptoms provoked by hyperventilation are common in general and psychiatric practice. They are a cause of much distress and contribute to a variety of general medical conditions. These symptoms are easy to identify. They are straightforward and cheap to treat, with a consequent saving of time and resources. This is satisfying for the busy practitioner.

References

1. Walton, I. Will anxiety be the downfall of the NHS? *Journal of Primary Care Mental Health* 2003; 7: 26–28.
2. Kumar, P., Clark, M. *Clinical Medicine* (5th edition). Edinburgh: WB Saunders, 2002.
3. Gelder, M., Gath, D., Mayou, R., Owen, P. *Oxford Textbook of Psychiatry* (3rd edition). Oxford: OUP, 1996.
4. Lum, L.C. Hyperventilation and Anxiety State. *Journal of the Royal Society of Medicine* 1981; 74: 1–4.
5. Klein, D.F. False suffocation alarms, spontaneous panics and related conditions: an integrative hypothesis. *Archives of General Psychiatry* 1993; 50: 306–317.
6. Clark, D.M., Salkovskis, P.M., Chalkley, A.J. Respiratory control as a treatment for 'panic attacks'. *Journal of Behaviour Therapy and Experimental Psychiatry* 1985; 16: 23–30.
7. Oliver, J.E. Successive generations of child maltreatment: the children. *British Journal of Psychiatry* 1988; 153: 543–553.

Overbreathing

Overbreathing (medical name 'hyperventilation') means a habit of breathing incorrectly and excessively. It can result from emotional stress and can cause tension or anxiety. Overbreathing upsets the chemistry of the body and can lead to many physical and emotional symptoms. Frequent sighing, yawning or swallowing air can add to the problem.

Symptoms

Dizziness, lightheaded, feeling faint; headaches; tension in your head; being easily tired; ringing in the ears; blurred vision; dry mouth; hard to swallow; sweating; shortness of breath; heart beating faster; palpitations; shaking hands; numbness or tingling of hands, feet or face; aches and pains in your limbs; bloated stomach; nausea; diarrhoea; passing wind up or down; apprehension; tension; agitation.

You can learn better breathing habits which will reduce many of these symptoms. However, it is not always easy to change habits and it may take some time. The actions outlined below have been useful to other people with this problem.

Treatment

Step 1   Breathe as slowly as you can using your stomach and not your chest. If possible, breathe only through your nose; in while counting 5 to yourself and then out while counting 5 to yourself.

Step 2   Sit or lie in a quiet place where you will not be interrupted and breathe like this for 5 minutes several times a day. Most people find this uncomfortable at first until the body is used to it.

Step 3   When you can do this easily then lengthen the time spent each day. Start to practise slow breathing when sitting quietly, for example watching TV or on a bus. Practise by speaking more slowly or by reading out loud.

Step 4   Eventually you will be able to breathe slowly all the time unless upset or frightened by something. Prepare for such times by breathing slowly beforehand and afterwards.

Interrupted breathing

Try taking a breath, then hold your nose with your mouth closed and push your breath as if you are trying to breathe out or are 'popping' your ears. Delaying your breathing in this way will calm your heart and your breathing within a few moments.

Rebreathing

If you find it difficult to start the above exercises or if you cannot control your breathing in certain situations, hold a paper bag (big enough for a loaf of bread) over your mouth and nose. Breathe as deeply as you like but only breathe the air inside the bag. You will begin to feel better after a few minutes of this. (It is not safe to use a plastic bag!)

Sighing, yawning or swallowing air

If you become aware of any of these habits try to take a single ordinary breath instead or hold your breath for five seconds.

Relaxation, yoga, tai chi or meditation may also help you to slow your breathing.

(Thanks to Helene Dellucci of Lyon for advice)
Dr A.J. Macdonald – 2010

References

Aaltonen, J., Seikkula, J., Alakare, B., Haarakangas, K., Keranen, J. and Sutela, M. (1997) 'Western Lapland Project: a comprehensive family- and network-centered community psychiatric project', *ISPS, Abstracts and Lectures*, 124: 12–16.

Adams, J.F., Piercy, F.P. and Jurich, J.A. (1991) 'Effects of solution-focused therapy's "formula first session task" on compliance and outcome in family therapy', *Journal of Marital and Family Therapy*, 17: 277–90.

Akchurin, M. (1992) *Red Odyssey: A Journey through the Soviet Republics*. London: Martin Secker and Warburg.

Allgood, S.M., Parham, K.B., Salts, C.J. and Smith, T.A. (1995) 'The association between pre-treatment change and unplanned termination in family therapy', *American Journal of Family Therapy*, 23: 195–202.

Andersen, T. (1991) *The Reflecting Team: Dialogues and Dialogues about the Dialogues*. New York: Norton.

Andersen, T. (1995) 'Reflecting processes: acts of informing and forming: you can borrow my eyes but you must not take them away from me!', in Friedman, S. (ed.) *The Reflecting Team in Action: Collaborative Practice in Family Therapy*. New York: Guilford Press. pp. 11–37.

APA (1994) *Diagnostic and Statistical Manual of Mental Disorders* (4th ed) (DSM-IV). Washington, DC: American Psychiatric Association.

Bagadia, V.N., Shah, L.P., Pradhan, P.V. and Gada, M.T. (1979) 'Treatment of mental disorder in India', *Progress in Neuro-Psychopharmacology*, 3: 109–18.

Bakker, J.M., Bannink, F.P. and Macdonald, A.J. (2010) 'Solution-focused psychiatry', *Psychiatric Bulletin*, 34: 297–300.

Bandler, R. and Grinder, J. (1979) *Frogs into Princes: Neuro Linguistic Programming*. Moab, UT: Real People Press. (UK edition 1990: London: Eden Grove Editions).

Banks, R. (2005) 'Solution-focused group therapy', *Journal of Family Psychotherapy*, 16(1/2):17–21. Special issue: Nelson, T.S. (ed.), *Education and Training in Solution Focused Brief Therapy*. Also published in book form: New York: Haworth Press.

Bannink, F. (2008) 'Solution-focused mediation'. Presentation, SOLWorld annual conference, Koln.

Bannink, F. (2010) *Handbook of Solution-Focused Conflict Management*. Cambridge, MA: Hogrefe & Huber.

Bargh, J.A., Chen, M. and Burrows, L. (1996) 'Automaticity of social behaviour: direct effects of trait construct and stereo-type activity on action', *Journal of Personality and Social Psychology*, 71: 230–44.

Bateson, G., Jackson, J.D., Haley, J. and Weakland, J. (1956) 'Toward a theory of schizophrenia', *Behavioural Science*, 1: 251–64.

Beck, A.T. (1967) *Depression: Clinical, Experimental and Theoretical Aspects*. New York: Harper and Row.

Bell, R., Skinner, C. and Fisher, L. (2009) 'Decreasing putting yips in accomplished golfers via solution-focused guided imagery: a single-subject research design', *Journal of Applied Sport Psychology*, 21: 1–14.

Berg, I.K. (1991) *Family Preservation: A Brief Therapy Workbook*. London: BT Press.

Berg, I.K. and DeJong, P. (1996) 'Solution-building conversations: co-constructing a sense of competence with clients', *Families in Society*, 77: 376–91.

Berg, I.K. and Reuss, N.H. (1995) *Solutions Step By Step: A Substance Abuse Treatment Manual*. New York: Norton.

Bertolino, B. and Thompson, K. (1999) *The Residential Youth Care Worker in Action: A Collaborative, Competency-Based Approach*. New York: Haworth Press.

Bettelheim, B. (1979) *Surviving the Holocaust*. London: Flamingo.

Beutler, L.E., Machado, P.P.P. and Neufeldt, S.A. (1994) 'Therapist variables', in Bergin, S.L. and Garfield, A.E. (eds) *Handbook of Psychotherapy and Behaviour Change* (4th ed). New York: Wiley. pp. 259–69.

Beyebach, M. and Carranza, V.E. (1997) 'Therapeutic interaction and drop-out: measuring relational communication in solution-focused therapy', *Journal of Family Therapy*, 19: 173–212.

Beyebach, M., Morejon, A.R., Palenzuela, D.L. and Rodriguez-Arias, J.L. (1996) 'Research on the process of solution-focused brief therapy', in Miller, S.D., Hubble, M.A. and Duncan, B.L. (eds), *Handbook of Solution-Focused Brief Therapy*. San Francisco, CA: Jossey-Bass. pp. 299–334.

Beyebach, M., Rodriguez Sanchez, M.S., Arribas de Miguel, J., Herrero de Vega, M., Hernandez, C. and Rodriguez-Morejon, A. (2000) 'Outcome of solution-focused therapy at a university family therapy center', *Journal of Systemic Therapies*, 19: 116–28.

Bierce, A. (1971) *The Enlarged Devil's Dictionary*. Harmondsworth: Penguin.

Bliss, E.V. and Edmonds, G. (2007) *A Self-determined Future with Asperger Syndrome: Solution Focused Approaches*. London: Jessica Kingsley Publishers.

Bond, T. (2000) *Standards and Ethics for Counselling in Action*. London: SAGE.

Bowie Youth & Family Services (1999) *Client Feedback Form*. Bowie, MD: Youth & Family Services.

Bowlby, J. (1969, 1973, 1980) *Attachment and Loss*, 3 vols. London: Hogarth.

Bowles, N., Mackintosh, C. and Torn, A. (2001) 'Nurses' communication skills: an evaluation of the impact of solution-focused communication training', *Journal of Advanced Nursing*, 36: 347–54.

Bostandzhiev, Vl. and Bozhkova, E. (2004–2006) 'SFBT in a Mental Health Day Center.' Presentations, Sofia University annual conferences of Clinical Psychology, Kiten, Bulgaria.

Brimstedt, L. (2002) 'Is risperidone the right choice in strongly drug-related psychoses?' *Lakartidning*, 95: 368. (Letter; original in Danish).

British Association for Counselling and Psychotherapy (2006) *Code of Ethics*. London: BACP.

Brown, G.W. and Harris, T.O. (1978) *Social Origins of Depression*. London: Tavistock.

Brumfitt, S. and Sheeran, P. (1999) *VASES: Visual Self-esteem Analogue Scale*. Bicester: Winslow.

Bryson, B. (1990) *Mother Tongue: The English Language*. London: Hamish Hamilton.

Burns, K. (2005) *Focus on Solutions: A Health Professional's Guide*. London: Whurr.

Burr, W. (1993) 'Evaluation der Anwendung losungsorientierter Kurztherapie in einer kinder- und jugendpsychiatrischen Praxis (Evaluation of the use of brief therapy in a practice for children and adolescents)', *Familiendynamik*, 18: 11–21. (German; abstract in English).

Bushman, B.J., Baumeister, R.F. and Stack, A.D. (1999) 'Catharsis, aggression, and persuasive influence: self-fulfilling or self-defeating prophecies?', *Journal of Personality and Social Psychology*, 76: 367–76.

Cade, B. and O'Hanlon, W.H. (1993) *A Brief Guide to Brief Therapy*. New York: Norton.

Callcott, A. (2003) 'Solution-focused assessment and interventions with suicidal or self-harming patients', *Journal of Primary Care Mental Health*, 7: 75–7.

Chung, S.A. and Yang, S. (2004) 'The effects of solution-focused group counseling program for the families with schizophrenic patients', *Taehan Kanho Hakhoe Chi (Journal of the Korean Academy of Nursing)*, 34: 1155–63. (Korean; abstract in English.)

Clark, D.M., Salkovskis, P.M. and Chalkley, A.J. (1985) 'Respiratory control as a treatment for "panic attacks"', *Journal of Behaviour Therapy and Experimental Psychiatry*, 16: 23–30.

Cockburn, J.T., Thomas, F.N. and Cockburn, O.J. (1997) 'Solution-focused therapy and psychosocial adjustment to orthopedic rehabilitation in a work hardening program', *Journal of Occupational Rehabilitation*, 7: 97–106.

Conoley, C.W., Graham, J.M., Neu, T., Craig, M.C., O'Pry, A., Cardin, S.A., Brossart, D.F. and Parker, R.I. (2003) 'Solution-focused family therapy with three aggressive and oppositional-acting children: an N=1 empirical study', *Family Process*, 42: 361–74.

Cook, C.C.H. and Thomson, A.D. (1997) 'B-complex vitamins in the prophylaxis and treatment of Wernicke-Korsakoff syndrome', *British Journal of Hospital Medicine*, 57: 461–5.

Corcoran, J.A. (2006) 'A comparison group study of solution-focused therapy versus "treatment-as-usual" for behavior problems in children', *Journal of Social Service Research*, 33: 69–81.

Corcoran, J.A. and Pillai, V. (2007) 'A review of the research on solution-focused therapy', *British Journal of Social Work*, 10: 1–9.

Crosby, P.B. (1981) *The Art of Getting Your Own Sweet Way* (2nd edn). New York: McGraw-Hill.

Cruz, J. and Littrell, J.M. (1998) 'Brief counseling with Hispanic American college students', *Journal of Multicultural Counseling and Development*, 26: 227–38.

Cuijpers, P., Riper, H. and Lemmers, L. (2004) 'The effects on mortality of brief interventions for problem drinking: a meta-analysis', *Addiction*, 99 (7): 839–45.

Dahl, R., Bathel, D. and Carreon, C. (2000) 'The use of solution-focused therapy with an elderly population', *Journal of Systemic Therapies*, 19: 45–55.

Daki, J. and Savage, R.S. (2010) 'Solution-focused brief therapy: impacts on academic and emotional difficulties', *Journal of Education Research*, 103: 309–26.

Darmody, M. and Adams, B. (2003) 'Outcome research on solution-focused brief therapy', *Journal of Primary Care Mental Health*, 7: 70–5.

de Hoogh, H. (2000) *Model Assessment Meeting (MAM)*. Unpublished. (Available at www.gingerich.net)

de Shazer, S. (1984) 'The death of resistance', *Family Process*, 23: 30–40.

de Shazer, S. (1985) *Keys to Solutions in Brief Therapy*. New York: Norton.

de Shazer, S. (1988) *Clues: Investigating Solutions in Brief Therapy*. New York: Norton.

de Shazer, S. (1991) *Putting Differences To Work*. New York: Norton.

de Shazer, S. (1994) *Words Were Originally Magic*. New York: Norton.

de Shazer, S. (2005) *Masterclass*, 8–9 September, BRIEF, London.

de Shazer, S. and Isebaert, L. (2003) 'The Bruges Model: a solution-focused approach to problem drinking', *Journal of Family Psychotherapy*, 14: 43–52.

de Shazer, S., Dolan, Y., Korman, H., Trepper, T., McCollum, E. and Berg, I.K. (2007) *More Than Miracles: The State of The Art of Solution-Focused Brief Therapy*. New York: Haworth Press.

de Shazer, S., Berg, I.K., Lipchik, E., Nunnally, E., Molnar, A., Gingerich, W. and Weiner-Davis, M. (1986) 'Brief therapy: focused solution development', *Family Process*, 25: 207–22.

DeJong, P. and Berg, I.K. (2001) *Interviewing for Solutions*. San Francisco, CA: Brooks/Cole.

DeJong, P. and Hopwood, L.E. (1996) 'Outcome research on treatment conducted at the Brief Family Therapy Center 1992–1993', in Miller, S.D., Hubble, M.A. and Duncan, B.L. (eds), *Handbook of Solution-focused Brief Therapy*. San Francisco, CA: Jossey-Bass. pp. 272–98.

Department for Education and Skills (2003) *Focusing on Solutions: A Practical Approach to Managing Behaviour*. London: HMSO.

Department of Health (2006) *The Common Assessment Framework for Children and Young People*. London: HMSO.

Department of Health (2007) *Improving Access to Psychological Therapies Implementation Plan: National Guidelines for Regional Delivery*. London: Department of Health. (www.dh.gov.uk/en/Publicationsandstatistics/Publications/PublicationsPolicyAndGuidance/DH_083150)

DeSisto, M., Harding, C.M., McCormick, R.V., Ashikaga, T. and Brooks, G.W. (1995) 'The Maine and Vermont three-decade studies of serious mental illness: I. Matched comparison of cross-sectional outcome; II. Longitudinal course comparisons', *British Journal of Psychiatry*, 167: 331–42.

Diderot, D. (2001 [1830]) 'Paradoxe sur le Comedien', in Diderot, D., d'Alembert, J. le R. and Proust, J. (eds), *L'Encyclopedie Diderot et d'Alembert*. Paris: Eddl/Soldeur.

Dolan, Y. (1991) *Resolving Sexual Abuse: Solution-focused Therapy and Ericksonian Hypnotherapy for Adult Survivors*. New York: Norton.

Dolan, Y. (2000) *Beyond Survival: Living Well is the Best Revenge*. London: BT Press. (Previous publication: Papier Mache Press: USA 1998.)

DSCF (2009) *Understanding Serious Case Reviews and their Impact – A biennial analysis of Serious Case Reviews 2005–2007*. London: Department for Schools, Children and Families.

Duncan, B. and Miller, S.D. (2000) *The Heroic Client: Doing Client-Directed, Outcome-Informed Therapy*. San Francisco, CA: Jossey-Bass.

Duncan, L., Ghul, R. and Mousley, S. (2007) *Creating Positive Futures: Solution-focused Recovery from Mental Distress*. London: BT Press.

Eakes, G., Walsh, S., Markowski, M., Cain, H. and Swanson, M. (1997) 'Family-centred brief solution-focused therapy with chronic schizophrenia: a pilot study', *Journal of Family Therapy*, 19: 145–58.

Emmelkamp, P.M.G. (1994) 'Behaviour therapy with adults', in Bergin, S.L. and Garfield, A.E. (eds), *Handbook of Psychotherapy and Behaviour Change* (4th edn). New York: Wiley. pp. 379–427.

Fisch, R., Weakland, J.H. and Segal, L. (1982) *The Tactics of Change: Doing Therapy Briefly*. San Francisco, CA: Jossey-Bass.

Fiske, H. (2008) *Hope in Action: Solution-focused Conversations about Suicide*. New York: Routledge.

Forrester, D., Copello, A., Waissbein, C. and Pokhrel, S. (2008) Evaluation of an intensive family preservation service for families affected by parental substance misuse. *Child Abuse Review*, 17: 410–26.

Franklin, C., Biever, J.L., Moore, K.C., Clemons, D. and Scamardo, M. (2001) 'The effectiveness of solution-focused therapy with children in a school setting', *Research on Social Work Practice*, 11: 411–34.

Franklin, C., Moore, K. and Hopson, L. (2008) 'Effectiveness of solution-focused brief therapy in a school setting', *Children and Schools*, 30(1): 15–26.

Franklin, C., Streeter, C.L., Kim, J.S. and Tripodi, S.J. (2007) 'The effectiveness of a solution-focused, public alternative school for dropout prevention and retrieval', *Children and Schools*, 29: 133–44.

Franklin, C., Trepper, T., Gingerich, W.J. and McCollum, E. (eds) (in press) *Solution-focused Brief Therapy: From Practice to Evidence-Informed Practice*. Oxford University Press: New York.

Freud, S. (1966 [1895]) *Project for a Scientific Psychology*, Standard Edition (vol. 1). London: Hogarth. (See also 23 subsequent volumes of Standard Edition.)

Froeschle, J.G., Smith, R.L. and Ricard, R. (2007) 'The efficacy of a systematic substance abuse program for adolescent females', *Professional School Counseling*, 10: 498–505.

Fujioka, K. (2010) *Becoming a Solution-building Psychiatrist*. Tokyo: Kongo Shuppan. (Japanese)

Furman, B. and Ahola, T. (1992) *Solution Talk: Hosting Therapeutic Conversations*. New York: Norton.

Gardner, R. (2008) *Developing an Effective Response to Neglect and Emotional Harm to Children*. Norwich: UEA/NSPCC.

Garfield, S.L. (1986) 'Research on client variables in psychotherapy', in Garfield, S.L. and Bergin, A.E. (eds), *Handbook of Psychotherapy and Behaviour Change* (3rd edn). New York: Wiley. pp. 213–56.

Garfield, S.L. and Bergin, A.E. (1971) 'Personal therapy, outcome and some therapist variables', *Psychotherapy: Theory, Research and Practice*, 8: 251–3.

Garfield, A.E. and Bergin, S.L. (eds) (1986) *Handbook of Psychotherapy and Behaviour Change* (3rd edn). New York: Wiley.

Gartrell, N., Herman, J., Olarte, S., Feldstein, M. and Localio, R. (1986) 'Psychiatrist–patient sexual contact: results of a national survey, I: prevalence', *American Journal of Psychiatry*, 143: 1126–31.

Gelder, M., Gath, D., Mayou, R. and Owen, P. (1996) *Oxford Textbook of Psychiatry* (3rd edn). Oxford: Oxford University Press.

George, E., Iveson, C. and Ratner, H. (1999) *Problem to Solution* (2nd edn). London: Brief Therapy Press.

Gingerich, W.J. and Eisengart, S. (2000) 'Solution-focused brief therapy: a review of the outcome research', *Family Process*, 39: 477–98. (2001 update available at www.gingerich.net)

Goffman, E. (1956) *The Presentation of Self in Everyday Life*. New York: Doubleday.

Goffman, E. (1968) *Asylums*. Harmondsworth: Penguin.

Goodall, J. (1990) *Through a Window: My Thirty Years with the Chimpanzees of Gombe*. New York: Houghton Miflin.

Gostautas, A., Cepukiene, V., Pakrosnis, R. and Fleming, J.S. (2005) 'The outcome of solution-focused brief therapy for adolescents in foster care and health institutions', *Baltic Journal of Psychology*, 6: 5–14.

Grant, A.M. and O'Connor, S.A. (2010) 'The differential effects of solution-focused and problem-focused coaching questions: a pilot study with implications for practice.' *Industrial and Commercial Training Journal*, 42: 102–11.

Grant, A.M., Curtayne, L. and Burton, G. (2009) 'Executive coaching enhances goal attainment, resilience and workplace well-being: a randomised controlled study', *Journal of Positive Psychology*, 4: 396–407.

Grant, A.M., Green, L.S. and Rynsaardt, J. (2010) 'Developmental coaching for high school teachers: executive coaching goes to school', *Consulting Psychology Journal: Practice and Research*, 62: 151–68.

Green, L.S., Grant, A.M. and Rynsaardt, J. (2007) 'Evidence-based life coaching for senior high school students: building hardiness and hope', *International Coaching Psychology Review*, 2: 24–32.

Green, L.S., Oades, L.G., Grant, A.M. (2006) 'Cognitive-behavioral, solution-focused life coaching: enhancing goal striving, well-being, and hope', *Journal of Positive Psychology*, 1: 142–9.

Greenberg, G.S. (1998) 'Brief, change-delineating group therapy with acute and chronically mentally ill clients: an achievement-oriented approach', in Ray, W.A. and de Shazer, S. (eds), *Evolving Brief Therapies*. Iowa City, IA: Geist and Russell. pp. 142–232.

Haley, J. (1973) *Uncommon Therapy: The Psychiatric Techniques of Milton H. Erickson*. New York: Norton.

Haley, J. (1976) *Problem Solving Therapy*. New York: Jossey-Bass.

Hanton, P. (2008) 'Measuring solution-focused brief therapy in use with clients with moderate to severe depression using a "bricolage" research methodology', *Solution Research*, 1(1): 16–24.

Harding, C.M., Brooks, G.W., Ashikaga, T., Strauss, J.S. and Breier, A. (1987) 'The Vermont longitudinal study of persons with severe mental illness: I. Methodology, study sample and overall status 32 years later', *American Journal of Psychiatry*, 144: 718–26.

Harkness, D. (1997) 'Testing interactional social work theory: a panel analysis of supervised practice and outcomes', *Clinical Supervisor*, 15: 33–50.

Harris, M.B. and Franklin, C. (2009) 'Helping adolescent mothers to achieve in school: an evaluation of the taking charge group intervention', *Children and Schools*, 31: 27–34.

Hausdorff, J.M., Levy, B.R. and Wei, J.Y. (1999) 'The power of ageism on physical function of older persons: reversibility of age-related gait changes', *Journal of the American Geriatrics Society*, 47: 1346–9.

Hawkes, D., Marsh, T.I. and Wilgosh, R. (1998) *Solution-focused Therapy: A Handbook for Health Care Professionals*. London: Butterworth Heinemann.

Hayes, S.C., Follette, V.M. and Linehan, M.M. (2004) *Mindfulness and Acceptance: Expanding the Cognitive-behavioural Tradition*. New York: Guilford Press.

Health Professions Council (2008) Standards of conduct, performance and ethics. (www.hpc-uk.org/aboutregistration/standards/standardsof conductperformanceandethics/)

Henden, J. (2005) 'Preventing suicide using a solution-focused approach', *Journal of Primary Care Mental Health*, 8: 82–8.

Henden, J. (2008) *Preventing Suicide: The Solution-focused Approach.* Chichester: Wiley.

Henden, J. (2011) *Beating Combat Stress.* London: Wiley-Blackwell.

Herrero de Vega, M. and Beyebach, M. (2007) 'Solutions for "stuck cases" in solution-focused therapy'. Workshop, European Brief Therapy Association annual conference, Bruges, Belgium.

Hester, R.K. and Miller, W.R. (eds) (1995) *Handbook of Alcoholism Treatment Approaches: Effective Alternatives* (2nd edn). Boston, MA: Allyn Bacon.

Hinde, R.A. (1989) 'Reconciling the family systems and the relationships approaches to child development', in Kreppner, K. and Lerner, R.M. (eds), *Family Systems and Life-span Development.* Hillsdale, NJ: Lawrence Erlbaum.

Hjerth, M. (2008) 'Microtools'. Presentation, SOLWorld annual conference, Koln.

Hoffman, K., Lueger, G. and Luisser, P. (2006) 'Effects of solution-focused training on productivity and behaviour', in Lueger, G. and Korn, H-P. (eds), *Solution-focused Management.* Munchen: Rainer Hampp. pp 89–97. (Proceedings of 5th International Conference on Solution Focused Practice in Organisations, Vienna 2006).

Hogg, V. and Wheeler, J. (2004) 'Miracles R Them: Solution-focused practice in a social services duty team', *Practice*, 16: 299–314.

Holmes, P. and Karp, M. (eds) (1991) *Psychodrama Inspiration and Technique.* London: Routledge.

Hosany, Z., Wellman, N. and Lowe, T. (2007) 'Fostering a culture of engagement: a pilot study of the outcomes of training mental health nurses working in two UK acute admission units in brief solution-focused therapy techniques', *Journal of Psychiatric and Mental Health Nursing*, 14: 688–95.

Howard, K.L., Kopta, S.M., Krause, M.S. and Orlinsky, D.E. (1986) 'The dose-effect relationship in psychotherapy', *American Psychologist*, 41: 159–64.

Howard, L., Flach, C., Leese, M., Byford, S., Killaspy, H., Cole, L., Lawlor, C., Betts, J., Sharac, J., Cutting, P., McNicholas, S. and Johnson, S. (2010) 'Effectiveness and cost-effectiveness of admissions to women's crisis houses compared with traditional psychiatric words: pilot patient-preference randomised controlled trial', *British Journal of Psychiatry*, 197: s32–s40.

Hubble, M.A., Duncan, B.L. and Miller, S.D. (eds) (1999) *The Heart and Soul of Change: What Works in Therapy.* Washington, DC: American Psychological Association.

Isebaert, L. (1997) 'Follow-up of solution-focused therapy with alcohol users'. Presentation, European Brief Therapy Association World Conference, Bruges, Belgium.

Isebaert, L. (2005) *A Protocol for Depression and Anxiety.* Presentation, European Brief Therapy Association World Conference, Salamanca, Spain, 23–24 September.

Iveson, C. (1993) *Whose Life? Community Care of Older People and Their Families*. London: Brief Therapy Press.

Iveson, C. (2002) 'Solution-focused brief therapy', *Advances in Psychiatric Treatment*, 8: 149–57.

Jackson, P.Z. and McKergow, M. (2002) *The Solutions Focus: The Simple Way to Positive Change*. London: Nicholas Brealey.

Jackson, P.Z. and Waldman, J. (2010) *Positively Speaking: The Art of Constructive Conversations with a Solutions Focus*. St Albans: The Solutions Focus.

Jacob, F. (2001) *Solution-focused Recovery from Eating Distress*. London: BT Press.

James, W. (1988 [1902]) *The Varieties of Religious Experience*. New York: Library of America.

Janes, K. and Trickey, K. (2005) '"Looking ahead": discharge in an older adult psychiatric day hospital', *Context: news magazine for family therapy*, 77: 27–30.

Johnson, L.D. and Shaha, S. (1996) 'Improving quality in psychotherapy', *Psychotherapy*, 33: 225–36.

Johnson, L.N., Nelson, T.S. and Allgood, S.M. (1998) 'Noticing pre-treatment change and therapeutic outcome: an initial study', *American Journal of Family Therapy*, 26: 159–68.

Jones, M. (1968) *Beyond the Therapeutic Community: Social Learning and Social Psychiatry*. New Haven, CT: Yale University Press.

Jorm, A.F., Korten, A.E., Jacomb, P.A., Rodgers, B., Pollitt, P., Christensen, H. and Henderson, S. (1997) 'Helpfulness of interventions for mental disorders: beliefs of health professionals compared with the general public', *British Journal of Psychiatry*, 171: 233–7.

Kesey, K. (1962) *One Flew Over the Cuckoo's Nest*. London: Picador. (Film version 1975).

Kim, J.S. (2006) 'Examining the effectiveness of solution-focused brief therapy: meta-analysis using random effects modeling'. Unpublished doctoral dissertation, University of Michigan database.

Kim, J.S. (2008) 'Examining the effectiveness of solution-focused brief therapy: a meta-analysis', *Research on Social Work Practice*, 18: 107–16.

Kim, J.S. and Franklin, C. (2009) 'Solution-focused brief therapy in schools: a review of the outcome literature', *Children and Youth Services Review*, 31: 464–70.

Kingston, K., Szmukler, G., Andrewes, B.T. and Desmond, P. (1996) 'Neuropsychological and structural brain changes in anorexia nervosa before and after refeeding', *Psychological Medicine*, 26: 15–28.

Klerman, G.L., Dimascio, A., Weissman, M., Prusoff, B. and Paykel, E.S. (1974) 'Treatment of depression by drugs and psychotherapy', *American Journal of Psychiatry*, 131: 186–91.

Klingenstierna, C. www.solutionwork.com/arkiv/Uppsatsstudie1.pdf (accessed April 2010).

Knekt, P. and Lindfors, O. (2004) 'A randomised trial of the effect of four forms of psychotherapy on depressive and anxiety disorders: design, methods and results on the effectiveness of short-term psychodynamic psychotherapy and solution-focused therapy during a one-year follow-up', *Studies in Social Security and Health*, No. 77. The Social Insurance Institution, Helsinki, Finland.

Knekt, P., Lindfors, O., Härkänen, T., Välikoski, M., Virtala, E., Laaksonen, M.A., Marttunen, M., Kaipainen, M., Renlund, C. and the Helsinki Psychotherapy Study Group (2008) 'Randomized trial on the effectiveness of long-and short-term psychodynamic psychotherapy and solution-focused therapy on psychiatric symptoms during a 3-year follow-up', *Psychological Medicine*, 38: 689–703.

Ko, M-J., Yu, S-J. and Kim, Y-G. (2003) 'The effects of solution-focused group counseling on the stress response and coping strategies in the delinquent juveniles', *Journal of Korean Academy of Nursing*, 33: 440–50.

Koss, M.P. and Shiang, J. (1994) 'Research on brief therapy', in Garfield, A.E. and Bergin, S.L. (eds), *Handbook of Psychotherapy and Behaviour Change* (4th edn). New York: Wiley. pp. 644–700.

Koumtsidis, C., Schifano, F., Sharp, T., Ford, L., Robinson, J. and Magee, C. (2006) 'Neurological and psychopathological sequelae associated with a lifetime intake of 40,000 ecstasy tablets', *Psychosomatics*, 47(1): 86–7.

Kral, R. (1988) *Strategies that Work: Techniques for Solution in the Schools*. Milwaukee, WI: Brief Therapy Family Center.

Kumar, P. and Clark, M. (2002) *Clinical Medicine* (5th edn). Edinburgh: Saunders.

Kvarme, L.G., Helseth, S., Sørum, R., Luth-Hansen, V., Haugland, S. and Natvig, G.K. (2010) 'The effect of a solution-focused approach to improve self-efficacy in socially withdrawn school children: a non-randomized controlled trial', *International Journal of Nursing Studies*, 47 (11): 1389–96. (doi:10.1016/j.ijnurstu.2010.05.001)

LaFountain, R.M. and Garner, N.E. (1996) 'Solution-focused counselling groups: the results are in', *Journal for Specialists in Group Work*, 21: 128–43.

Lambert, M.J. (1992) 'Implications of outcome research for psychotherapy integration', in Norcross, J.C. and Goldfried, M.R. (eds), *Handbook of Psychotherapy Integration*. New York: Basic Books. pp. 94–129.

Lambert, M.J. (2004) *Bergin and Garfield's Handbook of Psychotherapy and Behaviour Change* (5th ed). New York: Wiley.

Lambert, M.J., Bergin, S.L. and Garfield, A.E. (2004) 'Introduction and historical overview', in Lambert, M.J. (ed), *Bergin and Garfield's Handbook of Psychotherapy and Behaviour Change* (5th ed). New York: Wiley. pp. 3–15.

Lambert, M.J., Okiishi, J.C., Finch, A.E. and Johnson, L.D. (1998) 'Outcome assessment: from conceptualization to implementation', *Professional Psychology: Research & Practice*, 29: 63–70.

Lambert, M.J., Whipple, J., Smart, D., Vermeersch, D., Nielsen, S. and Hawkins, E. (2001) 'The effects of providing therapists with feedback on patient progress during psychotherapy: are outcomes enhanced?', *Psychotherapy Research*, 11: 49–68.

Lamprecht, H., Laydon, C., McQuillan, C., Wiseman, S., Williams, L., Gash, A. and Reilly, J. (2007) 'Single-session solution-focused brief therapy and self-harm: a pilot study', *Journal of Psychiatric and Mental Health Nursing*, 14: 601–2.

Lee, M.Y. (1997) 'A study of solution-focused brief family therapy: outcomes and issues', *American Journal of Family Therapy*, 25: 3–17.

Lee, M.Y., Greene, G.J., Uken, A., Sebold, J. and Rheinsheld, J. (1997) 'Solution-focused brief group treatment: a viable modality for domestic violence offenders?', *Journal of Collaborative Therapies*, IV: 10–17.

Lee, M.Y., Greene, G.J., Mentzer, R.A., Pinnell, S. and Niles, D. (2001) 'Solution-focused brief therapy and the treatment of depression: a pilot study', *Journal of Brief Therapy*, 1: 33–49.

Lee, M.Y., Sebold, J. and Uken, A. (2003) *Solution-focused Treatment of Domestic Violence Offenders*. New York: Oxford.

Lee, M.Y., Sebold, J. and Uken, A. (2007) 'Roles of self determined goals in predicting recidivism in domestic violence offenders', *Research on Social Work Practice*, 17: 30–41.

Li, S., Armstrong, S., Chaim, G., Kelly, C. and Shenfeld, J. (2007) 'Group and individual couple treatment for substance abuse clients: a pilot study', *American Journal of Family Therapy*, 35: 221–33.

Lindforss, L. and Magnusson, D. (1997) 'Solution-focused therapy in prison', *Contemporary Family Therapy*, 19: 89–104.

Linehan, M.M. (1993) *Cognitive Behavioural Treatment of Borderline Personality Disorder*. New York: Guilford Press.

Lipchik, E. and Kubicki, A.D. (1996) 'Solution-focused domestic violence views: bridges toward a new reality in couples therapy', in Miller, S.D., Hubble, M.A. and Duncan, B.L. (eds), *Handbook of Solution-Focused Brief Therapy*. San Francisco, CA: Jossey-Bass. pp. 65–98.

Littrell, J.M., Malia, J.A. and Vanderwood, M. (1995) 'Single-sessions brief counseling in a high school', *Journal of Counseling and Development*, 73: 451–8.

Knutsson, C., Norrsell, E., Johansson, C., Öhman, U. and Ericson, B. (1998) *The Lonnen Study*. European Brief Therapy Association. (Available at www. ebta.nu/page2/page6/page20/page20.html)

Lum, L.C. (1981) 'Hyperventilation and anxiety state', *Journal of the Royal Society of Medicine*, 74: 1–4.

Luttwak, E. (1969) *Coup d'Etat: A Practical Handbook*. Harmondsworth: Penguin.

Macdonald, A.J. (1994a) 'Brief therapy in adult psychiatry', *Journal of Family Therapy*, 16: 415–26.

Macdonald, A.J. (1994b) 'A paper that changed my practice: reversible mental impairment in alcoholics', *British Medical Journal*, 308: 1678.

Macdonald, A.J. (1995) 'Eating Disorders', *Journal of Family Therapy*, 17: 356. (Letter)

Macdonald, A.J. (1997) 'Brief therapy in adult psychiatry: further outcomes', *Journal of Family Therapy*, 19: 213–22.

Macdonald, A.J. (2000) 'Recommended reading for trainees', *Psychiatric Bulletin*, 24: 154. (Letter)

Macdonald, A.J. (2004) 'Hyperventilation: a curable cause of symptoms of anxiety', *Journal of Primary Care Mental Health and Education*, 7: 105–8.

Macdonald, A.J. (2005) 'Brief therapy in adult psychiatry: results from 15 years of practice', *Journal of Family Therapy*, 27: 65–75.

Macdonald, A.J. (2006a) 'Does cannabis really cause psychosis?', *British Medical Journal*, 332: 303. (Letter)

Macdonald, A.J. (2006b) 'Solution-focused situation management: finding cooperation quickly', in Lueger, G. and Korn, H-P. (eds), *Solution-focused Management*. Munchen: Rainer Hampp. pp 89–97. (Proceedings of 5th International Conference on Solution Focused Practice in Organisations, Vienna).

Måhlberg, K. and Sjöblom, M. (2004) *Solution-focused Education*. Stockholm: Måhlberg & Sjöblom. (Swedish edition Stockholm: Mareld 2002.)

Marks, I.M. (1987) *Fears, Phobias and Rituals: Panic, Anxiety and their Disorders*. London: Oxford University Press.

Masserman, J.H. (1972) 'Psychotherapy as the mitigation of uncertainties', *Archives of General Psychiatry*, 26: 186–8.

Mathers, J. (1974) 'The gestation period of identity change', *British Journal of Psychiatry*, 125: 472–4.

McAllister, M., Zimmer-Gembeck, M., Moyle, W. and Billett, S. (2008) 'Working effectively with clients who self-injure using a solution-focused approach', *International Emergency Nursing*, 16: 272–9.

McAskill, N. (1988) 'Personal therapy in the training of the psychotherapist: is it effective?', *British Journal of Psychotherapy*, 4: 219–26.

McGilton, K., Irwin-Robertson, H., Boscart, V. and Spanjevic, L. (2006) 'Communication enhancement: nurse and patient satisfaction outcomes in a complex nursing continuing care facility', *Journal of Advanced Nursing*, 54: 35–44.

McKeel, A.J. (1996) 'A clinician's guide to research on solution-focused therapy', in Miller, S.D., Hubble, M.A. and Duncan, B.L. (eds), *Handbook of Solution-focused Brief Therapy*. San Francisco, CA: Jossey-Bass. pp. 251–71.

McKeel, A.J. (1999) 'A selected review of research of solution-focused brief therapy'. (Available at www.solutionsdoc.co.uk/mckeel.htm)

McKergow, M. and Clarke, J. (eds) (2005) *Positive Approaches to Change: Applications of Solutions Focus and Appreciative Inquiry at Work*. Cheltenham: Solutions Books.

McKergow, M. and Clarke, J. (eds) (2007) *Solutions Focus Working: 80 real life lessons for successful organisational change*. Cheltenham: Solutions Books.

McNamara, J.R., Tamanini, K. and Pelletier-Walker, S. (2007) 'the impact of short-term counseling at a domestic violence shelter', *Research on Social Work Practice*, 18: 132–6.

Mehrabian, A. (1981) *Silent Messages: Implicit Communication of Emotions and Attitudes* (2nd edn). Belmont, CA: Wadsworth.

Mental Capacity Act (2005) (www.opsi.gov.uk/acts/acts2005/ukpga_20050009_en_1)

Metcalf, L. (1997) *Parenting Towards Solutions: How Parents Can Use Skills They Already Have to Raise Responsible, Loving Kids*. Paramus, NJ: Prentice-Hall.

Metcalf, L. (1998a) *Teaching Towards Solutions: Step-By-Step Strategies for Handling Academic, Behaviour and Family Issues in the Child*. New York: Center for Applied Research in Education/Simon and Shuster.

Metcalf, L. (1998b) *Solution Focused Group Therapy*. New York: Simon and Shuster.

Metcalf, L. (2004) *The Miracle Question: Answer It and Change Your Life*. Carmarthen: Crown House Publishing.

Metcalf, L., Thomas, F.N., Duncan, B.L., Miller, S.D. and Hubble, M.A. (1996) 'What works in solution-focused brief therapy', in Miller, S.D., Hubble, M.A. and Duncan, B.L. (eds), *Handbook of Solution-focused Brief Therapy*. San Francisco, CA: Jossey-Bass. pp. 335–49.

Milner, J. (2001) *Women and Social Work: Narrative Approaches*. Basingstoke: Palgrave Macmillan.

Milner, J. and Jessop, D. (2003) 'Domestic violence: narrative and solutions', *Probation Journal*, 50: 127–41.

Milner, J. and O'Byrne, P. (1998) *Assessment in Social Work*. Basingstoke: Palgrave Macmillan.

Milner, J. and Singleton, T. (2008) 'Domestic violence: solution-focused practice with men and women who are violent', *Journal of Family Therapy*, 30: 27–51.

Mintoft, B., Bellringer, M.E. and Orme, C. (2005) 'Improved client outcome services project: an intervention with clients of problem gambling treatment', *ECOMMUNITY: International Journal of Mental Health and Addiction*, 3: 30–40.

Morral, A.R., McCaffrey, D.F., Ridgeway, G., Mukherji, A. and Beighley, C. (2006) *The Relative Effectiveness of 10 Adolescent Substance Abuse Treatment Programs in the United States*. Santa Monica, CA: RAND.

Morgan, C. (1982) Personal communication, 21 October.

Morgan, H.G. and Priest, P. (1984) 'Assessment of suicide risk in psychiatric inpatients', *British Journal of Psychiatry*, 145: 467–9.

Morrison, J.A., Olivos, K., Dominguez, G., Gomez, D. and Lena, D. (1993) 'The application of family systems approaches to school behaviour problems on a school-level discipline board: an outcome study', *Elementary School Guidance & Counselling*, 27: 258–72.

Murphy, J.J. (1997) *Solution-focused Counselling in Middle and High Schools*. Alexandria, VA: American Counselling Association.

Mussman, C. (2006) 'Solution-focused leadership: the range between theory and practical application', in Lueger, G. and Korn, H-P. (eds), *Solution-focused Management*. Munchen: Rainer Hampp. pp. 99–110. (Proceedings of 5th International Conference on Solution Focused Practice in Organisations, Vienna 2006).

National Institute for Clinical Excellence (NICE) (2004) *Improving Supportive and Palliative Care for Adults with Cancer*. London: NICE.

Nelson, T.S. and Kelley, L. (2001) 'Solution-focused couples group', *Journal of Systemic Therapies*, 20: 47–66.

Newsome, W.S. (2004) 'Solution-focused brief therapy groupwork with at-risk junior high school students: enhancing the bottom line', *Research on Social Work Practice* 14: 336–43.

Norman, H., Hjerth, M. and Pidsley, T. (2005) 'Solution-focused reflecting teams in action', in McKergow, M. and Clarke, J. (eds), *Positive Approaches to Change: Applications of Solutions Focus and Appreciative Inquiry at Work*. Cheltenham: Solutions Books. pp. 67–80.

Nowicka, P., Pietrobelli, A. and Flodmark, C-E. (2007) 'Low-intensity family therapy intervention is useful in a clinical setting to treat obese and extremely obese children', *International Journal of Pediatric Obesity*, 2: 211–17.

Nowicka, P., Haglund, P., Pietrobelli, A., Lissau, I. and Flodmark, C-E. (2008) 'Family Weight School treatment: 1-year results in obese adolescents', *International Journal of Pediatric Obesity*, 3: 141–7.

Nylund, D. and Corsiglia, V. (1994) 'Becoming solution-focused in brief therapy: remembering something we already know', *Journal of Systemic Therapies*, 13: 5–11.

Nystuen, P. and Hagen, K.B. (2006) 'Solution-focused intervention for sick-listed employees with psychological problems or muscle skeletal pain: a randomised controlled trial', *BMC Public Health*, 6: 69–77.

O'Callaghan, K. and Mariappanadar, S. (2008) 'Restoring service after an unplanned IT outage', *IT Professional*, 10: 40–45.

O'Connell, B. (2005) *Solution-focused Therapy* (2nd edn). London: Sage.

Office of National Statistics (2001) *Regional Trends No. 26*. London: Office of National Statistics.

Osborn, D.P.J., Lloyd-Evans, B., Johnson, S., Gilburt, H., Byford, S., Leese, M. and Slade, M. (2010) 'Residential alternatives to acute in-patient care in England: satisfaction, ward atmosphere and service user experiences', *British Journal of Psychiatry*, 197: s41–s45.

Palazzoli, M.S., Boscolo, L., Cecchin, G. and Prata, G. (1978) *Paradox and Counterparadox*. New York: Jason Aronson.

Panayotov, P., Anichkina, A. and Strahilov, B. (in press) 'Solution-focused brief therapy and long-term medical treatment compliance/adherence with patients suffering from schizophrenia: a pilot naturalistic clinical observation', in Franklin, C., Trepper, T., Gingerich, W.J. and McCollum, E. (eds), *Solution-focused Brief Therapy: From Practice to Evidence-Informed Practice*. New York: Oxford University Press.

Park, E.S. (1997) 'An application of brief therapy to family medicine', *Contemporary Family Therapy*, 19: 81–8.

Parkinson, C.N. (1965) *Inlaws and Outlaws*. Harmondsworth: Penguin.

Parry, G. and Richardson, A. (1996) *Psychotherapy Services in England: Review of Strategic Policy*. London: Department of Health, NHS Executive.

Patel, V. and Saxena, S. (2003) 'Psychiatry in India', *International Psychiatry: Bulletin of the Board of International Affairs of the Royal College of Psychiatrists*, 1: 16–18.

Pavlov, I.P. (1926) *Lectures on Conditioned Reflexes: Twenty-Five Years of Objective Study of the Higher Nervous Activity Behaviour of Animals*. English edition: New York: Liveright Publishing (1928).

Peacock, F. (2001) *Water the Flowers, Not the Weeds*. Montreal: Open Heart Publishing.

Perez Grande, M.D. (1991) 'Evaluacion de resultados en terapia sistemica breve' (Outcome research in brief systemic therapy), *Cuadernos de Terapia Familiar*, 18: 93–110.

Perkins, R. (2006) 'The effectiveness of one session of therapy using a single-session therapy approach for children and adolescents with mental health problems', *Psychology and Psychotherapy: Theory, Research and Practice*, 79: 215–27.

Perkins, R. and Scarlett, G. (2008) 'The effectiveness of single session therapy in child and adolescent mental health. Part 2: an 18-month follow-up study'. *Psychology & Psychotherapy: Theory, Research & Practice*, 81: 143–56.

Pope, K.S. and Bouhoutsos, J.C. (1986) *Sexual Intimacy between Therapists and Clients*. New York: Praeger.

Prochaska, J.O. (1999) 'How do people change, and how can we change to help many more people?', in Hubble, M.A., Duncan, B.L. and Miller, S.D. (eds), *The Heart and Soul of Change: What Works in Therapy*. Washington, CD: American Psychological Association. pp. 227–55.

Prochaska, J.O. and DiClemente, C.C. (1982) 'Transtheoretical therapy: toward a more integrative model of change', *Psychotherapy: Theory, Research and Practice*, 19: 276–88.

Prochaska, J.O., DiClemente, C.C. and Norcross, J.C. (1994) *Changing for Good*. New York: Morrow.

Proust, M. (2001 [1922]) *In Search of Lost Time*. (trans. Moncrieff/Kilmartin/Enright) Everyman: London.

Reicher-Rossler, A. and Rossler, W. (1993) 'Compulsory admission of psychiatric patients – an international comparison', *Acta Psychiatrica Scandinavia*, 87: 231–6.

Reinehr, T., Kleber, M., Lass, N. and Toschke, A.M. (2010) 'Body mass index patterns over 5 y in obese children motivated to participate in a 1-y lifestyle intervention: age as a predictor of long-term success', *American Journal of Clinical Nutrition*, 91: 1165–71.

Rhee, W.K., Merbaum, M. and Strube, M.J. (2005) 'Efficacy of brief telephone psychotherapy with callers to a suicide hotline', *Suicide and Life-Threatening Behaviour*, 35: 317–28.

Rhodes, J. and Ajmal, Y. (1995) *Solution-focused Thinking in Schools*. London: BT Press.

Rivers, W.H.R. (1917) 'Freud's psychology of the unconscious', *Lancet*, i: 912–14.

Roffe, D. and Roffe, C. (1995) 'Madness and care in the community: a medieval perspective', *British Medical Journal*, 311: 708–12.

Rohrig, P. (2005) 'Solution focused feedback in management development', in McKergow, M. and Clarke, J. (eds), *Positive Approaches to Change: Applications of Solutions Focus and Appreciative Inquiry at Work*. Cheltenham: Solutions Books. pp. 131–40.

Rosenkranz, M.A., Busse, W.W., Johnstone, T., Swenson, C.A., Crisafi, G.M., Jackson, M.M., Bosch, J.A., Sheridan, J.F. and Davidson, R.J. (2005) 'Neural circuitry underlying the interaction between emotion and asthma symptom exacerbation', *Proceedings of the National Academy of Sciences*, 102: 13319–24.

Rothwell, N. (2005) 'How brief is solution focussed brief therapy? A comparative study', *Clinical Psychology and Psychotherapy*, 12: 402–5.

Rowan, T. and O'Hanlon, B. (1999) *Solution-oriented Therapy for Chronic and Severe Mental Illness*. New York: Wiley.

Royal College of Psychiatrists (2004) *Psychotherapy and Learning Disability*. Council Report CR116. London: Royal College of Psychiatrists.

Rycroft, C. (1972) *A Critical Dictionary of Psychoanalysis*. Harmondsworth: Penguin.

Ryle, A. (1990) *Cognitive Analytic Therapy: Active Participation in Change*. Chichester: Wylie.

Ryle, A. (1997) 'The structure and development of borderline personality disorder: a proposed model', *British Journal of Psychiatry*, 170: 82–7.

Sapolsky, R. (2002) *A Primate's Memoir: A Neuroscientist's Unconventional Life Among the Baboons*. New York: Touchstone.

Scottish Intercollegiate Guidelines Network (SIGN) (2002; reviewed 2007) *No. 57: Cardiac Rehabilitation*. Edinburgh: SIGN.

Seidel, A. and Hedley, D. (2008) 'The use of solution-focused brief therapy with older adults in Mexico: a preliminary study', *American Journal of Family Therapy*, 36: 242–52.

Seikkula, J., Alakare, B. and Aaltonen, J. (2000) 'A two-year follow-up on open dialogue treatment in first episode psychosis: need for hospitalization and neuroleptic medication decreases', *Social and Clinical Psychiatry*, 10: 20–29.

Seikkula, J., Arnkil, T.E. and Eriksson, E. (2003) 'Postmodern society and social networks: open and anticipation dialogues in network meetings', *Family Process*, 42: 185–203.

Seligman, M.E.P. (1995) 'The effectiveness of psychotherapy. The *Consumer Reports* study', *American Psychologist*, 50: 965–74.

Seligman, M.E.P. (2002) *Authentic Happiness*. New York: The Free Press/ Simon and Shuster.

Severin, B. (2001) *A Group for Sexual Offenders in Prison*. Presentation, European Brief Therapy Association Conference, Dublin.

Shapiro, F. (2001) *Eye Movement Desensitization and Reprocessing (EMDR): Basic Principles, Protocols, and Procedures* (2nd edn). New York: Guilford Press.

Sharry, J. (2001) *Solution-focused Groupwork*. London: Sage.

Sharry, J., Darmody, M. and Madden, B. (2002) 'A solution focused approach to working with clients who are suicidal', Symposium on Suicide. *British Journal of Guidance and Counselling*, 30: 383–99.

Shennan, G. (2003) 'The early response project: a voluntary sector contribution to CAMHS', *Child and Adolescent Mental Health in Primary Care*, 1: 46–50.

Shephard, B. (2000) *A War of Nerves: Soldiers and Psychiatrists 1914–1994*. London: Jonathan Cape.

Shilts, L. (2008) 'The WOWW program', in DeJong, P. and Berg, I.K. (eds), *Interviewing for Solutions* (3rd ed). San Francisco, CA: Brooks/Cole.

Shilts, L., Rambo, A. and Hernandez, L. (1997) 'Clients helping therapists find solutions to their therapy', *Contemporary Family Therapy*, 19: 117–32.

Shin, S-K. (2009) 'Effects of a solution-focused program on the reduction of aggressiveness and the improvement of social readjustment for Korean youth probationers', *Journal of Social Service Research*, 35: 274–84.

Short, E., Kinman, G. and Baker, S. (2010) 'Evaluating the impact of a peer coaching intervention on well-being amongst psychology undergraduate students', *International Coaching Psychology Review*, 5: 27–35.

Sladden, J. (2005) 'Psychotherapy skills in the real world', *British Medical Journal: Career Focus*, 22 January, 33–5.

Smith, M.J. (1981) *When I Say No, I Feel Guilty*. New York: Dial Press/Bantam Books.

Smock, S.A., Trepper, T.S., Wetchler, J.L., McCollum, E.E., Ray, R. and Pierce, K. (2008) 'Solution-focused group therapy for level 1 substance abusers', *Journal of Marital and Family Therapy*, 34: 107–20.

Sparks, P.M. (1989) 'Organizational tasking: a case report', *Organization Development Journal*, 7: 51–7.

Spence, G.B. and Grant, A.M. (2007) 'Professional and peer life coaching and the enhancement of goal striving and well-being: an exploratory study', *Journal of Positive Psychology*, 2: 185–94.

Springer, D.W., Lynch, C. and Rubin, A. (2000) 'Effects of a solution-focused mutual aid group for Hispanic children of incarcerated parents', *Child and Adolescent Social Work*, 17: 431–42.

Stams, G.J., Dekovic, M., Buist, K. and de Vries, L. (2006) 'Efficacy of solution-focused brief therapy: a meta-analysis', *Gedragstherapie (Dutch Journal of Behavior Therapy)*, 39 (2): 81–95. (Dutch)

Steinhelber, J., Patterson, V., Cliffe, K. and LaGoullon, M. (1984) 'An investigation of some relationships between psychotherapy supervision and patient change', *Journal of Clinical Psychology*, 40: 1346–53.

Sterne, L. (1967 [1759]) *Tristram Shandy*. London: Aimont. p. 327.

Stith, S.M., Rosen, K.H., McCollum, E.E. and Thomsen, C.J. (2004) 'Treating intimate partner violence within intact couple relationships: outcomes of multi-couple versus individual couple therapy', *Journal of Marital and Family Therapy*, 30: 305–18.

Stoddart, K.P., McDonnell, J., Temple, V. and Mustate, A. (2001) 'Is brief better? A modified brief solution-focused therapy approach for adults with a developmental delay', *Journal of Systemic Therapies*, 20: 24–41.

Strupp, H.H. (1958) 'The performance of psychiatrists and psychologists in a clinical interview', *Journal of Clinical Psychology*, 14: 219–26.

Sundmann, P. (1997) 'Solution-focused ideas in social work', *Journal of Family Therapy*, 19: 159–72.

Suzuki, S. (1970) *Zen Mind, Beginner's Mind*. New York: Weatherhill.

Swartz, L. (1998) *Culture and Mental Health: A South African View*. Oxford: Oxford University Press.

Taylor, D., Paton, C. and Kapur, S. (2009) *The Maudsley Prescribing Guidelines* (10th ed). London: Informa Healthcare.

Thase, M.E. and Jindal, R.D. (2004) 'Combining psychotherapy and psychopharmacology for treatment of mental disorders', in Lambert, M.J. (ed), *Bergin and Garfield's Handbook of Psychotherapy and Behaviour Change* (5th ed). New York: Wiley. pp. 743–66.

Thomas, F. (1996) 'Solution-focused supervision: the coaxing of expertise', in Miller, S.D., Hubble, M.A. and Duncan, B.L. (eds), *Handbook of Solution-focused Brief Therapy*. San Francisco, CA: Jossey-Bass. pp. 128–51.

Thompson, R. and Littrell, J.M. (2000) 'Brief counseling with learning disabled students', *The School Counselor*, 2: 60–7.

Thorslund, K.W. (2007) 'Solution-focused group therapy for patients on long-term sick leave: a comparative outcome study', *Journal of Family Psychotherapy*, 18: 11–24.

Tilsen, J., Russell, S. and Michael (2005) 'Nimble and courageous acts: how Michael became the boss of himself', *Journal of Systemic Therapies*, 24: 29–42.

Tohn, S.L. and Oshlag, J.A. (1996) 'Solution-focused therapy with mandated clients: cooperating with the uncooperative', in Miller, S.D., Hubble, M.A.

and Duncan, B.L. (eds), *Handbook of Solution-focused Brief Therapy*. San Francisco, CA: Jossey-Bass. pp. 152–83.

Tomori, C. and Bavelas, J.B. (2007) 'Using microanalysis of communication to compare solution-focused and client centred therapies', *Journal of Family Psychotherapy*, 18: 25–43.

Triantafillou, N. (1997) 'A solution-focused approach to mental health supervision', *Journal of Systemic Therapies*, 16: 305–28.

Turnell, A. and Edwards, S. (1999) *Signs of Safety: A Solution and Safety Oriented Approach to Child Protection Casework*. New York: Norton.

United Kingdom Council for Psychotherapy (2005) *Code of Ethics*. London: UKCP.

Unwin, D. (2005) 'SFGP! Why a solution-focused approach is brilliant in primary care', *Solution News*, 1: 10–12.

van Baaren, R.B., Holland, R.W., Steenaert, B. and van Knippenberg, A. (2003) 'Mimicry for money: behavioral consequences of imitation', *Journal of Experimental Social Psychology*, 39: 393–8.

Vaughn, K., Webster, D.C., Orahood, S. and Young, B.C. (1995) 'Brief inpatient psychiatric treatment: finding solutions', *Issues in Mental Health Nursing*, 16: 519–31.

Vaughn, K., Young, B.C., Webster, D.C. and Thomas, M.R. (1996) 'A continuum-of-care model for inpatient psychiatric treatment', in Miller, S.D., Hubble, M.A. and Duncan, B.L. (eds), *Handbook of Solution-Focused Brief Therapy*. San Francisco, CA: Jossey-Bass. pp. 99–127.

Visser, C. (2009) http://solutionfocusedchange.blogspot.com/2010/07/limitations-and-contra-indications-for.html (accessed April 2011).

Von Economo, C. (1931) *Encephalitis Lethargica: Its Sequelae and Treatment*. (trans. K.O. Newman) Oxford: Oxford University Press.

Wade, A. (1997) 'Small acts of living: everyday resistance to violence and other forms of oppression', *Contemporary Family Therapy*, 19: 23–39.

Wainwright, G.W. (1985) *Teach Yourself Body Language*. London: Hodder and Stoughton.

Wake, M., Baur, L.A., Gerner, B., Gibbons, K., Gold, L., Gunn, J., Levickis, P., McCallum, Z., Naughton, G., Sanci, L. and Ukoumunne, O.C. (2009) 'Outcomes and costs of primary care surveillance and intervention for overweight or obese children: the LEAP 2 randomised controlled trial', *British Medical Journal*, 339: 1132.

Walker, L. and Greening, R. (2010) 'Huikahi Restorative Circles: a public health approach for reentry planning.' *Federal Probation*, 74. (www.uscourts.gov/FederalCourts/ProbationPretrialServices/FederalProbationJournal/FederalProbationJournal.aspx?doc=/uscourts/FederalCourts/PPS/Fedprob/2010-06/index.html)

Walker, L. and Hayashi, L. (2009) 'Pono Kaulike: reducing violence with restorative justice and solution-focused approaches', *Federal Probation*, 73.

Available at www.uscourts.gov/viewer.aspx?doc=/uscourts/FederalCourts/
PPS/Fedprob/2009-06/index.html (accessed April 2011).

Wallerstein, R.S. (1986) *Forty-two Lives in Treatment: A Study of Psychoanalysis and Psychotherapy*. New York: Guilford Press.

Walrond-Skinner, S. (1986) *A Dictionary of Psychotherapy*. London: Routledge and Kegan Paul.

Walter, L.J. and Peller, E.J. (1992) *Becoming Solution-focused in Brief Therapy*. New York: Brunner/Mazel.

Wampold, B.E. (2001) *The Great Psychotherapy Debate: Models, Methods and Findings*. Hillsdale, NJ: Lawrence Erlbaum.

Wampold, B.E. and Bhati, K.S. (2004) 'Attending to the omissions: a historical examination of evidence-based practice movements', *Professional Psychology, Research and Practice*, 35: 563–70.

Wampold, B.E., Minami, T., Baskin, T.W. and Tierney, S.C. (2002) 'A meta-(re)analysis of the effects of cognitive therapy versus "other therapies" for depression', *Journal of Affective Disorders*, 68: 159–65.

Warner, R.E. (2000) 'Solution-focused training: developing the "qualitative self-assessment practice standards"', *European Brief Therapy Association Web Newsletter*. (Available at www.ebta.nu)

Watzlawick, P., Weakland, J.H. and Fisch, R. (1974) *Change: Principles of Problem Formation and Problem Resolution*. New York: Norton.

Wells, A., Devonald, M., Graham, V. and Molyneux, R. (2010) 'Can solution focused techniques help improve mental health and employment outcomes?', *Journal of Occupational Psychology, Employment and Disability*, 12: 3–15.

Wells, R.A. and Gianetti, V.J. (eds) (1990) *Manual of the Brief Psychotherapies*. New York: Plenum.

Wettersten, K.B., Lichtenberg, J.W. and Mallinckrodt, B. (2005) 'Associations between working alliance and outcome in solution-focused brief therapy and brief interpersonal therapy', *Psychotherapy Research*, 15: 35–49.

Wheeler, J. (1995) 'Believing in miracles: the implications and possibilities of using solution-focused therapy in a child mental health setting', *ACPP Reviews & Newsletter*, 17: 255–61.

Whipple, J.L., Lambert, M.J., Vermeersch, D.A., Smart, D.W., Nielsen, S.L. and Hawkins, E.J. (2003) 'Improving the effects of psychotherapy: the use of early identification of treatment failure and problem-solving strategies in routine practice', *Journal of Counseling Psychology*, 50: 59–68.

White, M. and Epston, D. (1990) *Narrative Means to Therapeutic Ends*. New York: Norton.

Wilmshurst, L.A. (2002) 'Treatment programs for youth with emotional and behavioural disorders: an outcome study of two alternate approaches', *Mental Health Services Research*, 4: 85–96.

Wiseman, S. (2003) 'Brief intervention: reducing the repetition of deliberate self-harm', *Nursing Times*, 99: 34–6.

Wittgenstein, L. (1965) *The Blue and Brown Books: Preliminary Studies for the 'Philosophical Investigations'*. New York: Harper.

World Health Organisation (1994) *International Classification of Diseases (ICD)*, 10th edn. Geneva: World Health Organisation. (See also www.who.int/classifications/icd/en/)

Yang, F.-R., Zhu, S-L. and Luo, W-F. (2005) 'Comparative study of solution-focused brief therapy (SFBT) combined with paroxetine in the treatment of obsessive-compulsive disorder', *Chinese Mental Health Journal*, 19: 288–90. (Mandarin; abstract in English)

Young, S. (1998) 'The support group approach to bullying in schools', *Education Psychology in Practice*, 14: 32–9.

Young, S. and Holdorf, G. (2003) 'Using solution-focused brief therapy in referrals for bullying', *Education Psychology in Practice*, 19: 271–82.

Zabukovec, J., Lazrove, S. and Shapiro, F. (2000) 'Self-healing aspects of EMDR: the therapeutic change process and perspectives of integrated psychotherapies', *Journal of Psychotherapy Integration*, 10: 189–206.

Zhang, H-Y., Wu, W-E., Wen, W-J. and Zheng, Y-M. (2010) 'Application of solution focused approach in schizophrenia patients of convalescent period', *Medical Journal of Chinese People's Health*, 18: 2410–12. (doi CNKI:SUN:ZMYX.0.2010-18-079)

Ziffer, J.M., Crawford, E. and Penney-Wietor, J. (2007) 'The Boomerang Bunch: a school-based multifamily group approach for students and their families recovering from parental separation and divorce', *The Journal for Specialists in Group Work*, 32: 154–64.

Zimmerman, T.S., Jacobsen, R.B., MacIntyre, M. and Watson, C. (1996) 'Solution-focused parenting groups: an empirical study', *Journal of Systemic Therapies*, 15: 12–25.

Zimmerman, T.S., Prest, L.A. and Wetzel, B.E. (1997) 'Solution-focused couples therapy groups: an empirical study', *Journal of Family Therapy*, 19: 125–44.

Zunin, L. (1972) *Contact: The First Four Minutes*. London: Tamly Franklin.

There have been several special issues of journals on solution-focused therapy:

Journal of Family Therapy (UK) (1997), 19: 117–232.
Contemporary Family Therapy (USA) (1997), 19: 1–144.
Journal of Systemic Therapies (1999), 18: 1–88 and (2000), 19: 1–13.
Journal of Family Psychotherapy (2005), 16:1/2 (*Education and Training in Solution-focused Brief Therapy*; published simultaneously in book form; Nelson, T.S. (ed.)).

Index